SIKO

THE AVIATION CAREERS OF IGOR SIKORSKY

DOROTHY COCHRANE

VON HARDESTY

RUSSELL LEE

PUBLISHED FOR THE NATIONAL AIR AND SPACE MUSEUM
BY THE
UNIVERSITY OF WASHINGTON PRESS
SEATTLE AND LONDON

The Aviation Careers of Igor Sikorsky
was produced for the University of Washington Press
by Perpetua Press, Los Angeles

Designed by Dana Levy
Production administration by Letitia O'Connor
Typeset in Galliard and Univers by Andresen Typographics, Tucson
Printed and bound by Dai Nippon, Tokyo

Library of Congress Cataloging-in-Publication Data

Cochrane, Dorothy.
    The aviation careers of Igor Sikorsky/Dorothy Cochrane, Von
Hardesty, Russell Lee.
        p.   cm.
    Bibliography: p.
    Includes index.
    ISBN 0-295-96842-7 (cl.)
    ISBN 0-295-96916-4 (pbk.)
    1. Sikorsky, Igor Ivan, 1889–1972—Exhibitions.   I. Hardesty,
Von, 1939–   .   II. Lee, Russell, 1956–   III. National Air and
Space Museum.   IV. Title.
TL506.U6W3732   1989
629.1 ' (092—dc20
[B]   89-34809
                                                       CIP

COVER ILLUSTRATION AND PAGES 4–5: Painting by James Dietz of
Sikorsky's epic flight from St. Petersburg to Kiev in 1914 in his four-
engine *Il'ya Muromets*.

PAGE 1: In 1976 the Soviet Union honored the Il'ya Muromets aircraft
with a commemorative stamp. Soviet histories of aviation have been slow
to acknowledge Igor Sikorsky as the designer of the Il'ya Muromets, the
world's first four-engine airplane. (NASM)

PAGE 3: The Winged-S company emblem adorned Sikorsky aircraft
beginning in 1926. It was designed by Russian emigré Andrei Avinoff,
an employee of the Pittsburgh Museum of Fine Arts and consultant
to the Mellon Art Foundation.

CONTENTS

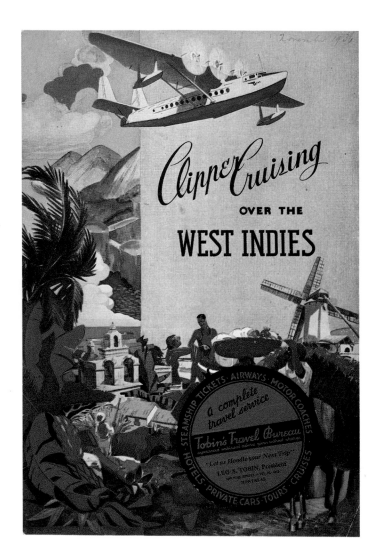

Pan American's "Clipper Cruises" of 1936 were described in the New York Times as the "Hit of the Year in Travel World." This November 1936 brochure offered flights by the Sikorsky S-42 to Port-au-Prince, Jamaica, Trinidad, San Juan, and Havana. (NASM)

Pan American's travel brochure of August 1936 described its "Flying Clipper Cruises" to Rio. The passengers flew in the Sikorsky S-42 and, for $665 each, could spend two weeks in Brazil. (NASM)

The large cockpit and spacious compartments of the S-40 are clearly evident in this cutaway painting of the aircraft skimming the waves. The original painting by V. N. Drashhil hangs in the United Technologies Archives Building in Hartford, Connecticut. (UTC Archives, AS-414)

PREFACE

The conquest of the air, Igor Sikorsky observed in his autobiography, *The Story of the Winged-S*, was one of the singular accomplishments of the twentieth century. Sikorsky himself played no small role in shaping the development of aviation, as a designer of airplanes, flying boats, and helicopters. His career as an active designer spanned a half century and included contributions to both Russian and American aviation.

Igor Sikorsky identified his contributions in the tradition of Thomas Edison and Henry Ford, seeing in these men a synergism of bold vision, belief in technology, and the practical skills of an inventor. Sikorsky brought to his work considerable personal energy and self-confidence. Coming of age at the turn of the twentieth century, he shared the previous century's faith in material progress. His upbringing had stressed reading and intellectual development. As a boy he avidly read Jules Verne, whose writings made an enduring impact on him. Sikorsky's vision and boldness as a designer in part can be traced to this formative influence.

Throughout his long career Sikorsky was at the leading edge of aviation development. As early as 1913, at the age of twenty-four, he had designed and flown in Russia the world's first four-engine airplane, known as the *Grand*. This same historic design became the world's first long-range bomber in World War I. Before he left Russia in 1918, he had designed a whole sequence of advanced monoplanes and biplanes, the "S" series. The triumph of the Bolsheviks in the Russian Revolution compelled him to emigrate, first to France and then to America.

Sikorsky's pursuit of an aviation career in America proved remarkable for its breadth and diverse accomplishments. In the 1920s, he emerged in America as an important pioneer, finding a profitable niche for himself in the production of flying boats. Once the flying boat era ended for Sikorsky in the late 1930s, he returned to an older obsession, the design of a helicopter. His success with the single-rotor VS-300 in 1939 signaled a whole new era of vertical flight.

The year 1989 marks the one hundredth anniversary of the birth of Igor Sikorsky and the fiftieth anniversary of the first flight of the VS-300. For this occasion the National Air and Space Museum (NASM) of the Smith-sonian Institution has prepared a special exhibition, a project supported by a grant from the United Technologies Corporation (UTC).

As part of this centennial celebration, the National Air and Space Museum has produced this publication to address the major themes of Igor Sikorsky's life through historical narrative, photographs, and documentary materials.

Right
Aviation photographer Hans Groenhoff is behind the camera as Les Morris looks skyward from the cockpit of the VS-300A, March 29, 1943. (NASM)

Opposite Right
Sikorsky flies the VS-300 near the factory parking lot in the summer of 1940. His flying attire includes a white cap and sunglasses instead of his characteristic upturned homberg. (UTC Archives, AS-452)

Below Right
Test pilot Les Morris hovers the VS-300A in 1943 as a man places a bundle in the nose basket. Such demonstrations occurred often to show the precise control characteristics of the Sikorsky helicopter. (NASM)

Below
The November 16, 1953, issue of *Time* magazine featured the Russian helicopter pioneer on the cover. Four months earlier, hostilities had ended in Korea where large numbers of Sikorsky military helicopters were successfully operated under combat conditions. (Courtesy *Time* magazine)

IGOR IVANOVICH SIKORSKY
With the oldest flying machine, a new era of flight.

ACKNOWLEDGMENTS

The authors wish to acknowledge the generous assistance of several individuals who made a significant contribution to the preparation of the Igor Sikorsky exhibition and to the publication of this book. Robert F. Daniell, Chairman and Chief Executive Officer, United Technologies Corporation, and Robert Stangarone, former Director of Communications, Sikorsky Aircraft, provided generous support for the exhibition and publication. Sergei Sikorsky, Vice President for Special Projects, Sikorsky Aircraft, served as a special advisor for the project. Anne Millbrooke, Corporate Archivist at United Technologies, played a pivotal role during the research phase. Her collaboration in obtaining photographs, drawings, and historical materials on the career of Igor Sikorsky is appreciated. Also, we are grateful to Harvey Lippincott who served as a technical advisor on the Sikorsky aircraft and helicopters.

Special thanks to Carl Bobrow for preparation of the appendices and numerous other materials, and to Harry Woodman, Paul Behrens, and Chuck Davis for providing their technical knowledge and expert drawings of aircraft.

Many other individuals participated in support roles at various stages of the project: Barbara Brennan, Delores R. Briere, James Dietz, William Fleming, Nicholas G. Glad, Patricia Graboske, Nicole De Horatius, Anita Mason, Beatrice Matkovic, C. Lester Morris, Alexander Nicolsky, Diane Rogers, David Romanowski, Mary Schlizter, Ross Serafimovich, Igor Sikorsky, Jr., and Dimitri Viner.

Finally, we thank Harold K. Skramstad, Jr., Randy Mason, and the staff of the Henry Ford Museum and Greenfield Village. The loan of the VS-300 to the National Air and Space Museum provided an artifact closely associated with Sikorsky's career for the exhibition.

IGOR
SIKORSKY

The 1988 U.S. stamp celebrated the lifelong contributions
of Igor Sikorsky to aviation. (U.S. Postal Service)

I. THE RUSSIAN PERIOD, 1889–1919

The *Il'ya Muromets* in flight. This famous photograph, taken at Korpusnoi aerodrome in 1914, shows two figures on the top of the rear fuselage observation deck. (NASM)

I. THE RUSSIAN PERIOD, 1889 – 1919

Igor Ivanovich Sikorsky (1889 – 1972) occupies a special place in the history of aviation. Few individuals in the history of flight equal his diverse roles as an aircraft designer, pilot, and aviation pioneer. Sikorsky's career included major contributions to multi-engine aircraft designs, flying boats, and helicopters. His substantial legacy in pre-1917 Russia has been obscured for years, largely as a result of his emigration to the West at the time of the Bolshevik takeover. Subsequent Soviet accounts of aviation history, until quite recently, have either ignored Igor Sikorsky or distorted the importance of his contributions. Sikorsky's role in American aviation has been significant, in particular his contributions to helicopter design where the name Sikorsky has become almost synonymous with the technology of vertical flight.[1]

Igor Sikorsky grew up in a family of four children, including two sisters, Olga and Helen, and one brother, Sergei. His family lived in Kiev, where his father, Ivan A. Sikorsky, a renowned professor, pursued an academic career and research in the pioneering field of psychiatry. The elder Sikorsky earned a considerable reputation as a lecturer and writer, both in Russia and Western Europe. The Sikorsky home was filled with books and art, lively conversation, and an atmosphere that encouraged intellectual curiosity.

Igor Sikorsky's interest in aviation, to a significant degree, can be traced to his youthful fascination with the writings of Jules Verne. A French novelist of the late nineteenth century, Verne became a worldwide sensation with his romantic fiction on futuristic breakthroughs in science and technology. Translations of Verne's works appeared in Russia and the young Sikorsky read them eagerly. Verne's popular works—20,000 *Leagues Under the Sea, Five Weeks in a Balloon, A Journey to the Center of the Earth, From the Earth to the Moon, Around the World in Eighty Days,* and *Clipper of the Clouds*—captivated a broad readership that was truly global in scope.

The young Sikorsky was especially intrigued with Verne's *Clipper of the Clouds,* which described an aircraft capable of vertical flight. This imaginative flying machine stimulated Sikorsky to dream about building a helicopter, a vision that would have an enduring place in his long career. His interest in the helicopter was given further stimulus when he studied Leonardo da Vinci, who speculated about the construction of flying machines. Sikorsky first built a spring-driven model of a helicopter in

1899, at the age of ten. Sikorsky's boyhood experiences gave expression to his fascination with vertical flight as a youth and his commitment to seeking out practical ways to translate ideas into reality.

The same year the Wright brothers flew at Kitty Hawk, Igor Sikorsky entered the Imperial Russian Naval Academy at St. Petersburg. He spent three years, 1903–6 there, completing a general course of studies. A naval career held less appeal for him than some branch of practical engineering. Consequently, he resigned from the naval academy in 1906, and, after a brief six-month period of study in Paris, enrolled in the Polytechnic Institute of Kiev in 1907 to study electrical engineering. While engineering studies were congenial to Sikorsky, he was restive with purely theoretical work, preferring to spend his limited spare time in his workshop. Here he built various mechanical devices and designed a steam-powered motorcycle.

Russian interest in aeronautics at this time was largely focused on lighter-than-air technology. Ballooning was popular and enjoyed active government patronage. There was also a long tradition of Russian ballooning going back to the nineteenth century. The Imperial Russian

Technical Society had created its own aeronautical section in the 1880s. Dmitry I. Mendeleev, known today as a compiler of the periodic tables, became a ballooning enthusiast. Russia already had produced a number of important aeronautical theorists such as Konstantin Tsiolkovsky and Nicholas Zhukovsky, who were destined to play a prominent role in Soviet aerospace history. As early as 1885 the Russian Army had built a special school for ballooning at Volkov Field near St. Petersburg. During the Russo-Japanese War of 1904–5, the Russian Army fielded a ballooning battalion for aerial reconnaissance. Lighter-than-air enthusiasts in Russia in the first decade of the twentieth century lobbied for the construction of dirigibles, to match the impressive flights of Count Ferdinand von Zeppelin in Germany.[2]

In 1908, when he accompanied his father on a trip to Germany, Igor Sikorsky had an opportunity to observe the Zeppelin craft firsthand. Each flight by Zeppelin was given considerable press coverage; yet while Sikorsky found the flights inspiring, he resisted the prevailing enthusiasm at home and abroad for lighter-than-air technology. That same year in Germany, Sikorsky discovered a French newspaper account, written by an eyewitness, of the flight by the Wrights at Kitty Hawk in 1903. The account made a profound impression on Sikorsky, who now realized the vast potential of heavier-than-air flying machines. In 1908 the Wright brothers made their historic visit to Europe to demonstrate their flying machine. These flights, along with the appearance of other innovative designers, stimulated an intense popular interest in the airplane with France emerging as a new center for aviation.

Sikorsky began to think about a flying machine capable of vertical flight, "rising directly from the ground by the action of a lifting propeller."[3] This concept of a helicopter demonstrated his affinity for heavier-than-air flying machines, but not necessarily along the path of the Wright brothers who had designed a fixed-wing airplane. Sikorsky dreamed of building a workable helicopter, a machine that could rise vertically, hover, and fly under full control on any heading.

By January 1909, Sikorsky had returned to Western Europe, this time to France where he encountered some important figures, places, and events associated with the burgeoning aeronautical community. Going to Paris in the fateful year of 1909 allowed him to visit aero-

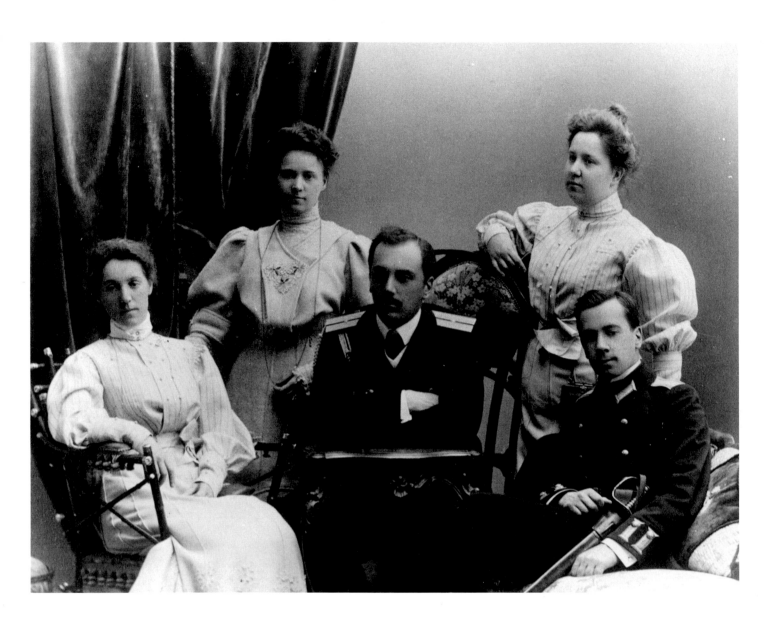

dromes and factories, to meet famed aviators Ferdinand Ferber and Louis Bleriot, and to seek out an aero-engine to power his proposed flying machine. His sister Olga had played a critical role at this juncture of his career, showing great interest in his ideas and offering financial support to purchase an engine. Originally he had planned to stay just briefly, but the excitement over aviation in Paris compelled him to stay on until May.

While in Paris, Sikorsky met Ferber and shared with the French aviator his plan to build a helicopter. Ferber was not encouraging at all, seeing correctly that the technology for such a flying machine did not exist at that time. Ferber told the young Sikorsky to find a more practical project. Such advice from Ferber, of course, was weighty, especially for the novice designer from Kiev, but Sikorsky persisted in his determination to construct a helicopter. Before Sikorsky left Paris, however, he met Louis Bleriot briefly and visited the flying fields at Issy les Moulineaux and Juvisy, where he observed short flights by Wright, Farman, and Bleriot airplanes.

This trip—meeting Ferber and Bleriot— validated Sikorsky's youthful devotion to aviation. Looking at these years later in life,

Sikorsky stated, "aeronautics was not an industry, not even a science, but an 'art' and a 'passion.'" The field of aviation with all its risks appealed to Sikorsky's pioneering spirit. His former plans to pursue a career in engineering were now abandoned in favor of aviation.

Sikorsky returned to Kiev in May 1909, with an Anzani 25-horsepower engine, the same engine used by Bleriot in his epic flight across the English channel in July of that year. Bleriot's remarkable feat stunned Europe and aroused a new wave of enthusiasm for the airplane. Grand Duke Alexander, for example, returned to Russia from France as a devotee of heavier-than-air machines, arguing that the airplane would revolutionize transportation and supply a new, perhaps decisive, weapon of war. The Grand Duke encouraged the Imperial All-Russian Aero Club (IRAC), founded in 1908, to give place to the airplane. Soon aero clubs took shape in many Russian cities, even as far away as Tashkent, and Russia began to mobilize its own aeronautical community. It was in this environment that Sikorsky would first try to build a helicopter.

The young Sikorsky pursued his new career as a designer with great enthusiasm. He was not

МАЙ 1910г. КИЕВ

alone in Europe, or even Russia. Many would-be designers constructed flying machines, but only a few emerged successful. "The greatest failure and the bitterest disappointments," Sikorsky later observed, "came from overconfidence and uncontrolled imagination which the unfortunate inventor mistook for intuition."[4] Sikorsky stood apart from many of his contemporaries because he understood that "intuition" in airplane design and testing must rest on practical experimentation. He shared the empirical hands-on approach that had enabled the Wright brothers to achieve success.

After two unsuccessful attempts to build a helicopter, Sikorsky shifted his energies to building airplanes. He launched his "S" series of aircraft in 1910, a sequence of new designs that would extend into World War I and earn Sikorsky a reputation as one of Russia's premier aircraft designers. The "S" series consisted of both monoplanes and biplanes. The S-1, with a modest 15-horsepower engine, did not actually fly but served as a test bed for perfecting longitudinal and directional control during high-speed ground runs. The S-2 and S-3, powered by 25- and 35-horsepower engines, respectively, followed and gave evidence of Sikorsky's evolving skill as a designer. Both the S-1 and the S-2 were destroyed in crashes;

however, Sikorsky survived the mishaps with little more than bruises.

By the spring of 1911, Sikorsky had built the S-4 and the S-5, each equipped with an Argus 50-horsepower engine. The S-5 represented his first real breakthrough; it was a flyable airplane that allowed Sikorsky to perfect his skills as a pilot as he made short cross-country flights at altitudes of up to 1,500 feet. That summer the young designer earned his pilot's license (no. 64) from the Imperial All-Russian Aero Club, an affiliate of F.A.I. (Fédération Aéronautique Internationale).

While the S-5 earned Sikorsky a reputation in Russia as a successful designer, his work, to date, had been largely derivative in nature. His aircraft clearly mirrored a dependence on French designs and technology. Despite the marginal performance of the S-5, Sikorsky flew the airplane in a number of air shows at Kiev and Kharkov, events that enabled him to establish himself as a serious experimenter.[5]

During the winter of 1911–12, Igor Sikorsky began the construction of a new airplane, the S-6. The new type went through several modifications as Sikorsky endeavored to build a larger airplane with greater power and range, and one that incorporated a streamlined de-

sign to reduce drag. The S-6-A could take aloft three passengers and cruise at seventy miles per hour, a new level of performance for Sikorsky aircraft. With the S-6-A, in fact a separate design, he set a number of records and won several prizes. His next variant, the S-6-B, won first prize in a field of Russian and foreign entries at a military-sponsored competition at Moscow in the summer of 1912. This milestone achievement demonstrated that Sikorsky's design equaled the performance of rival European types.

Sikorsky's design work soon caught the atten-

tion of M. V. Shidlovskiy, the director of the Russo-Baltic Wagon Company in Riga. Shidlovskiy, a highly successful Russian industrialist with influence in high government circles, became convinced that the airplane possessed considerable commercial potential. He recruited Sikorsky to move to St. Petersburg to head a new aviation branch factory to manufacture airplanes. Sikorsky eagerly accepted the offer, for the position provided freedom to continue work on his "S" series and to experiment with radically new designs. Shidlovskiy's patronage was pivotal, allowing Sikorsky to keep and to expand the small

The S-6-A biplane designed by Igor Sikorsky. A variant of the biplane, the S-6-B, flown by the designer, won the Russian military competition at Moscow in 1912.

group of engineers, mechanics, and workers who had made the "S" series a success.

At St. Petersburg, Sikorsky designed the S-10 and S-11 in the spring of 1913. These two aircraft established new benchmarks for Sikorsky and the Russo-Baltic Wagon Company. The S-10 and S-11 won first and second prizes in military competition against advanced French single-engine biplanes (Moranes, Nieuports, Farmans). More important, they suggested that the Russo-Baltic firm could manufacture modern airplanes for the growing Russian market.

During these early years the Tsarist government encouraged the growth of aviation. The Russian Ministry of War played a key role by purchasing aircraft, sponsoring competitions for advanced designs, and building the institutional foundations for military aviation. Igor Sikorsky's triumph at the Moscow military competition of 1912 with the S-6-B revealed the close interaction of civilian designers with their military patrons. The Russian Army trained its pilots at the large air park at Gatchina, twenty-five miles outside St. Petersburg. The Navy built a large naval aviation training facility at Sevastopol on the Black Sea. The Russians would be the first to organize a naval air arm that included hydroplanes

Igor Sikorsky (left) and V. S. Panasiuk, his mechanic.
(NASM)

The *Grand* rests on blocks at St. Petersburg in 1913. This historic aircraft, the world's first four-engine type, enabled Igor Sikorsky fo establish an important breakthrough in aircraft design. (UTC Archives)

launched from specially fitted transports. Older ballooning units would survive into World War I, but by 1912, heavier-than-air machines had gained the ascendancy.

Early flight in Russia was characterized by great vitality and Sikorsky participated actively in the aeronautical community. Nicholas Ye. Zhukovsky, the famed Russian aerodynamicist, directed construction of Russia's first powered wind tunnel (Europe's second) in 1902 at Moscow University. His 1912 lectures on aerodynamics at Moscow provided an important theoretical contribution to aeronautics. In the Soviet Union today he is remembered as the "father of Soviet aviation." Russian aircraft designers such as Yakob M. Gakkel and Dimitri Grigorovich had established reputations for excellence. While Russia possessed many talented aerodynamicists, designers, and pilots, the industrial base for aviation remained small.

Russians joined the pre-World War I mania for air races and air spectaculars. IRAC organized Russia's first big air race, the four-hundred-mile St. Petersburg-to-Moscow competition in 1911. This highly publicized air race was won by a native Russian pilot, A. A. Vasil'yev, in a field of foreign competitors.

Aviation plants first appeared in Russia in 1910, and Russian entrepreneurs soon built aircraft plants in St. Petersburg and Moscow. Most of these plants merely assembled foreign designed aircraft. No real industrial capacity emerged to manufacture engines, although Russians did experiment with engine designers. Aeronautical magazines proliferated, popularizing flying not only as a sport, but as a future means of transportation to tie together the vast domains of the Russian Empire.[6]

Igor Sikorsky proved to be one of the most creative pioneers in the history of early flight. His "S" series had established his reputation as a competent designer. He became convinced that the next logical step was to design a large multi-engine aircraft. His patron Shidlovskiy supported the project, although many contemporary aviation experts said such an undertaking would be foolhardy. Sikorsky's work with small airplanes suggested to him that a large airplane capable of carrying passengers over long distances was feasible. His conviction reflected personal intuition, based on considerable design and flying experience, not on any data about large aircraft. In 1913 there was little known about the performance charac-

teristics of large flying machines. There was the widespread notion, however, that any engine breakdown (always a high probability) would create asymmetrical propeller thrust, throwing the multi-engine aircraft into a spin.

Despite the uncertainties, Sikorsky devoted his energies during the winter of 1912−13 to building his behemoth aircraft. He named it the *Russkiy vityaz* (Russian knight), but it soon acquired the familiar name, the *Grand*. It was a huge aircraft, weighing about nine thousand pounds, and powered by four German-made Argus engines. The *Grand*'s fuselage suggested the silhouette of a ship. The building of the *Grand* prompted considerable skepticism within the aviation community, especially among foreigners who had profound suspicions about Russian engineering skill. The skeptics referred to the *Grand* as the "Petersburg Duck."[7]

Work on the multi-engine aircraft began in September 1912. It was completed early in 1913. For such a grandiose and risky undertaking Sikorsky required the approval of Shidlovskiy, his patron and director of the Russo-Baltic Wagon Company. Shidlovskiy was no stranger to bold projects, and as a result of his confidence in Sikorsky and his team of craftsmen, he endorsed the project.

Construction of the *Grand* took place during the cold winter of 1912–13 at the Russo-Baltic firm's St. Petersburg aviation factory. Sikorsky supervised the construction of the wood and fabric biplane. The airplane differed from contemporary designs in scale, a sort of scaled-up version of the S-6-B which had won the military competition. The fuselage was covered with plywood to increase rigidity. The wing span was 88 feet 7 inches, the fuselage length 65 feet 7 inches, a truly giant flying machine for its time. The wing configuration incorporated a high aspect ratio, long and narrow with minimum drag. The lower wing was fitted to accommodate four engines, initially in two tractor-pusher pods and finally four abreast, in tractor configuration. An observation balcony, at the nose of the *Grand*, was positioned forward of an enclosed cabin with large windows. A narrow folding door provided access from the cockpit to the balcony. Two control wheels with seats in the cockpit gave the pilot and co-pilot excellent forward and lateral vision. Behind the cockpit there was a passenger compartment equipped with a folding table, camp chairs, and overhead electric lights powered by a wind-driven generator. In many respects the *Grand* in silhouette and detail embodied a fanciful imagination worthy of Jules Verne.

Emperor Nicholas II joins Igor Sikorsky on the balcony to inspect the *Grand* in 1913 at Krasnoye selo near St. Petersburg. (NASM)

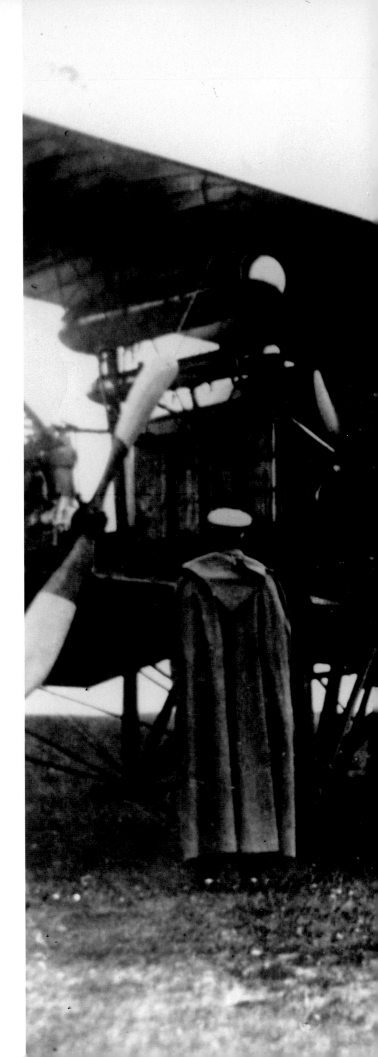

The *Grand* was constructed in sections and transported, piece by piece, to the Komendatskiy airfield north of St. Petersburg. Here it was assembled and fitted with the 100-horsepower Argus engines. Taxiing tests were made with two engines, allowing Sikorsky to attempt a few short hops to an altitude of 300 feet. Having established the fact that his giant airplane could fly, he then added two more Argus engines. On May 26, 1913, he made his first historic flight. The time selected for the flight was 10 P.M., to take advantage of the still air of St. Petersburg's fabled "White Nights." Sikorsky steered the aircraft to an altitude of 400 feet, gingerly turned to the left, and then, at a cruising speed of about fifty-eight miles per hour, climbed another 250 feet. While circling the large grass Komendatskiy Field rimmed with birch and pine trees, he noticed that a large crowd had gathered. For the landing, Sikorsky made an extended downwind approach, throttling back one of his outboard engines to measure its effect on directional control. Once satisfied he had sufficient rudder control even with the loss of one engine, he gradually descended toward the grass field. His landing was greeted with wild enthusiasm by the crowd. Sikorsky had been aloft a mere ten minutes; the *Grand*—the so-called Petersburg Duck—had flown.[8]

Igor Sikorsky seated at the controls of the *Grand* in 1913. This airplane had an enclosed cockpit (a radical innovation) and a forward observation balcony. (NASM)

By July, Sikorsky had made numerous adjustments in design, including the four-abreast engine configuration. The *Grand* was determined ready for a long-distance flight. Accordingly, Sikorsky flew to Krasnoye selo, the site for Russian Army maneuvers outside St. Petersburg, where Emperor Nicholas II inspected the *Grand* for the first time. A month later the *Grand* established a new record with a flight of one hour and fifty-four minutes with eight passengers.

Sikorsky's use of the high-aspect ratio theory in the design of the *Grand* was linked, in his own mind, to intuitive judgment. At the time aeronautical theory was largely undeveloped, especially the aerodynamics associated with the flying of large aircraft. This design feature was crucial because the four 100-horsepower, water-cooled Argus engines provided modest power, at best, to propel the enormous wood and fabric-covered machine into the air. The *Grand* soon demonstrated that a multi-engine airplane could fly safely with one, even two, engines shut down. The worst fears about the safety of large airplanes in flight had not materialized.

The *Grand* proved to be a highly stable airplane. Sikorsky flew the remarkable flying machine in a series of demonstrations in the spring of 1913. The citizens of St. Petersburg flocked to Komendatskiy Field to observe Sikorsky's unique aircraft. For the passengers who obtained rides with Sikorsky on those early flights, there were unparalleled comforts—an enclosed cabin with a table, wicker chairs, and a forward balcony to look down upon the fine boulevards, palaces, and stately public buildings of the imperial capital.

Sikorsky was compelled to build a successor to the *Grand* after it was damaged in a freak accident. (It had been parked on the flight line when an engine from another airplane flying over broke loose and fell through the *Grand*'s port wing.) Sikorsky called his new four-engined airplane the *Il'ya Muromets*, after a legendary folk hero. In July 1913, Sikorsky flew the *Il'ya Muromets* from St. Petersburg to Krasnoye selo for a demonstration flight. Emperor Nicholas II again met Sikorsky and inspected his latest design. An avid proponent of aviation and an admirer of Sikorsky, Nicholas II inspected the huge flying machine with great interest, asking numerous questions about its construction and flying capabilities.

The design of the *Il'ya Muromets* embodied a radical departure from its prototype, the *Grand*. Completed in late October 1913, the *Il'ya Muromets* had a larger wing span, nearly

20 percent greater, a new fuselage, and a blunt nose with a simple forward platform. The cabin area was spacious, over 5 feet wide and 6 feet high, and enclosed in a tapering 70-foot fuselage. The fuselage structure was wood, cross-braced with steel wires, and covered with fabric and plywood. The first *Il'ya Muromets* was fitted with an auxiliary wing, situated in the middle of the fuselage between the main wings and the tail. This peculiar structure was later removed once it was realized that the extra wing added too much lift.

After a series of flight tests, including one mishap at Komendatskiy Field in December 1913, Sikorsky launched a series of demonstration flights. In February 1914, he took sixteen passengers and his dog (the mascot of the aviation plant) for a flight at St. Petersburg. Several dozen flights followed in which the citizens of the Imperial capital were amazed to see the large flying machine make leisurely sweeps over the city. A second *Il'ya Muromets* was completed in April 1914. Press coverage in Russia was extensive and fragmentary reports reached the newspapers of Western Europe telling of the feats of the "Sikorsky airplane."

Sikorsky carried out a series of flights by the *Il'ya Muromets* during the winter and spring of 1914 to demonstrate the durability and range of his new aircraft. On one flight, he took eight passengers aloft and cruised above St. Petersburg at 3,300 feet for two hours and six minutes, setting a new world record. To attract potential governmental support, Sikorsky took five members of the Russian Duma (national parliament) for a short hop. By the summer of 1914, on the eve of World War I, Sikorsky's aerial feats continued to attract considerable attention abroad, prompting *Flight* magazine in England to describe his "aerial bus" as "the first successful attempt at a large, multipassenger machine."

In 1914, the young designer from Kiev planned an even bolder flight for the *Il'ya Muromets*—an aerial spectacular that would demonstrate beyond doubt the practicality of large aircraft. On June 30, at 1:00 A.M., with a crew of three (copilots Lieutenant G. I. Lavrov and Captain K. F. Prussis, and mechanic V. S. Panasiuk), took off from Komendatskiy Field for a round-trip flight to Kiev. The 1,200-mile trek across the broad expanse of European Russia subjected Sikorsky's design to its most severe test. To complete the flight, Sikorsky stored on board ample supplies of fuel, spare parts, and provisions. Except for a planned refueling near the city of Orsha, there were no emergency airfields along the way, only the unfolding beauty of the Russian landscape below: the

forests and swamps of North Russia, interspersed with cultivated fields and small villages, giving way at the end to steppe lands of the Ukraine with its flat expanse and meandering rivers. His well-planned route called for the *Il'ya Muromets* to fly over the cities of Vitebsk and Orsha and then to follow the winding Dnieper River southward to Kiev.

The *Il'ya Muromets* afforded Sikorsky and his crew unique comfort for the long flight. The box-shaped structure of the fuselage contained several compartments, including a cockpit with large windows and a forward balcony; a private cabin with bed, table, and cabinet; a toilet; and an observation platform above the rear fuselage. A generator powered the interior electric lights, and the exhaust gas from the two inboard motors passed through two steel tubes to provide heat for the enclosed cabins. For emergency in-flight repairs, Sikorsky designed side hatches that opened out to plywood ramps stretching across the lower wings. Instrumentation on the *Il'ya Muromets* was austere, but essential: a compass for navigation, four tachometers, a bank indicator, a primitive airspeed indicator, and a horizontal tube on the nose, which was aligned with the windshield so the pilot could measure climbs, descents, and turns.

The four-engine behemoth airplane departed from St. Petersburg on June 30, in the pre-dawn twilight, moving southward toward Kiev at an altitude of 5,000 feet and a cruising speed of about sixty-five miles per hour. For the first eight hours, the flight was uneventful and relaxed, with Sikorsky and his copilots alternating at the controls every hour. Crew members took their meals in the large cabin, and there was ample time to enjoy the breath-taking view. When the *Il'ya Muromets* passed over the city of Vitebsk, Sikorsky dropped two aluminum tubes with bright-colored streamers. In the tubes he had placed telegraph messages, one to his home, the other to the Russo-Baltic factory; both later reached their destinations. At 9:00 A.M. Sikorsky landed at an improvised airfield at Orsha, as planned, and refueled his four-engined aircraft. Taking off again required the intrepid Sikorsky to propel his aircraft down a gently inclined 1,200-foot slope, which ended abruptly over a 100-foot bluff facing the river and the city of Orsha beyond. The crew watched anxiously as Sikorsky guided them down this arduous take-off run. The aircraft cleared the bluff, dipped precariously, and then skimmed over the roof-tops of Orsha. Sikorsky then set the heading southward toward the city of Kiev.

The final leg of the flight proved more dangerous than anticipated. As the *Il'ya Muromets*

Igor Sikorsky's S-10. Manufactured in 1913, it went through several modifications, even being fitted out as a seaplane. (NASM)

approached the Dnieper River, one of the four engines caught fire, forcing Lavrov and Panasiuk out on the wing to beat out the flames with their trenchcoats. With some effort, Sikorsky managed to keep the aircraft in stable flight during these anxious moments, but his concern about the damaged engine compelled him to land again. The problem had been a broken fuel line. Since it was late in the day, Sikorsky decided to delay his takeoff until the next morning.

The following day brought rain, fog, and low clouds, but the *Il'ya Muromets* pushed onward. Again, the lumbering aircraft encountered air turbulence and Sikorsky had to steer through rain and clouds, flying blind for long periods of time. There were moments of extreme danger in these turbulent skies, violent pitching and steep dives, including one spin in which the aircraft fell 1,200 feet before Sikorsky regained control. This was Sikorsky's first experience with a spin and his survival rested on his good judgment to let the controls neutralize themselves; otherwise he might have stayed in the spin and crashed.

Finally, Sikorsky maneuvered the large craft upward and through the enveloping clouds to take full advantage of the serene and sunbathed void above the cloud layer. This breath-

taking vista above the immense layer of clouds that stretched to the horizon made an indelible impression on Sikorsky and his crew. The interlude also gave them a moment to reflect on the unique nature of their flight.

The moment for the *Il'ya Muromets* to begin the crucial descent to Kiev was a calculated guess, based on a rough estimate that the aircraft was over the city. After a long and undulating descent, the *Il'ya Muromets* suddenly broke out of a cloud bank above the Dnieper River. Ahead, Sikorsky saw the familiar outlines of his native Kiev and the golden domes of the Kiev-Pechersk Monastery. When Sikorsky landed, he and his crew were met by city officials and an enthusiastic crowd. Word

of the epic flight soon reached across the Russian empire. Total flying time had been twelve hours and fifty-seven minutes.

The return flight to St. Petersburg, no less a triumph, proved to be a more arduous undertaking. This second leg consumed thirteen hours, and again challenged Sikorsky's flying skill. When the *Il'ya Muromets* reached St. Petersburg, there were awards and public acclaim, including the special gratitude of Nicholas II who renamed the airplane the *Il'ya Muromets Kievskiy* in honor of the great flight.[9]

Igor Sikorsky's epic flight from St. Petersburg to Kiev riveted the attention of the Russian

The *Il'ya Muromets* in flight. This famous photograph, taken at Korpusnoi aerodrome in 1914, shows two figures on the top of the rear fuselage observation deck. (NASM)

aviation community. Before detailed news of the flight reached the West, another dramatic event intervened to obscure Sikorsky's accomplishment—the outbreak of World War I. The advent of war prompted Shidlovskiy, himself a former navy officer, to propose to the Ministry of War that a new squadron be created to fly the Il'ya Muromets (plural, Murometsy). He felt Sikorsky's aircraft possessed great potential as a long-range, four-engine bomber and reconnaissance aircraft. Russia, he argued, would be the first to operate a squadron of large, multi-engined strategic bombers.

The Ministry of War accepted Shidlovskiy's proposal in the chaotic period after the declaration of war in August 1914. Accordingly, Nicholas II approved the creation of the Squadron of Flying Ships (*Escadra vozdushnykh korablei*, or EVK). Shidlovskiy accepted an army commission to head the new squadron and his firm, the Russo-Baltic Wagon Company, received a contract to build military versions of the Il'ya Muromets. As the head of the aviation branch, Sikorsky led a workforce of over three hundred people to produce Murometsy for the war effort. Initially, the Imperial Russian Air Force (IRAF) viewed the newly created EVK with some suspicion. The

IRAF possessed in 1914 an inventory of about two hundred and fifty aircraft, all light and predominantly foreign in design. Most IRAF pilots admired Sikorsky as an individual, but many shared the fighter pilot's disdain for bombers. They also viewed dirigibles and lighter-than-air machines with equal disfavor, seeing the dirigible and balloon units as rivals within the army. These pilots were familiar with small biplanes and possessed little, if any, experience with large aircraft. Pre-war training and doctrine had not prepared them to comprehend the potential of new air weapons.[10]

The EVK, hurriedly organized and inexperienced, entered the war zone in September 1914. The squadron had decided to take the two existing Murometsy, including the *Il'ya Muromets Kievskiy*, the airplane that had made the flight from St. Petersburg to Kiev in July, and send them to the front. This was done after some minor field modifications of the airplanes to equip them for military service. The premature commitment of the squadron proved nearly fatal. Both aircraft were old and, in the hands of inexperienced pilots, failed to meet minimal altitude and performance standards. Many IRAF pilots—already predisposed to view the Il'ya Muromets as an oddity—quickly complained to the Ministry of War, asking that the aircraft be withdrawn. The headquarters staff of the Northwestern Front of the Russian Army, in fact, refused to accept any future deliveries of the Murometsy.

Despite these developments, the *Stavka* (Russian military headquarters) confirmed Shidlovskiy's appointment as commander and gave him the rank of major general. Given a reprieve, Shidlovskiy asked Igor Sikorsky to join the EVK at the front, near Warsaw, in January 1915. Sikorsky was asked to fly a series of tests of the Il'ya Muromets. He quickly demonstrated that the airplane could meet, even exceed, the military flight requirements.

The EVK went on after 1915 to make a significant contribution to the air war; flying bombing and reconnaissance missions, the squadron maintained high morale throughout the war, even on the eve of the Revolution, when the Russian Army was in retreat and many military units experienced mutinies. In 1915–16, the EVK operated with a total of thirty Murometsy. In combat, Sikorsky's flying fortress proved to be a formidable adversary of German fighters. While slow, the later model Il'ya Muromets bombers bristled with guns and, if attacked, gunners returned devastating defensive fire. Over seventy Murometsy were

manufactured and only three were lost during the war. The EVK systematically bombed enemy positions, specifically transport-communication facilities. The greatest contributions of the Il'ya Muromets, however, came in the area of aerial reconnaissance and photography: the ability to cruise at will over large sectors of the front, sometimes deep into the enemy rear, to gather photo intelligence available by no other means. While precise records do not exist, the combat record of the EVK was impressive—one Il'ya Muromets shot down, one lost through sabotage, another lost in training.

When well armed, the Il'ya Muromets presented a formidable challenge to German fighters who attempted to intercept them. In July 1916, for example, an Il'ya Muromets piloted by Captain G. I. Lavrov was attacked by four German fighters near Lvov. Three of the German fighters were shot down and the fourth abandoned the attack. Lavrov returned to his base on three engines. In another spectacular aerial duel in September 1916, an Il'ya Muromets was besieged by seven German fighters. The Russian aircraft shot down three of the attackers before it caught fire and crashed, killing four crew members. Among all the varied combat missions flown by

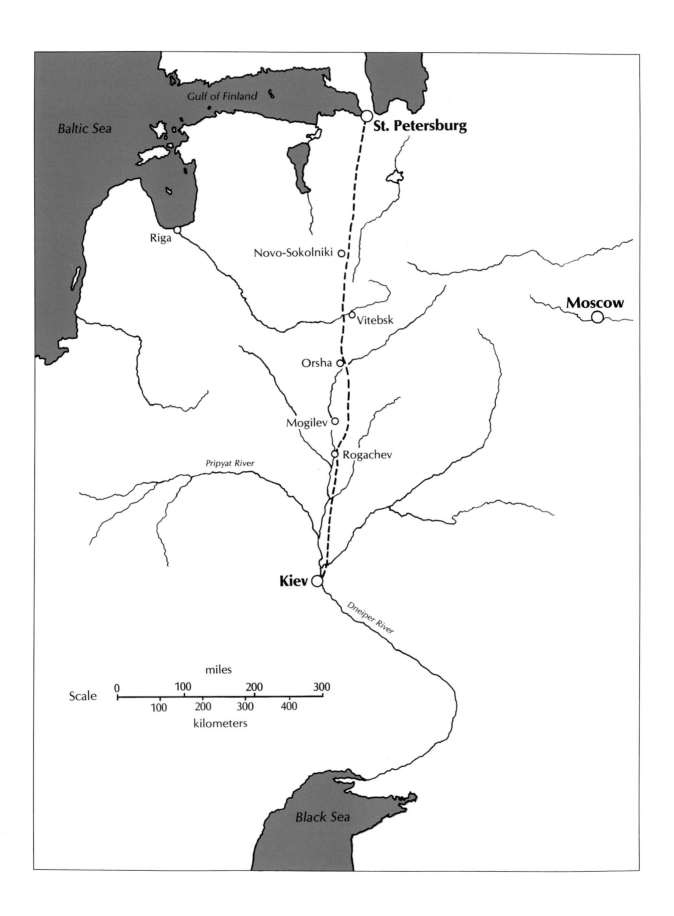

◄ In June 1914, Sikorsky and a crew of three made an arduous flight from St. Petersburg to Kiev and back, demonstrating the practicality of large, four-engine aircraft.

The *Il'ya Muromets* possessed a spacious interior compartment that included wicker chairs, table, and lights. Sikorsky incorporated into this aircraft the essential elements of a passenger airliner. (NASM)

Murometsy, this was a rare recorded instance of the Germans downing an Il'ya Muromets in air combat.

Sikorsky himself shuttled between the front and Petrograd (formerly St. Petersburg) during most of the war, attending to the management of the aviation branch, which built all of the Murometsy. The manufacture of the Il'ya Muromets aircraft was a complex process. There were constant design changes to meet the combat requirements at the front. The most acute problem was the absence of adequate aero engines. The original *Il'ya Muromets* had used German Argus engines, which became unavailable after 1914, so Sikorsky had to seek out a series of substitute power plants from British and French sources. Even the Russo-Baltic firm itself produced its own copy of the Argus engine to meet this critical shortage. Little is known of these wartime years, but it is apparent that Sikorsky and his small coterie of engineers and mechanics achieved considerable success in producing Il'ya Muromets aircraft for the EVK. Toward the end of World War I Germany produced its own copies of the "Sikorskies," as the Germans called the Il'ya Muromets. The deployment of Gotha bombers to attack London in 1917 confirmed the strategic potential of the "heavy," multi-engined bomber and gave enlarged scope to the Sikorsky design.

Wartime Russian drawing illustrating the Il'ya Muromets in combat against a German fighter. (NASM)

◄ Crew members of the *Il'ya Muromets Kievskiy* return to airfield at Yablonna after mission against the Germans in East Prussia, March 1915. (UTC Archives)

Previous Page
The Il'ya Muromets I (IM-1) with members of the EVK squadron at Yablonna, near Warsaw, in 1915. (NASM)

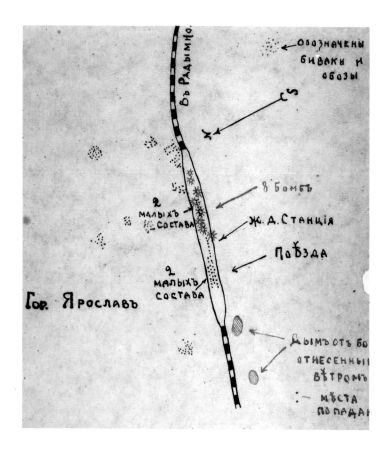

Bombs dropped by an Il'ya Muromets bomber fall on ▶ Yaroslav railway in 1915. (Sergei Sikorsky)

The photo interpretation of the railway bombing shows the accuracy of the attack. The Russians developed advanced aerial photography techniques during World War I. (Sergei Sikorsky)

The Revolution of March 1917 brought an end to the Romanov dynasty, and, eventually, an end to Russia's participation in World War I. Between March and November of that fateful year, a Provisional Government exercised formal power in competition with the "Soviets," the more radical centers of revolutionary activity set up in various cities. Igor Sikorsky found the Provisional Government the best hope for Russia to redirect its political future. But this new regime lacked a firm political base and, in the course of the spring and summer of 1917, unwisely renewed Russia's involvement in the war, even launching an offensive in July under Alexander Kerensky. Already discipline in the army and the navy had broken, as revolutionary agitation encouraged soldiers and sailors to abandon the war effort. In November 1917, Lenin led his Bolsheviks to power, toppling the Provisional Government, organizing his own revolutionary regime, and setting into motion a brutal civil war that would bring even greater misery to war-ravaged Russia.

The Grand Duke Alexander Mikhailovich (second from right) visits Major General M. V. Shidlovskiy (third from right) and the EVK squadron at Yablonna in 1915. Behind them is an Il'ya Muromets. The Murometsy bombers conducted numerous missions in winter of 1914—15. (NASM)

An Il'ya Muromets (Type B) equipped with Salmson engines. The photograph was taken at Petrograd shortly after the beginning of World War I. (NASM)

Igor Sikorsky in 1919. (UTC Archives)

Notes

1. For an overview of the career of Igor Sikorsky, see Igor I. Sikorsky, *The Story of the Winged-S: An Auto-biography*, 2d ed. rev. (New York: Dodd, Mead and Company, 1958); Frank J. Delear, *Igor Sikorsky: His Three Careers in Aviation* (New York: Dodd, Mead and Company, 1969); and K. N. Finne, *Igor Sikorsky: The Russian Years*, edited by Carl J. Bobrow and Von Hardesty (Washington, D.C.: Smithsonian Institution Press, 1987).

2. A basic Soviet account of the formative years, in particular, coverage of the nineteenth century, is *Vozdukhoplavaniye i aviatsiya v Rossii do 1907g, Sbornik dokumentov i materialov* [Aeronautics and aviation in Russia before 1907: Documents and materials], edited by V. A. Popov (Moscow, 1956). Another Russian-language work that covers the period up to World War I is P. D. Duz, *Istoriya vozdukhoplavaniya i aviatsii v Rossii* [History of aeronautics aviation in Russia] (Moscow, 1979). The introductory essay written by Von Hardesty in K. N. Finne's *Igor Sikorsky: The Russian Years* provides a general overview of Sikorsky's place in the development of aviation in Russia before 1917.

3. Sikorsky, *The Story of the Winged-S*, p. 15.

4. The Imperial All-Russian Aero Club became the center for civilian aviation activities. The organization existed until 1917. The Grand Duke Alexander survived the revolutionary period and emigrated to Paris, where he died in 1933.

5. Sikorsky, *The Story of the Winged-S*.

6. Throughout Russia's active involvement in World War I, military aviation faced an acute shortage of aero engines. This 1914−16 crisis would persist well into the Soviet period.

7. Sikorsky, *The Story of the Winged-S*, pp. 40−63; Delear, *Igor Sikorsky*, pp. 35−38.

8. Sikorsky, *The Story of the Winged-S*, pp. 83−94.

9. This same airplane, the *Il'ya Muromets Kievskiy*, was mobilized for the war effort and deployed on numerous combat operations, ending its career as a trainer.

10. For an account of the wartime operations of the EVK, see K. N. Finne, *Igor Sikorsky: The Russian Years*. Finne was a flight surgeon with the squadron and provided a detailed history of the Il'ya Muromets at war, 1914−17.

A rare photograph of the aviation branch factory of the
Russo-Baltic Wagon Company. The fuselage section of
an early model Il'ya Muromets contains one unidentified
workman. (NASM)

II. THE GOLDEN AGE OF FLIGHT, 1919–39

II. THE GOLDEN AGE OF FLIGHT, 1919–39

Igor Sikorsky found the Bolshevik regime unacceptable as an alternative to the Tsarist political order. The Bolsheviks also posed a direct threat to his safety. A worker warned Sikorsky that he would soon be brought to trial as an enemy of the working class and urged him to flee. Sikorsky decided to leave Petrograd for Paris in February 1918, but before he left he burned his military uniform and credentials as a general of the army, given to him in the war years. Now caught up in the vortex of revolution, he had left his family, friends, and homeland for the uncertainties of emigré life. Shidlovskiy, his old friend and wartime colleague, was less fortunate; while attempting to escape to Finland with his son, both were captured and executed.

Sikorsky's circuitous route to the West took him from Murmansk to Britain by steamer. He arrived in London to see the city bombed by German Gotha bombers and then went on to Paris, where he approached the French Air Service with a proposal to build a large bomber. The French accepted Sikorsky's offer, seeing a strategic air weapon in the proposed bomber. Sikorsky worked to design the large aircraft in his hotel room in Paris. He completed the project in short order and submitted it to the French government. The French quickly approved his design and ordered the construction of five of the new Sikorsky bombers. All this effort proved to be in vain, for no sooner had the contract been approved than World War I came to an end. The Armistice was signed on November 11, 1918, and Sikorsky's contract was cancelled.

Sikorsky considered staying on in France. His pre-war association with France was strong. However, France at the close of the war offered few real opportunities for aeronautical research. Emigration to the West had meant unaccustomed poverty for Sikorsky. In his mind America offered greater opportunities to rebuild his life, so on March 14, 1919, Sikorsky sailed for the United States on the French liner *Lorraine*.

It had been a decade since he launched his aviation career in Kiev. He was now thirty years old, and few men his age could point to a career with such singular accomplishments. He arrived in America with little money and no real prospects for a job. He did come to New York with a few letters of recommendation, including one from General Mason Patrick, commander of the U.S. Army Air Service of the American Expeditionary Forces in Europe.

His arrival in America coincided with demobilization and the return to a peacetime economy. America, like France, offered few opportunities. There were vast surpluses of Curtiss JN-4 Jennies and other World War I aircraft, creating a glut of airplanes for the small American aviation market. Civil aviation was still in its infancy and commercial air transport remained a dream. Against these formidable obstacles, Igor Sikorsky launched his second career in aviation.

His first venture involved the organization of an aviation company in New York with a group of Russian emigrés. Called the Hannevig-Sikorsky Aircraft Company, the fledgling firm established its headquarters in Wantagh, Long Island. The firm aimed to design and construct a new airplane capable of transporting a payload of 12,000 pounds at ninety miles per hour. Despite the grandiose goals, the firm failed to coalesce. Sikorsky again faced a future of uncertain employment.

In late September 1919, Sikorsky completed the drawings for the *Avion Atlas*, the bomber he originally had designed for the French. Now called the Sikorsky Battleplane, Type I.S. 27, the *Avion Atlas* appeared on paper as a large four-engine bomber with a wingspan of

85 feet. Sikorsky submitted his design to the U.S. Army Air Service in Washington, D.C., where he met with Lt. Colonel B. Q. Jones of the Office of the Director of the Air Service. Jones responded favorably to the Sikorsky project, sending him to the Engineering Division at McCook Field in Dayton, Ohio. In describing the project, Colonel Jones gave a positive recommendation: "Inasmuch as the Air Service is at present particularly interested in the design of a superbomber, there is no doubt but that the arrival of the most experienced designer of super machines in the world, will be of very great interest to the Engineering Division."[1] McCook Field was the Air Service's test center, where the research and development of aircraft took place.

Sikorsky's proposal to the Air Service called for him to produce "general views of two types of multi-seater airplane with three 700 H.P. engines each."[2] The Air Service formally accepted his proposal on November 10, 1919. Sikorsky moved to Dayton and by Christmas, he had produced ten detailed drawings of a bomber. Both versions of the Sikorsky M.S.N.B. (night bomber), if built, would have had wingspans of 130 feet. Type A would have incorporated a third engine placed at the center section of the rear of the fuselage, while

Type B called for a third engine on the top wing. Both types had two engines mounted on the lower wing. However, citing lack of money as the problem, Colonel Thurman Bane, chief of the Engineering Division, decided to discontinue the project. For the work on these multi-engine bomber designs, Sikorsky earned $1,500, the admiration of the Engineering Division, and a couple of news columns in the Dayton press. His quest to find secure employment remained as elusive as ever.

Upon his return to New York City, Sikorsky resumed his efforts to gain a foothold in the aviation business. His most recent experience at McCook Field confirmed the fact that military contracts offered minimal opportunity. By contrast, the design of aircraft for the civilian market appeared more promising. Aviation remained a high-risk economic venture in the immediate postwar years, although the idea of a commercial air transport system persisted as a powerful vision of the future. Sikorsky was one of the proponents of such a system—a man who clearly saw the need for a long-range air transportation network to promote commerce and travel. Sikorsky firmly believed that the potential market existed; the task was to design large, safe commercial air transports to make the concept a reality.

The final paper version of the *Avion Atlas*, originally designed as a French bomber, was completed in New York in 1919 as the Sikorsky Battleplane, I.S. 27. This bomber drew the interest of the U.S. Army Air Service which offered Sikorsky the opportunity to submit a design for a bomber. (UTC AS-2)

Accordingly, Sikorsky joined with Ivan Pro-kofieff and Joseph Michael in February 1920 to form a partnership to manufacture "aero-planes for freight or passenger transporta-tion."[3] Sikorsky already had designed his S-28, a four-engine transport aircraft, in late 1919, and the partnership would have allowed him to head a new company and to develop the S-28 as well as other new designs. The finan-cial backing for the project, however, did not materialize and the partnership was dissolved. Again Sikorsky was on his own.

Now Sikorsky encountered a more grim reality—how was he to find employment to pay for the necessities of life? His small finan-cial reserves had been nearly exhausted. The prospects for immediate employment as an aircraft designer appeared remote. Where to turn? Living in New York, Sikorsky had met many Russian emigrés who then had intro-duced him to a larger Russian community in the city. One member of this community, Leo Trofimov, encouraged Sikorsky to teach some night courses at the Russian Collegiate In-stitute in New York City. Here Sikorsky en-tered the unfamiliar domain of the classroom, teaching mathematics and astronomy. Despite his inexperience as a teacher, he quickly won the affection of his students.

Throughout 1921–22 Sikorsky lived a rather austere life, renting a modest apartment and forced to embrace a diet of beans and bread. The rigors of his life in America, however, did not bring personal disillusionment or despair. He retained his essential optimism throughout these difficult days. His lectures allowed him to meet a large number of people and he soon expanded his lecture itinerary to include the Nauka (Science) Society, where there was an opportunity to discuss his ideas about aviation with an informed and enthusiastic audience.

It was at the Nauka Society that Igor Sikorsky met Elizabeth Semion, a teacher in the chil-dren's program. She had also recently arrived in the United States, having escaped from Si-beria at the time of the Russian Revolution. Her father had been a professional soldier in the Russian Army before the Revolution, and both of her parents had disappeared in the chaotic days of the Civil War after the Bolshe-vik seizure of power in 1917. Her friendship with Igor Sikorsky deepened over time and they were married in January 1924. Eventually, they raised a family of four sons, Sergei, Nikolai, Igor, Jr., and George.

For the many Russian emigrés in New York, Igor Sikorsky was a source of community

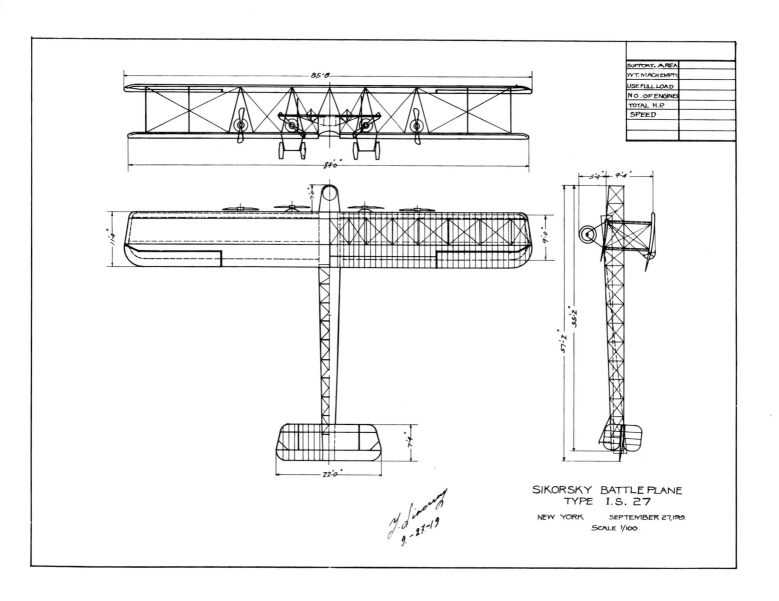

SUPPORT. AREA	
WT. MACH EMPTY	
USE FULL LOAD	
NO. OF ENGINES	
TOTAL H.P.	
SPEED	

85'-8"

84'-0"

7'-6"

1'-4"

9'-0"

57'-2"

55'-2"

5'-4"   9'-4"

7'-6"

22'-0"

SIKORSKY BATTLE PLANE
TYPE I.S. 27

NEW YORK   SEPTEMBER 27, 1919.
SCALE 1/100.

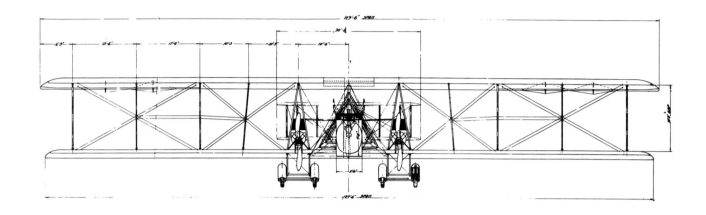

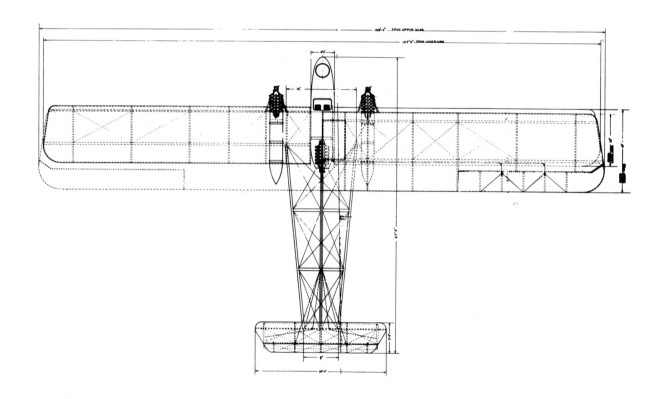

◄ The Sikorsky M.S.N.B., Type A, drawn for the Air Service at McCook Field, Ohio, December 1919. Citing lack of funds, the Air Service did not offer Sikorsky a contract. (UTC AS-184)

Baron Nicholas Solovioff, left, and Jimmy Viner, Sikorsky's nephew, in the chicken coop/machine shop at the Utgoff farm on Long Island. (UTC AS-120)

pride, a survivor of the pre-Revolution days who symbolized the character and achievement of the Russian aeronautical community. The paradox for Sikorsky, however, was that events had conspired to obscure in America his achievements in Tsarist Russia. Only a few individuals were intimately acquainted with his accomplishments in Russia. Sikorsky's epic flight from St. Petersburg to Kiev in 1914, his numerous aircraft designs, his many record-breaking flights, and his contributions to the EVK, the world's first bomber squadron, had slipped into historical obscurity. The Bolsheviks who gained power in 1917 ignored Sikorsky, largely for political reasons, because

Sikorsky had emigrated to the West in opposition to the Communist regime. Other members of the old Russian aviation community, Nicholas Zhukovsky, for example, embraced the revolutionary government and found a new place for themselves. Igor Sikorsky, by contrast, had to start over.

Sikorsky's sequence of ill-fated commercial ventures ended on March 5, 1923, when he joined with a group of financial backers to organize the Sikorsky Aero Engineering Corporation. Unlike the earlier efforts, this new corporation, with Sikorsky as president, possessed (just barely) the requisite financial base

in the forms of cash and pledges for stock to enter the very competitive and highly risky field of airplane manufacturing.

In reality, Sikorsky's backers possessed more enthusiasm than money, and as a group they demonstrated a solid confidence in the undertaking and in Igor Sikorsky's abilities as a designer. Many were Russian emigrés, a substantial number being former Russian naval officers, who were willing to invest a sufficient amount of money to allow the building of the Sikorsky prototype. Attached to the enterprise were a group of Russian engineers, pilots, and mechanics who would give continuity to the work: Michael and Serge Gluhareff, Michael Buivid, Robert Labensky, Nicholas Solovioff, Nicholas Glad, D. D. Viner, Victor Koodroff, and Boris Sergievsky. Their loyalty—even in the absence of regular paychecks—sustained the effort.

Victor Utgoff, a naval officer and friend of Sikorsky, provided the first "factory" for the Sikorsky Aero Engineering Corporation—a chicken farm near Roosevelt Field, Long Island. At first, only a small band of Russians worked on the aircraft and lived at the farm in communal fashion. Besides the Utgoff family, there were Sikorsky and his family and a small

The S-29-A takes shape on rural Long Island. The company moved a short distance away to a rented hangar at Roosevelt Field in late 1923. (UTC AS-79)

number of workers. Sikorsky's family included his sisters, Olga and Helen, and Helen's two children, Dimitri (Jimmy) Viner, Jr., and Galina Viner, and Igor's daughter, Tania, from a brief first marriage, all of whom had just recently arrived from Russia.

The project prompted local curiosity and before long interested onlookers found themselves drawn there as volunteers, some working full time, others assisting on nights or weekends. The workforce ebbed and flowed, but stabilized at between twelve and fourteen men. Former Russian officers and other unemployed veterans, all of whom had fled the Bolshevik Revolution, gravitated to the project. Despite their economic plight, they were highly educated and possessed a great deal of mechanical and engineering talent. As a group, they exhibited enormous faith in Igor Sikorsky and his vision. These intangible factors were critical, because the corporation required dedicated work for little and intermittent pay.

The building of the fourteen-passenger S-29-A ("A" for America) became the one and only objective of the Sikorsky team gathered on Long Island. Hospital bedsteads, retrieved from junkyards, yielded angle iron which formed 90 percent of the structure of the aircraft. The pieces were bolted together and, when combined with wire bracing, produced an unusually strong structure. The chicken coop served as the machine shop where handmade tools and parts were fashioned. The duralumin fuselage and wings, supported by wooden horses, were assembled in the open. Workers and chickens vied for precious rivets, the former for the airplane and the latter for digestive purposes. The budget was so strained that these digestive aids were later retrieved from the chickens who then graced the dinner table each Saturday night.[4]

With the approach of winter in 1923, Sikorsky rented hangar space at nearby Roosevelt Field, where the S-29-A was finally assembled. The shift in location was made possible by a gift of $5,000 from the famous Russian composer Sergei Rachmaninoff. Work continued throughout the winter in this cold, leaky hangar, but there were times when the work crew went without pay for weeks. When assembled, the sesquiplane transport was 49 feet 10 inches long, 13 feet 6 inches high, and had a span of 69 feet on the upper wing and 62 feet 6 inches on the lower wing.

On May 4, 1924, the S-29-A was ready for its

first flight. Sikorsky permitted eight workers to board because, even though he suspected the airplane was underpowered, he felt he owed these dedicated people the privilege of participating in the first flight. As Sikorsky feared, the two Hispano Suiza engines (each generating only 300 horsepower) were unable to provide sufficient power for safe flight. He took the S-29-A to an altitude of only about 100 feet, negotiated a brief touch-and-go at Mitchel Field, and then when one engine failed, crash landed on the nearby Salisbury golf course. No one was injured, but the S-29-A suffered substantial damage. The next day the airplane was carried back to Roosevelt Field and repairs began.

The aircraft was repaired over the summer. Liberty engines of 400 horsepower were located to replace the Hispano Suizas; however, their price tag nearly exhausted the company's resources. In a long and intense meeting with his stockholders, Sikorsky managed to persuade them to contribute the necessary funds to continue the project. Then he unlocked the door and let them out.

The first successful flight of the S-29-A occurred finally on September 25, 1924. This time Sikorsky took only three men on the flight. The flight proved to be an unqualified success, prompting a New York newspaper to describe it as a triumph of Russian ingenuity and perseverance.[5] It was apparent that the Liberty engines had supplied more than enough power to make the S-29-A a success. Over the next few days, Sikorsky treated his stockholders and crew to well-deserved flights in the S-29-A, his first successful American design.

Sikorsky realized that publicity would be crucial to his success and therefore granted demonstration flights for the public, the military, and the press. By the end of 1924, the fourteen-passenger S-29-A had made forty-five flights and clocked a total time in the air of fifteen hours and thirty-seven minutes.[6] The large cockpit area and the comfortable passenger seats in the roomy cabin gave the aircraft a unique appearance. Over 420 passengers flew with Sikorsky in 1924, including Lieutenant Cecil E. Archer of the U.S. Army Air Service and Alexander Klemin, professor of aeronautics at New York University. During his flight, Professor Klemin and five of his students observed a series of performance tests, including cruising with only one engine. The favorable results of these test flights were reported in *Aviation* magazine.[7] By the end of

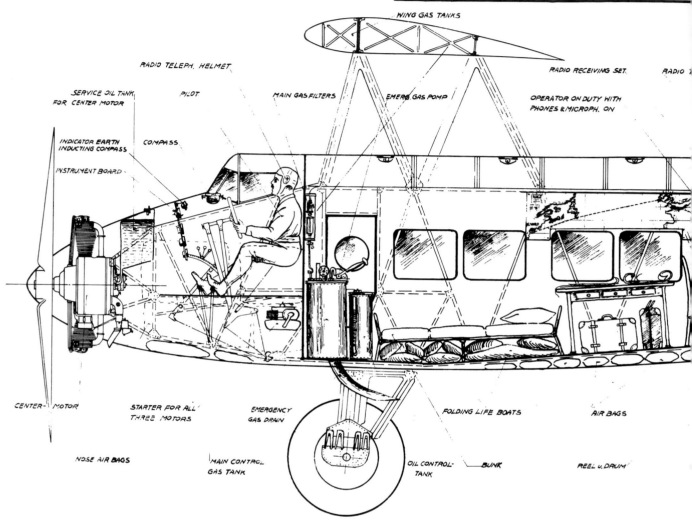

WING GAS TANKS

RADIO RECEIVING SET. RADIO

RADIO TELEPH. HELMET

SERVICE OIL TANK
FOR CENTER MOTOR

PILOT

MAIN GAS FILTERS

EMERG. GAS POMP

OPERATOR ON DUTY WITH
PHONES & MICROPH. ON

INDICATOR EARTH
INDUCTING COMPASS

COMPASS

INSTRUMENT BOARD

CENTER MOTOR

STARTER FOR ALL
THREE MOTORS

EMERGENCY
GAS DRAIN

FOLDING LIFE BOATS

AIR BAGS

NOSE AIR BAGS

MAIN CONTROL
GAS TANK

OIL CONTROL
TANK

BUNK

REEL v. DRUM

Detailed drawing of the S-35. Originally envisioned as a
large transport aircraft, the S-35 was enlarged and
modified for the transatlantic attempt by René Fonck in
1926. (UTC AS-36)

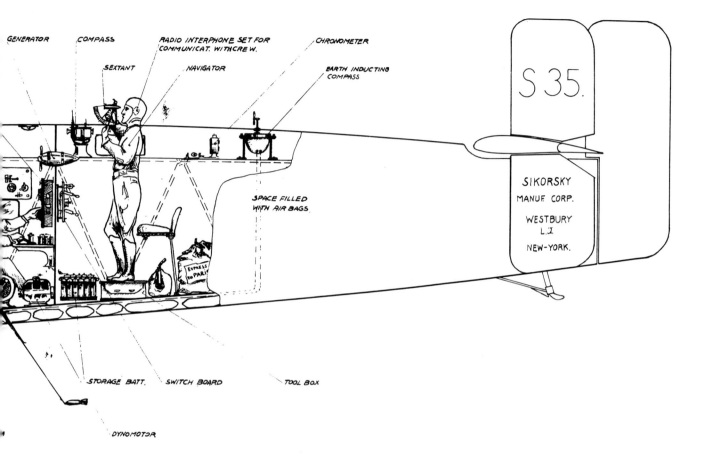

GENERATOR COMPASS RADIO INTERPHONE SET FOR COMMUNICAT. WITH CREW. CHRONOMETER

SEXTANT NAVIGATOR EARTH INDUCTING COMPASS

S 35.

SIKORSKY MANUF CORP. WESTBURY L.I NEW-YORK.

SPACE FILLED WITH AIR BAGS

EXPRESS TO PARIS

STORAGE BATT. SWITCH BOARD TOOL BOX

DYNOMOTOR

the year, Sikorsky made the S-29-A available for lease to earn some monetary return on the stockholders' investment.

Demonstration flights continued throughout 1925. Harold Hartney, a World War I ace, had visions of using the S-29-A design for his proposed airline that would link Boston, New York, Detroit, Chicago, Minneapolis, and St. Paul. The Sikorsky Aero Engineering Corporation's first real paying job was the transportation of two baby grand pianos from New York to Washington, D.C., which generated favorable publicity for Sikorsky. A variety of publicity stunts followed, ranging from air photography to airborne radio broadcasts from

inside the S-29-A. When a request was received from a member of the press to take photographs of New York City from the wingtip of the aircraft, Sikorsky agreed, but first made a trial run to see how the airplane would handle. He enlisted the services of his nephew, Jimmy Viner, who sat on a wingtip while he flew around the countryside. Viner made a wonderful photograph of his uncle flying the plane and attracted a bit of attention from pilots at nearby Mitchel Field.[8]

Sikorsky himself piloted the S-29-A more than two hundred times. In addition, his two associates, Nicholas Solovioff and Michael Gluhareff, also became accomplished S-29-A

Crowds gather to inspect the newly rolled-out S-35. Public interest was high because French aviator Fonck was hoping to win the $25,000 Orteig prize for the first non-stop transatlantic crossing. (UTC 140)

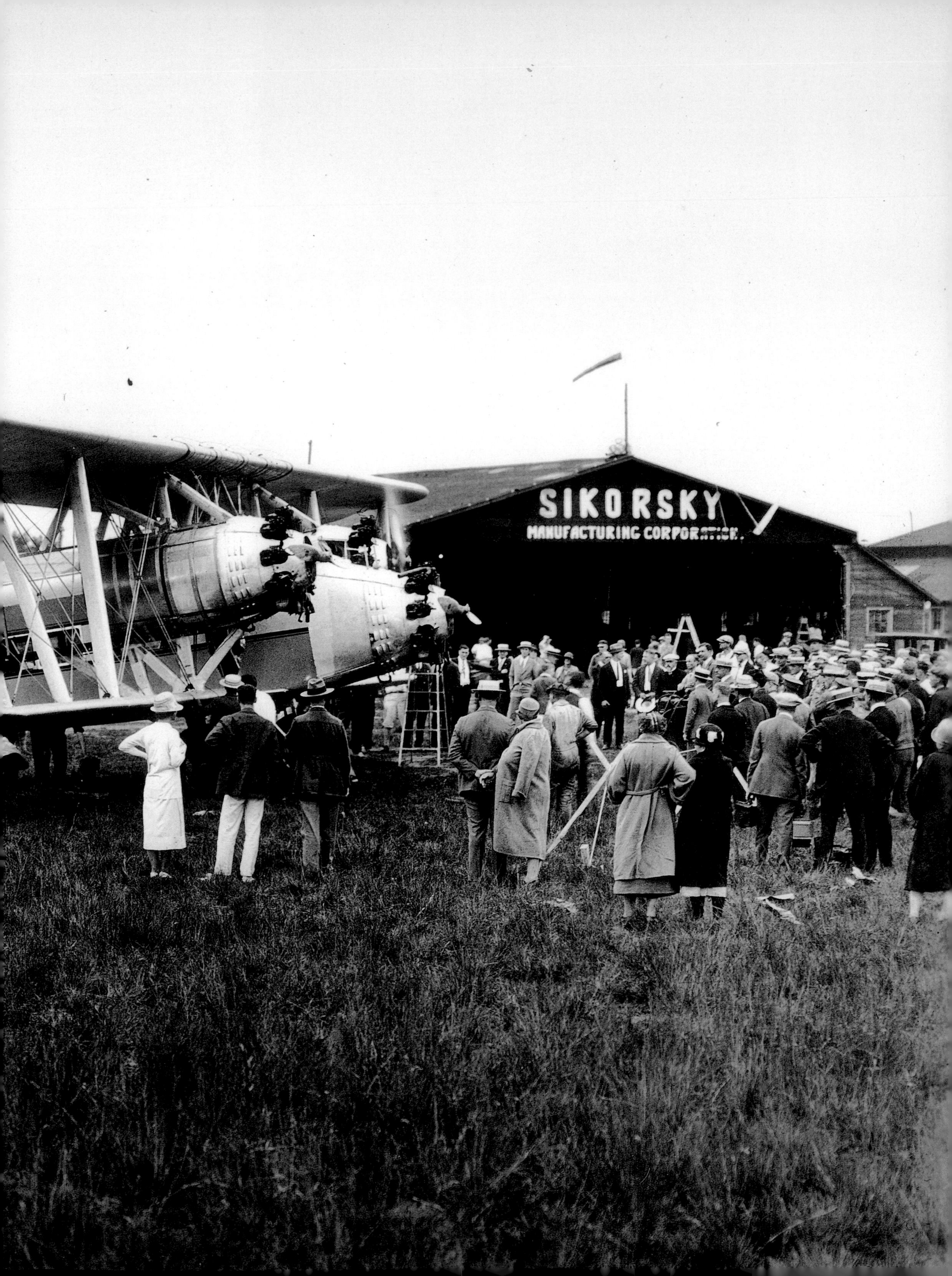
SIKORSKY
MANUFACTURING CORPORATION

pilots. The S-29-A proved to be a durable aircraft and the impressive passenger logs illustrated the broad public attention focused on the project.

Crashes were still an all too familiar part of aviation, as Sikorsky found out one evening when returning from a flight to Staten Island. The S-29-A was not equipped for night flight, and they had left Staten Island late in the day. Dusk descended upon the aircraft and its passengers. Through a mix-up with the ground crew, who failed to light a signal flare, Sikorsky overshot Roosevelt Field and flew on into the darkness. Realizing he had missed the field, he decided to land. He began his descent, and while he searched for a landing site in the gray landscape below, there was a sudden bump. Sikorsky continued on and made a safe landing in a field. Later he discovered a tree limb protruding from one wing and surmised that he had clipped the branches of some trees on his way down. This sobering event illustrated how close the aircraft had come to disaster. Its loss would have been fatal to the company. Sikorsky saved the tree limb and placed it in his office as a symbol of fate.

The Sikorsky Aero Engineering Corporation, with its investors and the S-29-A design team, hoped a new era in commercial air transportation was near at hand. The S-29-A was an excellent aircraft, but the company received no contracts. The anticipated market for large transport aircraft had not appeared. To recover some of the investment, Sikorsky decided in 1926 to sell the S-29-A to the flamboyant racing pilot Roscoe Turner. Turner flew the aircraft for advertising and charter flights, and kept in touch with Sikorsky regarding performance, hours, and miles flown. In 1928 Turner sold the S-29-A to Howard Hughes for use in the movie *Hell's Angels*. The airplane was modified to resemble a German Gotha bomber and was destroyed in a spectacular crash.[9]

Even as these events unfolded, the economic context for the aviation industry began to change. The role of the federal government proved to be crucial. In February 1925, the Contract Air Mail Act, more commonly known as the Kelly Act, authorized the Post Office Department to award airmail service contracts to private airlines. The Act, sponsored by Representative Melville Clyde Kelly of Pittsburgh, stimulated the airline industry and gave it a sense of stability, with a promise for the future, by awarding domestic contracts for three to five years with guaranteed subsidy for each mile flown.[10] Aviation now had a base

Sikorsky stands beside a wooden mock-up of the S-38 at the College Point plant. The mock-up served as the model for the cockpit and controls, and was used as a form against which metal parts could be hand beaten into shape. (UTC 632)

upon which to build, as the lucrative contracts attracted entrepreneurs who suddenly viewed aviation as a worthwhile investment opportunity. The altered environment provided Sikorsky with contracts for smaller aircraft and this, coupled with the success of the S-29-A as a prototype commercial aircraft, attracted new investors to his company.

On July 21, 1925, the company was reorganized as the Sikorsky Manufacturing Corporation, with Arnold Dickinson of Fitchburg, Massachusetts, as president and Igor Sikorsky as vice-president. The new corporation blended the old Russian design team with experienced American businessmen anxious to exploit the new aviation market. Dickinson took over daily management of the company, a job Sikorsky was eager to relinquish, and, even more important, Dickinson assumed responsibility for the task of raising capital.

While Sikorsky now had more time to devote to design work, his close associate, Michael Gluhareff, had already produced a set of new, more efficient wings for the old World War I JN-4D Jenny. His redesigned wing provided a dramatic increase in the rate of climb and in the speed of the aircraft. About twenty pairs of G-S-1 (Gluhareff-Sikorsky) wings were sold

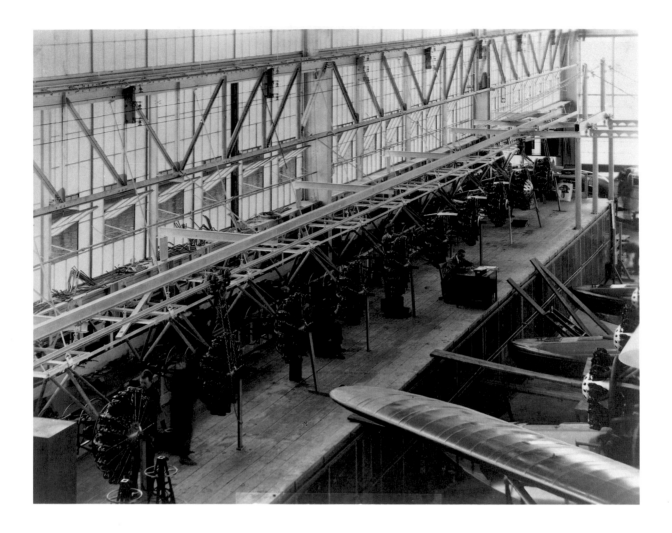

for Jennies, the Curtiss Oriole, and other popular aircraft. This special project provided much needed income and prestige for the company, and was only the beginning of a long line of airfoils and wings designed by Gluhareff for Sikorsky aircraft.

Sikorsky now gambled on the production of a number of smaller designs aimed at garnering some of the airmail market. His S-30, which never made it past the blueprint stage, was designed as a light transport or mail airplane with a range of six hundred miles. Next came the S-31, a small all-metal transport plane with a 45-foot wingspan and a single Wright Whirl-

wind J-4 engine. The S-31 boasted a cruising speed of 110 miles per hour and was offered in four configurations: mail, observation/bomber, four-passenger, or photographic. The only S-31 produced had a two-place, open cockpit and a central cabin area configured for photographic work, as it was built for the Fairchild Flying Corporation. Following its flight tests with Bert Acosta and Homer Berry, in September of 1925, the S-31 was flown in the New York Air Races in October. Piloted by Richard Depew, Fairchild's chief pilot, the S-31 flew in two separate races, placing seventh and ninth, respectively. The S-31 was then flown to South America by Fairchild for aerial

A long line of Pratt & Whitney Wasp engines destined for Sikorsky S-38s. The factory at College Point, Long Island, offered the first modern facility for the Sikorsky company. However, the immediate success of the S-38 swamped the plant and forced Sikorsky to relocate. (UTC AS-532)

photographic work in the jungles and mountainous terrain.

The S-32 followed, and, again, only one was built—for the Andean National Corporation, a subsidiary of the Standard Oil Company operating in Colombia. The *Ancol*, as the S-32 was named, was a five-place observation plane equipped with pontoons, and it flew, in one year, a total of 42,000 miles up and down the Magdalena River, ferrying supplies, payroll, and personnel. Although the S-32 had a good performance record, the rigors of the damp climate in South America played havoc with the fabric-covered wings and wooden pontoons, and it proved to be short-lived as a transport.

Sikorsky's next design was the S-33 Messenger, a wooden biplane with a wingspan of 32 feet and a cruising speed of 110 miles per hour. One of the two S-33s built flew in the 1925 Glenn H. Curtiss Trophy Race with, among others, the Waco 9, the Bellanca CE, and the Thomas Morse S4E. The Thomas Morse was piloted by Basil Rowe, who would later become a Pan American captain and fly the S-40 on its maiden flight from Miami to the Canal Zone. Also in the race was an Oriole-Sikorsky, featuring the Gluhareff-Sikorsky wings. The

S-33 was piloted by Sikorsky worker Alexander P. Krapish, and was fitted with a Lawrance L-4 engine which developed trouble, forcing Krapish out of the race. Unfortunately, the S-33, as with its immediate predecessors, slipped into obscurity. Despite considerable effort, Sikorsky had failed to penetrate the market or carve out a logical and profitable niche in the aviation field.

At this juncture, Sikorsky designed his first amphibian, the S-34. The twin-engined S-34, powered by two Wright J-4 radial engines, carried seven people and flew at a top speed of 125 miles per hour. The sesquiplane's upper wing had a span of 56 feet, while the fuselage of the aircraft looked more like a boat hull. Unfortunately, during a test flight over Long Island Sound, one engine failed and the S-34 crashed and sank; all aboard, including Igor Sikorsky, escaped injury and were rescued.[11] Although the S-34 was lost, its design and production were an important phase for Sikorsky in his quest for a practical transport, as the S-34 was the forerunner of the S-38, ultimately Sikorsky's most successful aircraft design.

Sikorsky's dream of developing a large transport aircraft remained in the forefront of his

An Inter-Island Airways S-38 soaring over the spectacular scenery of the Hawaiian Islands. (UTC D-117)

mind. By 1926, he had his next opportunity to begin design work on such a large aircraft. The new S-35 was designed as a sixteen-passenger, twin-engine aircraft with a crew of three. At the time there was a competition under way to see who could fly the first non-stop flight across the Atlantic Ocean to win the $25,000 prize offered by Raymond Orteig, a wealthy New York hotel owner. The S-35 design appealed to René Fonck, a French ace of World War I, who with his backers was seeking a multi-engine airplane to make the Atlantic crossing and win the prize. Fonck convinced Sikorsky to redesign the S-35 to attempt this record flight. Substantial modifications of the original S-35 followed. The most prominent change was the addition of a third engine for power and safety. Fonck chose three 425-horsepower Gnome-Rhone Jupiter engines.

Brief performance tests of the S-35 proved that the aircraft could climb with two engines and even maintain flight on one engine. The upper wings, originally projected to be 76 feet long, were extended to 101 feet, while the lower wings were extended to 76 feet. Sikorsky continued his use of duralumin frame construction, with internal wire bracing and an exterior fabric covering. No welding was used;

Osa and Martin Johnson's S-38, *Osa's Ark*, settles in for the evening on the African plain. (UTC AS-129)

Next Page
The *American Clipper* over New York City. (NASM)

instead, as with the S-29-A, steel bolts and rivets held the aircraft together. The S-35 had three self-compensating rudders, allowing the plane to fly with any two of the three engines. Extra fuel tanks were added along with an auxiliary landing gear that would help support the heavily loaded aircraft on its takeoff and then be jettisoned. The projected range of the aircraft was over 4,000 miles; takeoff weight was estimated at 24,000 pounds. The enclosed cockpit, equipped with dual controls, was in front of the large cabin (4 feet wide by 6 feet high and 15½ feet long), which now contained extra fuel tanks.

While the aircraft was hailed as a triumph of engineering, the seeds of a future disaster had been planted. The promoters of the Fonck flight bickered over money and the selection of the flight crew. These disputes created considerable confusion in the Fonck camp, and Sikorsky was alarmed over these developments. The promoters of the Fonck flight clamored for an early flight, before winter weather set in, but such pressure ran against the orderly procedures Sikorsky normally insisted upon.

Modifications to the S-35 at Roosevelt Field were time-consuming. When the aircraft was

The *American Clipper* perches on the edge of its ramp, wheels still down, as it is prepared for its next flight. (UTC AS-43)

completed in August, Sikorsky planned a long series of flight tests to ensure that all systems would perform properly and to obtain the final desired flight performance parameters. By September 14, the S-35 had made twenty-three flights covering a total of about 2,500 miles in twenty-three hours and fifty minutes. But none of these flights had been made at the estimated fully loaded weight of 24,200 pounds. Sikorsky would have preferred delaying the flight until spring of 1927, but the promoters rejected his proposal and ended his testing program. Meanwhile, the press hovered and reported every move.[12]

Plans to launch the flight on September 16 were foiled by a fuel leak. By the night of September 20, the weather had cleared again and the extended forecast predicted a window of opportunity for the next day. Following a night of fueling, using fifty barrels of gasoline, the aircraft was weighed and found to be nearly 4,000 pounds heavier than expected. At daybreak, the wind suddenly shifted, becoming a tailwind moving down the length of the runway which had been hurriedly extended across several small roads. The S-35 began its takeoff roll before a large crowd of spectators lining the field, with pilot René Fonck, co-pilot Lieutenant William Curtin, mechanic and Sikorsky employee Jacob Islamoff, and radio operator Charles Clavier. As the heavily laden plane rolled down the runway, it crossed the first bumpy road, damaging the auxiliary landing gear and then the tail skid. With the tail now dragging on the ground, the S-35 swerved, narrowly missing the crowd, as Fonck tried to maintain control. Fonck managed to steer the aircraft back on the runway, but now he lacked sufficient takeoff speed. Failing to gain altitude, the S-35 plunged down an embankment, and after a dramatic pause, burst into flames. Fonck and Curtin were able to escape, but Islamoff and Clavier were trapped and killed in the inferno.[13]

Rene Fonck's hopes of a transatlantic flight had been crushed, while the loss of the two crewmen deepened the tragedy of the day. Beyond the loss of life, Sikorsky now had to face the loss of a beautiful and expensive airplane, and his company was again in deep financial trouble. No one directly blamed Sikorsky or the S-35 for the crash, but the end of the S-35 constituted a major blow to the company.

Despite all the negative publicity from the crash, the company was still able to move its manufacturing operations to more modern fa-cilities at College Point, New York, in late 1926. There, in a rented factory where the S-34 was assembled and tested, parts for the new S-37 were produced. Fonck and Sikorsky agreed to try again, and work began in earnest on the S-37 *Ville de Paris*. Conceived from the outset as a transatlantic plane, the S-37 was a twin-engine sesquiplane with a cruising speed of 120 miles per hour, similar in construction to the S-35 and S-29-A before it. The aircraft was built to accommodate gross loads of 15,000 pounds and the undercarriage was to sustain a gross load of up to 21,000 pounds.

Unfortunately, Lindbergh's solo transatlantic flight of 1927 ended the plans of Fonck and Sikorsky for the S-37, and the aircraft was sold to American Airways International, Inc. Christened the *Southern Star*, the S-37 began the Sikorsky tradition of making survey flights for future commercial air routes. In 1929, after a 7,000-mile flight from New York to Santiago, Chile, the *Southern Star* blazed a trail across the Andes, flying as high as 19,000 feet above sea level, to Buenos Aires, Argentina. However, as with the S-29-A, there still was no market for a transport with such a large payload. A second S-37, the *Guardian*, was tested as a night bomber for the Army Air Corps, but did not win a contract.

The Lindbergh flight signaled a new era for the aviation industry. A so-called "Lindbergh Boom" followed with the rise of new aviation companies, airlines, and a flurry of corporate mergers, and it appeared that new markets for aircraft were about to open.

Sikorsky was already working on new designs, and by the summer of 1927, he had tested his latest design, an open-cockpit, eight-seat amphibian. The S-36, a modified and enlarged version of the S-34, was aimed at capturing a share of the small cargo and passenger market in the now highly charged aviation environment.

The decision to build an amphibian was based on several factors. Sikorsky reasoned that most large cities and centers of industry were located on large bodies of water or rivers. Established airports were rare and new ones were expensive to build. Lindbergh's flight had proven the aircraft a viable means of transportation, but many felt that traveling long distances over open water in land planes was inherently dangerous. Also, overland aircraft were being produced in abundance but no one had yet designed a successful amphibian. Sikorsky decided to gamble on producing an amphibian that carried a smaller useful load than his previous large transports.

The plush, paneled interior of the S-40, complete with backgammon table. Sikorsky Clippers set the standard for airline interiors. (Finne Collection, NASM)

The S-36, as opposed to earlier Sikorsky designs, went beyond the prototype stage. Six S-36 amphibian-sesquiplanes were ordered, each boasting a boat-hull silhouette with retractable landing gear and two powerful Wright Whirlwind J-5 engines that gave the S-36 a cruising speed of 100 miles per hour.

One S-36 was sold to Frances Grayson, a wealthy real estate broker from Long Island, who planned to be the first woman to fly across the Atlantic. Grayson felt secure with her S-36, which she christened *The Dawn*, as the amphibian appeared ideal for long-distance flight. If mechanical troubles should occur, she reasoned that she and her crew could land on the water, make repairs, and continue the flight. Unlike Lindbergh, Grayson was going only as a passenger, having hired Oscar Omdahl as her pilot. After two false starts terminated by mechanical and weather problems, she took off on December 23, 1927, with Omdahl and two other crew members, never to be seen again. Grayson however, was the first of a number of sport pilots to purchase Sikorsky aircraft for adventure.

The Andean National Corporation, the same company that had purchased the only S-32,

bought an S-36 for continued operations up and down the Magdalena River in Colombia. Here the S-36 proved its value as a sturdy corporate transport capable of flying under primitive conditions. The Navy purchased an S-36 for testing as a patrol plane in 1927. Designated the XPS-1, the aircraft was used primarily as a utility transport, but the Navy was interested in future Sikorsky designs, as was the U.S. Army Air Corps. A fourth S-36 went to the newly formed Pan American Airways on December 7, 1927, to survey the Caribbean, along with two Fokker F-VIIs, laying the groundwork for proposed routes.

The purchase of the S-36 was the beginning of a long relationship between Sikorsky and Pan American. Juan Trippe, the twenty-seven-year-old president of Pan American Airways, was building an airline. An ambitious man whose interest in flying dated back to his days at Yale, Trippe aimed to build his own airline that would establish transoceanic routes. He was already a veteran of the domestic scene, having founded Long Island Airways and done a brief stint at Colonial Air Transport. In 1928, Trippe's Aviation Corporation of America merged with Pan American, which had recently won the Key West–Havana airmail contract, and Trippe lost no time taking control. Leav-

ing the domestic routes to others, Trippe and
Pan American looked south for expansion.
Lindbergh had just completed a triumphant
9,000-mile goodwill tour of the Caribbean in
early 1928. The Postmaster General established
airmail routes along Lindbergh's flight path, as
a result of the Foreign Air Mail Act of 1928,
and Trippe eventually engineered a Pan American monopoly of all Caribbean air routes. His
plans enjoyed favor in Washington, D.C.,
where some politicians and military officials
were alarmed by European sponsored airlines,
through which Germans in particular were
gaining a foothold in Latin America. Washington decided, with plenty of help from
Trippe, that one strong American airline was a
good foreign policy.[14]

To achieve his ambitions Trippe needed dependable aircraft with long-range capabilities, and
he turned to the new Sikorsky S-38 as a solution. The S-38 represented for Igor Sikorsky a
major step toward his dream of designing and
building a successful line of transport aircraft
in the United States. The S-38 was born out of
the success of the S-36 and Sikorsky's correct
hunch that there would be a place for larger
amphibians in the growing aviation market.
The S-38 carried eight passengers and two
crew members, with its more powerful 420-

horsepower Pratt & Whitney Wasp engines, at
100 miles per hour. The unique-looking aircraft had a long nose, a boat-shaped wooden
hull covered in aluminum, and twin tails set
on high outriggers. There was a cluttered appearance of struts and wires between the 71-
foot upper parasol wing and the lower wing,
but it proved to be a record-breaking aircraft
when Sikorsky's pilot, Boris Sergievsky, a former Russian fighter pilot in World War I, set a
world altitude record of 19,065 feet carrying a
load of 4,409 pounds. The S-38 was the first
twin-engine aircraft to maintain level flight at
gross weight using only one engine. Three
S-38As were built, followed by the S-38B with
its more gently sloped forward window.

Pan American Airways selected the S-38 for
the inaugural airmail flight from Miami to the
Panama Canal, beginning February 4, 1929,
with Lindbergh, as the new Pan American
technical advisor, piloting the aircraft. While
Lindbergh preferred landplanes and saw them
as the future of air transportation, he acknowledged that no aircraft in 1929 was reliable for
long flights over water. The S-38 amphibian
was the prudent choice. Pan American's chief
engineer, André Priester, shared this view. He
was an advocate of air safety and felt that an
amphibian was the only means of providing

safe, scheduled airmail and passenger service in the Caribbean. In September of 1929, Charles and Anne Lindbergh and Juan and Betty Trippe made a spectacular flight throughout the Caribbean in an S-38. The press followed the S-38 from Miami as it island-hopped to Paramaribo, Dutch Guyana, where Lindbergh dropped off the mail, and then back along the northern coast of South America and up into Central America, where Trippe was making arrangements for the expansion of Pan American into Latin America. Huge crowds greeted the S-38 everywhere. Sikorsky could not have asked for a better public relations program. A total of thirty-eight S-38s

were purchased by Pan American for the Caribbean fleet and Latin American subsidiaries.

The S-38 amphibian became the aircraft of choice for numerous airlines including Colonial Western Airways, Northwest Airlines, Inter-Island Airways of Hawaii, and New York Rio & Buenos Aires Lines, which was swallowed by Pan American. Sikorsky sold 111 S-38s to commercial airlines, operators of business aircraft, private owners, and the military (navy designation XPS-2, PS3; army designation C-6). It became *the* corporate aircraft for many highly successful businesses, performing transport duties for employees as well as corporate executives. The S-38 was used for charter flights by the Curtiss Flying Service, for geological surveys and exploration by Creole Petroleum Corporation in South America, and for the transportation of officials and for sales promotions by Pan American Petroleum Company. The Andean Corporation purchased an S-38, its third Sikorsky aircraft.

Private owners of the S-38 included Martin and Osa Johnson, whose spectacular expeditions took them to Africa and Borneo. The Johnsons were authors and photographers, whose popular articles, books, and films quite often featured their Sikorsky aircraft as well as wildlife. They had two amphibians, *Osa's Ark*, an S-38 (painted in zebra stripes) and the smaller *Spirit of Africa*, an S-39 (painted in leopard spots). Martin Johnson wrote to Sikorsky in 1933, "It was a wonderful day for us when we bought *Osa's Ark* and *Spirit of Africa*, we just cannot understand why all air minded people don't buy them in preference to any other planes."[15] Other private owners included Charles R. Walgreen, president of Walgreen and Company, John Hertz, founder of a prominent taxi company, New York financier James C. Wilson, New York sportsman Harry Payne Whitney, and Joseph Patterson, publisher of *Liberty* magazine.

The S-38 had proven to be an instant success, and it was immediately clear that the small Sikorsky factory at College Point, Long Island, would not be able to handle the anticipated production schedule. Sikorsky was compelled to search for new plant facilities. His investors prevailed upon him to relocate closer to them in New England, and eventually they settled on Stratford, Connecticut, on the north shore of Long Island Sound. The mouth of the Housatonic River and the Sound provided the needed access to calm waters necessary for the testing of Sikorsky's flying boats. The new factory became the firm's first truly modern factory capable of handling the increased number of production orders. Boat-hull testing on the Housatonic and the Sound became an integral part of the testing program that went into the design of each flying boat. In addition, a vertical wind tunnel was built for model spin testing. At Stratford, twenty-one S-39s were also produced. A smaller, single-engine version of the S-38, the S-39 carried four or five people and appealed to sport and executive pilots of the day, as well as to commercial airlines.

The expansion of the company resulted in a reorganization as the Sikorsky Aviation Company early in 1929. More important, the immediate success of the S-38 design attracted the attention of the large and powerful United Aircraft and Transport Corporation. In July of 1929, Sikorsky Aviation became one of many divisions of this holding corporation which, among others, included Pratt & Whitney engines, Hamilton Standard propellers, Chance-Vought aircraft, and Boeing Air Transport. However, production at the new plant coincided with the stock market crash, and a resulting cancellation of orders.

Sikorsky's business ties with United Aircraft and Pan American Airways proved fortuitous throughout the Depression and, while some cost-cutting and belt-tightening were prudent, the production of S-38s and new designs continued. Eugene E. Wilson, formerly of Hamilton Standard, was given the task of melding an "Old World" Russian community and a modern aircraft manufacturing plant and he succeeded to a remarkable degree. Nonetheless, the S-38 was still a maintenance problem because mismatched metals corroded one another and the salt water environment of the amphibian took its toll.

Juan Trippe required a new, larger amphibian, but in the early 1930s technology was not keeping pace with his vision of a global airline.

Pan American was rapidly expanding its routes around Latin America and required aircraft with a larger payload and range. Sikorsky designed the S-40 to meet these requirements, at least temporarily. The S-40 was nicknamed the "clipper" ship by Trippe, who saw flying boats such as the S-40 as reminiscent of the great sailing vessels of the past, capable of reaching distant ports of the earth. Performance and payload were the key as the horizons of air travel continued to expand over greater and greater distances. Pan American was directly involved with the design of the S-40, and provided for consultation not only its head engineer, André Priester, but also its technical advisor, Charles Lindbergh, and the president, Juan Trippe. The design team included Sikorsky's wing specialist, Michael Gluhareff, as well. During the design phase, Sikorsky and Lindbergh discussed various locations for the cockpit, hoping to avoid the negative aspects of its aft placement on the S-38s (during take-off, the engines blew water back onto the window of the cockpit, causing a temporary loss of forward vision). Placement of the cockpit in the rear of the aircraft had been a traditional practice in the aviation community. Lindbergh suggested moving the cockpit forward, about a third of the way between the wing and the

front of the hull, for better visibility, and the design was completed.[16]

Trippe was in a hurry for his new flying boat for Latin America and the S-40 temporarily suited his purposes. The S-40 carried up to forty passengers and cruised at a speed of 115 miles per hour. Four Pratt & Whitney T2D1 Hornet engines powered the flying boat, which had a range of up to nine hundred miles. Three S-40s were built. The first, the *American Clipper*, was christened on October 12, 1931, by Mrs. Herbert Hoover. It was followed shortly by the *Caribbean Clipper* and the *Southern Clipper*. The *American Clipper* made its maiden voyage from Miami to the

Canal Zone on November 19, 1931, flown by Pan American pilot Basil Rowe and copiloted by Charles Lindbergh and Igor Sikorsky. These three flying boats successfully completed the expansion of Pan American Airways throughout South America. In addition, the S-40 established numerous flying records and, before and after retirement from Pan American, continued to serve as charter aircraft and trainers.

The S-40 offered its passengers unusual luxury and comfort. It featured upholstered chairs, backgammon tables, and spacious compartments. Hot meals, prepared in a small galley, were served by a uniformed steward. For ap-

Pan American officials seated on the tail of an S-42 on the Housatonic River. At left is Grover Loening, a member of the Board of Directors, third from the right is President Juan Trippe, next to him his wife Betty, and at the far right, Technical Advisor Charles Lindbergh. The three other individuals are unidentified. (UTC AS-534)

pearance, the ship's crew adopted handsome naval-style uniforms. The elegance of a flight in an S-40 made air travel romantic as well as safe. Pan American obtained considerable publicity, and even inspired the 1933 movie *Flying Down to Rio*, an RKO film that included shots of the S-40 and introduced the dance team of Fred Astaire and Ginger Rogers.

But the S-40 was only a stopgap measure for Trippe, who now sought a longer-range flying boat to extend the Pan American overseas routes into the Atlantic and the Pacific. The scope and rigors of these routes demanded larger, more advanced flying boats with increased payload capabilities. Therefore, in the summer of 1931, he asked six aircraft manufacturers to submit designs for a large flying boat. In 1932, Trippe accepted the designs of Glenn L. Martin and Igor Sikorsky, and ordered three flying boats from each. Sikorsky's S-42 design was not only cheaper than Martin's ($210,487 versus $417,000), but it was promised for the spring of 1934 while the Martin was not expected until the fall of 1934 (and subsequently was delayed much later than that).[17]

Sikorsky's successful design was a four-engine, all-metal, high-wing monoplane. Lindbergh and Sikorsky had made preliminary plans for

the S-42 while flying the S-40 on the Miami–Canal Zone flight in 1931 (using the backs of menus), and continued the collaboration throughout the design phase, which included, once again, André Preister and Michael Gluhareff, as well as experts from Pratt & Whitney and Hamilton Standard. Everything about the S-42 was impressive. The largest aircraft of its day, the S-42 was an imposing 69 feet long and 21 feet 9 inches high, with a wingspan of 118 feet 2 inches. With a cruising speed of 150 miles per hour, the S-42's four 750-horsepower Pratt & Whitney engines provided a range of 1,200 miles when loaded with thirty-two passengers. Hamilton Standard provided radically new variable pitch propellers that allowed the angle of the propellers to be set at takeoff for maximum power and then adjusted in flight to fewer revolutions per minute for lower fuel consumption at cruising speed. Modern flush riveting, fully cowled engines, and a streamlined, all-metal hull added to the performance of the S-42.

The key to the success of the S-42, however, lay in its high wing-loading, the highest of the day—28.5 pounds per square foot. The bare weight of the S-42 was just under that of the S-40 (the wing area was also less); however, Sikorsky's refinements in the design and con-

The S-42 rising from the water. This sleek flying boat surprised the aviation industry with its remarkable performance. (UTC AS-208)

Next Page
The *Pan American Clipper* flies over San Francisco Bay, and the construction of the San Francisco-Oakland Bay Bridge, on its way to Hawaii. (UTC AS-125)

struction of the S-42 resulted in an aircraft capable of lifting much more payload (16,055 versus 13,000). For example, in rejecting the fashionable cantilever wing and using a braced wing, Sikorsky was able to reduce the weight of the wing, and thus the airframe. Two penalties of high wing-loading—a long takeoff run and a high landing speed—were offset with the design of a new variable wing flap which increased lift. The high wing-loading, in combination with all the other features, produced a comfortable flight for the passengers and phenomenal performance that allowed the S-42 to outperform any other transport aircraft.[18] In a stunning lecture before the Royal Aeronautical Society in London in 1934, Sikorsky explained how the S-42 was able to carry 1,000 pounds more payload and still have a better rate of climb than the British flying boat, the Short S.17 *Kent*. The lecture and subsequent publication demonstrate a marvel of engineering talent.[19] For its time, the S-42 was the premier flying boat.

Boris Sergievsky took the S-42 up for its first flight on March 29, 1934, and shortly thereafter set two world records. On August 1, 1934, the S-42 set a total of eight world records with Sergievsky, Captain Ed Musick of Pan American, and Charles Lindbergh in the cockpit.

The course of the S-42 took it from the Stratford lighthouse to the New Jersey side of the George Washington Bridge, down to Staten Island, up to Block Island and Point Judith, Rhode Island, and back to Stratford. During the eight-hour, 1,200-mile flight, the aircraft set records in speed and payload categories, bringing the total world records for the S-42 to ten. The record-setting Sikorsky aircraft was christened the *Brazilian Clipper* and was immediately put into Pan American service in South America, where Trippe had completed his acquisition of airmail contracts. The S-42 reduced the travel time from Miami to Buenos Aires from eight to five days.

Trippe committed his second S-42 to a different task. Stymied in his attempts to establish air service across the Atlantic, he eagerly shifted his attention to the Pacific, where Pan American would achieve its greatest successes with flying boats. Having gained permission to survey routes in a stepping stone pattern across the Pacific, he enlisted the help of the U.S. Navy to build seaplane bases at Wake and Midway islands. Initially, Trippe had counted on using the Martin 130 flying boats, which promised a longer range than the S-42, for survey flights from California to China; however, the Martin was delayed and Trippe had to go with the S-42.

On April 16, 1935, Captain Ed Musick took off from San Francisco for Hawaii flying a specially modified S-42 for transoceanic flight. The aircraft had been completely stripped inside and carried extra fuel tanks to extend its range, along with new navigational equipment. It made the 2,400-mile flight, and the first Pacific airmail flight, in eighteen hours and thirty-seven minutes and returned to San Francisco on April 22. While the flight to Hawaii was made in record time, the return flight proved to be much more harrowing as the crew battled headwinds and arrived five hours late (twenty-three hours and forty-one minutes) and nearly out of fuel.[20] The S-42

The *Bermuda Clipper* upon its arrival in Bermuda, on June 18, 1937, following the inaugural flight from New York. (NASM)

continued the survey hops across the Pacific: June 12, Honolulu-Midway (1,380 miles); August 9, Midway-Wake (1,260 miles); October 5, Wake-Guam, arriving back in San Franciso on October 24, 1935. Each flight made headline news for both Pan American and Sikorsky, and eventually the S-42 extended its survey flights all the way to Manila. However, it was the Martin 130, not the S-42, which lacked the range for passenger service, that made the inaugural commercial airmail flight from San Francisco to Honolulu on November 22, 1935.

Another S-42 and four S-42As, with a longer wing and uprated Hornet engines, were flown in Pan American service throughout the Ca-ribbean and Latin America. Three S-42Bs, with a wing-loading of thirty-three pounds per square foot and further improved engines, performed survey flights across the Pacific and Atlantic oceans. The S-42B carried twenty-four passengers 1,800 miles. Captain Ed Musick flew the S-42B, *Samoan Clipper,* on island-hopping survey flights from San Francisco to New Zealand in 1937 and was later killed in the crash of this aircraft near Pago Pago in January 1938.

Trippe's conquest of the Atlantic was proving much more difficult than his earlier exploits in Latin America. In Europe he faced already established government airlines which were not

The XPBS-1 (S-44), Navy patrol boat, and prototype for the VS-44 long-range transport. (UTC 6658)

about to give exclusive landing rights to a U.S. carrier. They demanded reciprocal landing rights in the United States, something Pan American was not authorized to give. Pan American, while the only U.S. international carrier, was not a state-owned government airline, although Trippe depended on the support of the U.S. Government to attain his objectives. Further complications arose with Imperial Airways of Great Britain with whom Trippe was bidding for reciprocal airmail contracts. Imperial did not have an aircraft anywhere near equal in performance to the S-42, thus transatlantic service was delayed indefinitely, or at least until a comparable British aircraft could be built.

Moreover, Pan American was under intense scrutiny from Senator Hugo L. Black, whose committee was investigating abuses in the airmail contracts system. Black, a Democrat from Alabama, convened his investigation in January 1934. He initially reviewed the domestic airmail contract system managed by former Postmaster General Walter F. Brown under the Hoover Administration. The investigation revealed a lack of competitive bidding and a tight circle of investors controlling the entire aviation industry. The Black Committee reflected the mood of President Franklin Roosevelt's New Deal, which aimed to break up the large aviation holding companies, including Sikorsky's own parent company United Aircraft and Transport (which was split into three new corporations: Boeing Aircraft, United Airlines, and United Aircraft, including Sikorsky, Pratt & Whitney, Chance Vought, and Hamilton Standard). The Black Committee then turned to foreign airmail contracts, but Trippe eventually managed to diffuse the issue by claiming further investigation might result in embarrassment for the United States.[21]

Due to these political delays, Pan American did not inaugurate commercial airline service with the S-42B *Bermuda Clipper* between Port Washington, New York, and Bermuda until June 1937. The *Bermuda Clipper* later extended Pan American service to Hong Kong, completing Trippe's conquest of the Pacific. Five Atlantic survey flights with the *Pan American III* began in 1937, but even then, full scheduled service did not become a reality until 1939. By the end of the decade, the S-42s had been surpassed by new, larger flying boats with longer range and greater passenger capabilities. In the end, Pan American purchased a total of ten S-42s.

This level of interest did not provide a broad economic base for further Sikorsky designs, although the company endeavored to be competitive. In 1935, Pan American offered a

$50,000 prize to aircraft manufacturers for the design of a large transoceanic flying boat capable of carrying fifty passengers over a distance of 5,000 miles. Sikorsky accepted the challenge, and by October, he and Michael Gluhareff presented preliminary drawings and specifications to Pan American. The plan fell short of Trippe's requirements. Sikorsky suggested a project for two planes, one to carry twenty-four passengers, the other to carry fifty passengers. In a memorandum to Sikorsky, dated November 25, 1935, Gluhareff reported that André Priester, as anticipated, would not accept anything smaller than the original specifications. Ultimately, Trippe decided to order the rival Boeing 314.

Sikorsky continued to advocate the development of a long-range flying boat. One article by Sikorsky in the *Journal of the Aeronautical Sciences* in 1936 prompted a response from Lindbergh, then living in England.[22] Lindbergh deeply admired Sikorsky, but saw the future of air transportation linked to the landplane. The flying boat had performed well during the formative years of air travel, although landplanes alone would possess the range to connect the major population centers of the world. Lindbergh predicted that future air travel would follow Great Circle routes, necessitating the use of northern airports year-round, a problem that flying boats, needing ice-free ports, could not overcome. Sikorsky cheerfully received his old friend's views and replied that he would indeed study potential designs of landplanes and even a flying wing.[23]

While the production of the large clipper ships occupied much of the Sikorsky factory's time, smaller flying boats were also being designed. The S-41, developed in 1931, was a twin-engine amphibian/monoplane which saw only limited success. Seven were constructed; three became navy transport/patrol aircraft, designated RS-1, while two others joined the Pan American fleet. This design lacked a clear commercial market and therefore was abandoned.

Later, in 1935, Sikorsky produced the S-43, a fifteen-passenger amphibian. Slightly larger that the S-41, and with more powerful, 750-horsepower Pratt & Whitney Hornet engines, the S-43 had a top speed of 182 miles per hour. With 400 gallons of fuel and a useful load of about 6,000 pounds, the S-43 had a range of 800 miles. The size and performance of the S-43 recaptured some of the old S-38 market for the company. Pan American and the U.S. Navy purchased nearly two-thirds of the fifty-three S-43s between them, while Inter-Island Airways happily began flying a Sikorsky amphibian once again. A French airline, Chargeurs Réuni, flew the S-43 along the west coast of Africa, while an affiliate airline of KLM flew S-43s in the Dutch East Indies. The army ordered six S-43s. Howard Hughes purchased a modified S-43-W, sporting two 760-horsepower Wright Cyclone engines, which he briefly considered using for his round-the-world flight before settling on the Lockheed 14. The S-43 continued Sikorsky's record-making tradition by setting four altitude records in April of 1936. Also in keeping with tradition, Pan American flew the S-43 for survey flights from Seattle to Juneau, Alaska.

Sikorsky's final venture into the production of large transport aircraft was the VS-44A (Vought-Sikorsky). Designed as a patrol bomber for the navy (designated XPBS-1) and first flown on August 13, 1937, the S-44 *Flying Dreadnought* lost out in competition to the Consolidated PB2Y. Subsequently, three VS-44A aircraft were produced in 1942 for American Export Airlines, which, with the help of the Roosevelt Administration, had finally broken Pan American's monopoly on international airline service. Powered by four Pratt & Whitney Wasp engines, these thirty-nine-passenger aircraft, dubbed the "Flying

Aces," flew non-stop across the North and South Atlantic over distances of nearly five thousand miles. During World War II, American Export Airlines operated a transatlantic service for the U.S. Navy, using VS-44As. Throughout their careers, the VS-44As established a number of long-distance firsts as well as a transatlantic record. The airline replaced the *Excalibur*, the *Excambian*, and the *Exeter* with Douglas C-54s (DC-4s) in September of 1945. The last surviving VS-44A, *Excambian*, was flown by Avalon Air Transport, which operated a twelve-mile shuttle service between Long Beach Harbor and Catalina Island in California between 1957 and 1967. In 1968, the *Excambian* moved to the Caribbean, the first home of Sikorsky flying boats, as a member of the Antilles Air Boats fleet. This aircraft is now being restored by a volunteer staff based at the Sikorsky Memorial Airport in Stratford, Connecticut.

The flying-boat era drew to a close in the late 1930s. Sikorsky produced plans for the AX-244-A and the AX-245-AB, featuring a fully cantilevered wing with six engines and a gracefully refined hull line, to meet Pan American's requirements for a transoceanic aircraft capable of a non-stop, 5,000-mile flight. The interior was a double-deck arrangement of private sleeper compartments and lounge areas,

connected with staircases. Neither design was accepted, however, as the era of the flying boat, to which Sikorsky had contributed so much, came to an end. Flying boats, with their dependence on warm-water ports, had not proven profitable on either ocean and the development of faster, dependable landplanes capable of landing at ever-multiplying airports around the world pushed the elegant flying boat from center stage. In 1940, Pan American sold the rights to Boeing 314s still on order to British Overseas Airways and placed an order for twenty Lockheed L-049 Constellations for transatlantic service, signaling the end of the flying boat era. The premier international air carrier was out of the flying-boat business.

In 1938, Pan American had already gone to Martin and Boeing flying boats and no new Sikorsky designs had been accepted. The company was obviously in trouble. Eugene Wilson, now senior vice-president of United Aircraft, delivered his speech to Igor Sikorsky, citing the reasons that the Sikorsky division should be closed. After listening intently, Sikorsky shocked Wilson with a counter-proposal right on the cutting edge of technology—the development of the helicopter. Wilson, exhibiting enormous faith and confidence in Sikorsky, agreed to give the Russian designer and his company a new lease on life.

Notes

1. Lt. Col. B. Q. Jones to Chief of Engineering Division, McCook Field, October 28, 1919, Igor I. Sikorsky Papers, Library of Congress, Washington, D.C.

2. Major R. H. Fleet to Igor I. Sikorsky, November 20, 1919, Sikorsky Papers, Library of Congress.

3. Contract between Ivan Prokofieff, Joseph Michael, and Igor Sikorsky, February 1920, Igor I. Sikorsky Papers, New England Air Museum, Windsor Locks, Connecticut.

4. Nicholas Glad, interview, July 7, 1988, Stratford, Connecticut.

5. "Russian Exiles Here Successful in Test of Plane," *New York Herald Tribune*, September 26, 1924, and "Big Plane Tested Again," *New York Times*, September 26, 1924, in personal scrapbook, Igor I. Sikorsky Papers, United Technologies Corporation (UTC) Archives, East Hartford, Connecticut.

6. Design Books, nos. 20, 27, 28, Sikorsky Papers, UTC Archives.

7. Alexander Klemin, "The Sikorsky S29A Twin-Engined Transport Plane," *Aviation*, vol. 18, pp. 182–84.

8. Dimitri Viner, interview, July 7, 1988, Stratford, Connecticut.

9. Design Books, nos. 20, 27, and 28, and Roscoe Turner file, Sikorsky Papers, UTC Archives; also Sikorsky Papers, Library of Congress.

10. R. E. G. Davies, *Airlines of the United States Since 1914* (Washington, D.C.: Smithsonian Institution Press, 1982), p. 33.

11. S-34 derivative, the "Airco," detailed in "Sikorsky Sales," *Aviation*, vol. 20 (April 19, 1926), p. 592, and "A New Twin Engine Amphibian," *Aviation*, vol. 20 (April 19, 1926), p. 603.

12. Mitch Mayborn, "The Sikorsky S-35 and the First New York to Paris Attempt," *American Aviation Historical Society Journal*, vol. 3 (Fall 1959), pp. 119–28.

13. Ibid.

14. Marilyn Bender and Selig Altschul, *The Chosen Instrument* (New York: Simon and Schuster, 1982); and Robert Daley, *An American Saga* (New York: Random House, 1980).

15. Martin Johnson to Igor Sikorsky, October 7, 1933, Sikorsky Papers, Library of Congress.

16. Frank J. Delear, *Igor Sikorsky: His Three Careers in Aviation* (New York: Dodd, Mead and Co., 1969), pp. 145–46; and Bender and Altschul, *The Chosen Instrument*, pp. 187–88.

17. Bender and Altschul, *The Chosen Instrument*, p. 225.

18. Richard K. Smith, "The Superiority of the American Transoceanic Airliner, 1932–1939," *American Aviation Historical Society Journal*, vol. 2 (Summer 1984), pp. 82–94, and H. A. Franchimont, "Basic Design Features of the S-42," *Aero Digest*, August 1934, pp. 54–56, September 1934, pp. 24–26, October 1934, pp. 50, 52.

19. Igor I. Sikorsky, "The Development and Characteristics of a Long-Range Flying Boat: The S-42," *Journal of the Royal Aeronautical Society*, vol. 39 (1935), pp. 263–81.

20. Bender and Altshul, *The Chosen Instrument*, p. 239.

21. Von Hardesty, "Aviation and the New Deal," manuscript, National Air and Space Museum, Washington, D.C.; and Bender and Altschul, *The Chosen Instrument*, pp. 218–23, 239–48.

22. "Problems of the Transoceanic Airplane," *Journal of the Aeronautical Sciences*, vol. 3, no. 9 (July 1936), pp. 318–21; Charles A. Lindbergh to Igor I. Sikorsky, October 2, 1936, Sikorsky Papers, Library of Congress.

23. Igor I. Sikorsky to Charles A. Lindbergh, November 17, 1936, Sikorsky Papers, UTC Archives, file SA-3, no. 522.

III. VERTICAL FLIGHT, 1939–57

III. VERTICAL FLIGHT, 1939–57

As the flying-boat production began to taper off in 1938, the stage was set for Igor Sikorsky to enter a new arena of activity—vertical flight. Building a helicopter was an attractive idea in the interwar years, and there was already an intense competition underway in France, Germany, and the United States to design the first successful flying machine capable of vertical flight. Autogiros, a hybrid aircraft with the properties of an airplane and a helicopter, had flown in the early 1920s and represented a rival type of vertical flight.

The management of United Aircraft Corporation, however, had informed Igor Sikorsky that they would allow him to pursue research on the helicopter project, as long as it did not become burdensome financially. The offer was timely, for Sikorsky had been interested in designing a helicopter for many years. United Aircraft also made a crucial concession; Sikorsky would be allowed to keep his talented engineering team together for this new endeavor. The initial locale for the work was the Vought-Sikorsky plant at Stratford, Connecticut. Later, during the war years, the project was shifted to Bridgeport.

Previous Page
The crash of the VS-300 in December 1939 resulted in a massive reconfiguration which Sikorsky is flying in the spring of 1940, tethered safely to the ground by heavy ropes. Collective pitch control is retained in the main rotor but cyclic blade pitch actuation is now gone, replaced by a pair of smaller rotors turning in a horizontal plane and carried on lateral outriggers at each side of the tail, for control of pitch and roll. The antitorque tail rotor (rotating in a vertical plane) was retained. (NASM)

Sikorsky approached his new project with an enthusiasm that could be traced to his boyhood and first years as a designer. Building a helicopter had been an enduring visionary idea. "The idea of a vehicle that could lift itself vertically from the ground and hover motionless in the air," he once remarked, "was probably born at the same time that man first dreamed of flying."[1]

His first effort to build a practical helicopter was in Kiev, in May–June 1909. At the time Sikorsky was twenty years old. Working alone, he took an Anzani 25-horsepower engine, purchased that same year in Paris with money borrowed from his sister, and mounted it on a rectangular frame constructed of wood and braced with wire. This wooden cage, without wheels, incorporated a transmission system of wooden pulleys and belts that drove coaxial shafts topped with two twin-bladed rotors. The rotor blades were fashioned with steel pipes and wooden ribs, and covered with linen. The rotors were secured to the shaft by wire, and turnbuckles were employed to allow change in pitch.

After two months of experimentation, frequent modifications, and testing, Sikorsky's prototype helicopter failed to fly. He then abandoned the effort. There had been considerable problems with vibration and control. The Anzani engine could generate around 150 pounds of thrust, but the total weight of the machine was 450 pounds. The arithmetic working against the young Sikorsky was formidable.

By February 1910, Sikorsky was ready to try again. His new machine was lighter, by design, weighing just under 400 pounds, but again powered by a 25-horsepower Anzani engine. This time Sikorsky used three blades on each rotor, a total of six, hoping the new configuration would provide additional thrust. The machine generated more thrust, but failed once more to hover. The design also lacked an effective mechanism for lateral or longitudinal control.[2] Faced with these frustrations, Sikorsky decided to abandon vertical flight experiments for fixed-wing designs. Looking back on these formative designs, Sikorsky remarked that they were "very fine except for one thing—they couldn't fly."[3]

Sikorsky learned many things from these false starts. With a relatively modest investment in time and money he discovered what many con-

Igor Sikorsky alongside the second helicopter in the spring of 1910. His second attempt at flight, the machine was reported capable only of lifting itself on short hops off the ground. A single 25-horsepower Anzani engine powered counter-rotating rotors. (NASM)

temporary helicopter experimenters learned, often after sinking personal fortunes and spending years of work on their projects: the powerplants of the day were too inefficient to permit sustained vertical flight. A successful helicopter, Sikorsky stated in his autobiography, had to await "better engines, lighter material and experienced mechanics."[4]

The quest to build a helicopter continued during the next two decades, in Russia, in Western Europe, and in the United States. Another Russian named Boris N. Yuriev, as early as 1912, had designed a single-rotor helicopter. He, too, failed, but his design showed great ingenuity. Emile Berliner, a talented inventor in America, worked on several helicopter configurations between 1908 and 1925. Other early experimenters included Louis Breguet, Jacob Ellehammer, and George de Bothezat. These numerous helicopter designs brought meager results. The U.S. Army, for example, spent $200,000 in the 1920s to bankroll de Bothezat's ill-fated giant "helicopter," consisting of a massive metal tube-and-wire structure supporting four rotors. The failure of the de Bothezat project soured the army on the helicopter for many years.

Even while a number of experimenters worked on helicopter designs in the 1920s, Igor

This 1930 drawing by Sikorsky depicts a helicopter design with the general characteristics of the aircraft he successfully flew nine years later. The side view is noteworthy; it resembles the boat fuselage and boom-braced empennage of the S-38 seaplane. (UTC AS-183)

Sikorsky devoted his energies to building fixed-wing aircraft, amphibians, and flying boats. Throughout these years, he remained convinced that a practical helicopter could be built. Economic necessity, however, dictated that his interest in helicopter design remain theoretical. There was little time or opportunity for Sikorsky to give concrete expression to his enduring vision of designing a vertical flying machine.

In 1930, he urged United Aircraft to consider building a helicopter. The onset of the Depression and the marginal character of Sikorsky's flying-boat program precluded any financial support for such a risky venture. Nevertheless, Sikorsky persisted in thinking about the problem of vertical flight. In 1931 he applied for a patent for a single-rotor design helicopter. This patent was approved, and in many respects anticipated his successful design at the end of the decade.

The decade of the 1930s saw new advances in helicopter design worldwide. The context was highly competitive and Sikorsky, in fact, would find his entry into the field in 1939 to be somewhat belated.

Henrich Focke, a former military pilot in World War I, built the Fa-61 helicopter. First flown in 1936, the Fa-61 with its twin rotors established a number of endurance and altitude records. There was also the Breguet-Dorand *Gyroplane*, another multi-rotor design, that made its initial flight in 1933 and competed with the Fa-61. Focke also designed the Fa-223. Larger than its predecessors, the Fa-223 had a 1,000-horsepower engine to power two triple-bladed rotors mounted on outriggers. The Fa-223 was equipped with an enclosed cabin that seated four persons. There also was Anton Flettner, who designed a number of helicopters, including the highly successful Fl-282 Kolibri (Hummingbird) which entered military service in Germany in 1940.

Unlike his competitors, Sikorsky was dedicated to developing the single-rotor configuration because it represented a major step toward the solution of a fundamental problem, designing the most efficient placement of major components to provide the best compromise between hovering capability, horizontal speed, and precise control.

Sikorsky's single-rotor design became the VS-300 helicopter. The origins of the VS-300 could be traced to 1930 when Sikorsky sketched in his large notebook, called "Various Developments," a helicopter with one main

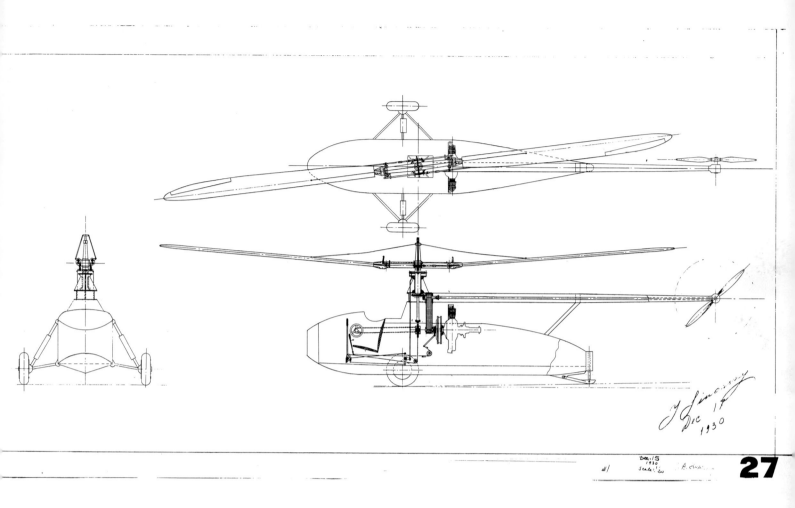

27

Lift and torque forces could be studied and recorded in detail after Sikorsky and the helicopter design team built this test stand in 1938. The scale on the end of the pipe at left was anchored or held by hand, and torque readings were taken directly from it. Torque, acting in a horizontal plane opposite to the rotation of the rotor (note the single-blade with counterbalance for this application), was an immense obstacle to designers of the helicopter. It was conquered by the tail rotor. (NASM)

Sikorsky stands next to the VS-300 on September 14, ►
1939, when he was able to make the first short hops off the ground. A total of about ten seconds flight time was accumulated. (NASM)

rotor and one smaller rotor on the tail of an airplane-style fuselage. This design was basically a fixed-wing layout with helicopter devices substituted for fixed-wing equipment. The similarity in layouts represented a parallel between the development history of airplanes and helicopters. In the beginning, both technologies used multiple, cumbersome lifting surfaces, for example, triplanes and biplanes with canard elevators and dual rudders and multi-rotor helicopter configurations with co-axial and outrigger rotors. As both technologies evolved, the trend toward simplicity became apparent. Externally braced multi-planes gave way to streamlined monoplanes with simple, cruciform tails; multi-rotor helicopters became single-rotor types.

Once Sikorsky had determined the general fuselage and rotor layout, he then focused on the challenge of precise control. "The main problem," Sikorsky observed, "was control and the difficulty was threefold. First, we had little knowledge of helicopters in general; second, we were building the first helicopter in the world with a single main rotor; and third, we knew practically nothing about how to pilot a helicopter."[5] Sikorsky was not aware that a fellow countryman, Yuriev, had experimented with a single-rotor helicopter in 1912.

One of the key developments in the control of rotary-wing aircraft is attributed to the Spaniard Juan de la Cierva who developed the autogiro that first flew in 1923. An American aviation entrepreneur, Harold F. Pitcairn, manufactured Cierva autogiros. He improved upon and then patented a Cierva main-rotor design which Sikorsky used to solve the problem of precise helicopter control. Sikorsky ultimately adapted this control concept into a practical machine. His VS-300 could not only make hovering takeoffs and landings, but could also convert to horizontal flight and back to a hover, all under positive control.

Sikorsky gathered a small, skilled team of employees to build the VS-300. This group consisted of Michael Gluhareff and his brother Serge, Alexander Mashinsky, Michael Buivid, J. Russell Clark, Adolph Plenefisch, J. Walker, and Robert Labensky. Alexis ("Prof") Sikorsky joined the team and provided expertise on rotor-wing aerodynamics. The team quickly recognized the need for two pieces of equipment: a test device to measure main-rotor torque; and a simulator for training pilots to fly the helicopter. The VS-300 team fashioned both devices from scratch, using spare parts and surplus materials.

Interestingly, the simulator was equipped with

three tail rotors, while the prototype VS-300 had a single tail rotor. When the VS-300 crashed, it, too, was rebuilt to the three-tail rotor configuration. Finding the proper tail configuration was a major problem that haunted the design team for many months.

The first VS-300 flight took place on September 14, 1939, with little notice. Public attention was focused elsewhere, on Europe (as it was in 1914 just after Sikorsky flew the *Il'ya Muromets Kievskiy* from St. Petersburg to Kiev) where World War II had begun just weeks before. Three decades had passed since Igor Sikorsky had attempted to build his first helicopter, so the day represented for him the renewal of an old challenge.

The machine was tethered to heavy weights on the ground outside the factory in Stratford. It had a primitive look—a welded steel tube frame (left uncovered to make modification easier) with an undercarriage of four wheels and a three-blade main rotor. A 75-horsepower Lycoming engine drove the single-blade, counterbalanced, wooden tail rotor, as well as the main rotor. Each main rotor blade was constructed much like an airplane wing. Thirty-eight wooden ribs were evenly spaced and glued along the trailing edge of a wooden box,

or spar. The ribs and spar formed an airfoil shape which, when glued together, formed an assembly that was covered with fabric and painted with a flexible, waterproof finish. Strong, noncorrosive wire was used inside the trailing edge fabric for strength and retention of shape.

The main rotor shaft protruded from a transmission box constructed with old truck gears. Connected to the engine by five belts, the transmission reduced the engine RPM (about 3,000 at full throttle) to a rate low enough to operate the main rotor. In flight, the main rotor turned at approximately 255 RPM while the shaft-driven tail rotor revolved at 1,700 RPM.[6]

Igor Sikorsky, seated in the open cockpit and wearing a large overcoat and fedora, made the first flight in the VS-300. Starting the engine prompted the VS-300 to vibrate awkwardly. After taking a few minutes to familiarize his senses with the sights and sounds of a helicopter about to fly, Sikorsky pulled up on the collective control lever at his left side. The VS-300 cleared the ground, became airborne for a second or two, then landed. More hops were made that same day, several with Serge Gluhareff as pilot. While the altitude was min-

Sikorsky and Captain H. Franklin Gregory of the U.S. Army Air Corps, in charge of rotorcraft procurement for all branches of the United States military. (UTC AS-364)

imal, just a few feet, the fact remained that the VS-300 had flown in a marginally controlled fashion.

In the months that followed, other tethered flights took place with either Sikorsky or one of his engineering associates at the controls. Each flight was not only a test of the prototype helicopter, but a training exercise: "It was a wonderful chance to relive one's own life," Sikorsky recalled, "to design and construct a new type of flying machine without really knowing how to do it, and then climb into the pilot's seat and try to fly it . . . without ever having flown a helicopter before!"[7]

There were real dangers. Serge Gluhareff, at the controls on December 9, 1939, attempted to land on the downwind side of a large hanger. As he approached, a sudden crosswind flipped the VS-300 on its side. Gluhareff escaped injury, but the damage to the helicopter was extensive.

Control remained the critical problem. Sikorsky spent the winter of 1939–40 rebuilding the VS-300 with two additional rotors that revolved in a horizontal plane and were mounted on outriggers, one on each side of the antitorque tail rotor. These new rotors would control the helicopter pitch by simul-

taneously varying the blade pitch of both rotors: more pitch gave greater thrust, raising the tail and lowering the nose for forward flight; less pitch lowered the tail for reverse flight. Helicopter roll was achieved by varying differentially the blade pitch of each rotor. More pitch on the left rotor rolled the helicopter to the right; likewise, more pitch for the right rotor rolled the machine to the left.

The new post-crash configuration removed cyclic (direction) control from the main rotor entirely, transferring it to the two new tail rotors. Collective (lift) control remained in the main rotor. Separating cyclic and collective control actions allowed Sikorsky to analyze, understand, and fine tune each control action. The VS-300 was subject to continual modification and redesign—in fact, eighteen distinct major revisions prior to October 1943, when the historic helicopter made its final flight.

By May 1940, Sikorsky had acquired considerable expertise as a helicopter pilot. He was now able to put the redesigned VS-300 through a series of increasingly complex maneuvers. A new 90-horsepower Franklin engine replaced the Lycoming engine in July, giving the VS-300 a needed boost in power. At this juncture, Sikorsky put the machine

through extended flights of twenty minutes or more, hovering and moving sidewards and backwards with ease.

Forward flight, however, at twenty to twenty-five miles per hour, triggered instability and rapid loss of control. This phenomenon was explained by main rotor downwash on the horizontal tail rotors. Continued modifications followed as Sikorsky and his engineers made incremental refinements. The outriggers supporting the two tail rotors, for example, were extended outward and raised to escape the downwash. This was an improvement but the problem was not totally eliminated.

The U.S. Army Air Corps was taking more interest in the VS-300. Captain H. Franklin Gregory, who had visited Sikorsky in 1939 and examined the simulator, returned to the Sikorsky plant in July 1940. Gregory headed the program to develop rotorcraft for all U.S. military services, and the Sikorsky prototype was one of several experimental vertical flight machines competing for government funding. He played a crucial role in the development of the helicopter, combining a visionary confidence in Sikorsky's work with his own commitment to perfecting helicopter technology. Gregory first flew the VS-300 on July 24, 1940.

2684   VS-300-A   HELICOPTER & PILOT AFTER WORLD RECORD ENDURANC
FLIGHT.   TIME: I HOUR 32 I/2 MIN.   5-6-41

WORLDS RECORD BROKEN

Igor Sikorsky gave Charles H. Lindbergh a flying demonstration of the VS-300 on October 9, 1940. (UTC AS-310)

During this period of intensive test flights and public demonstrations, the VS-300 fell victim to a mishap on October 14, 1940, this time with Igor Sikorsky at the controls. One of the tail rotor support booms broke in flight, causing the helicopter to roll over and crash to the ground. Remarkably, Sikorsky emerged unhurt from the heavily-damaged machine. Again the VS-300 was quickly rebuilt. The reconstruction of the VS-300 provided another opportunity for design changes. The new version appeared in November 1940 and projected an altered appearance: all three tail rotors were lengthened again and positioned even higher. Flight tests of the rebuilt VS-300 followed in January 1941.

That same month the Army Air Corps, at Gregory's direction, approved a contract with Sikorsky Aircraft to build a two-place helicopter. The progress of the VS-300 convinced Gregory that Sikorsky stood the greatest chance of designing a helicopter to meet government specifications. Plans called for the new army helicopter to be powered by a Warner 165-horsepower radial engine. Initial plans specified a triple tail rotor configuration for the military version of the VS-300, to be called the XR-4.

Amid growing confidence in the VS-300, Sikorsky moved to establish some helicopter flight endurance records. On April 15, 1941, he hovered in the air for a record one hour, five minutes, and fourteen and one half seconds. This represented a dramatic advance over his first "flight" of several seconds in 1939. Later, in May, he set a world record of one hour, thirty-two minutes, and twenty-six seconds. This record-breaking flight attracted a large number of spectators and press coverage. The name of Sikorsky was increasingly identified with the helicopter and vertical flight.[8]

The year 1941 saw the VS-300 undergo further design changes. A new engine was installed in April. It was a more powerful Franklin that produced 100 horsepower. For aircraft registration purposes, the helicopter was redesignated VS-300A. In August, a single horizontal rotor, mounted atop a pylon, replaced the two horizontal tail rotors. This design change was important because it restored partial cyclic control in the main rotor. Fewer rotors also meant simpler operation with less aerodynamic interference and drag, and greatly reduced the number of gear boxes and transmissions required. Fewer moving parts meant greater reliability and safety. Full cyclic and

02077

Les Morris broke the American cross-country helicopter distance record by flying 761 miles in five days from Stratford, Connecticut, to Wright Field, Dayton, Ohio. This photograph was taken on May 15, 1942. Left to right: Ed Walsh, crew chief; Adolph Plenefisch, shop foreman; Igor Sikorsky; Orville Wright; Ralph Alex, assistant; Les Morris, pilot; Bob Labensky, project engineer. (NASM)

The Sikorsky R-4 was the first mass-produced helicopter. ► These R-4s being assembled in 1943 represent a series of orders that actually began on May 30, 1942, with official Army Air Corps acceptance of the XR-4. Orders for R-5 and R-6 helicopters followed. By the end of the war on September 2, 1945, three years and four months later, a total of 425 Sikorsky helicopters were accepted by the U.S. Air Corps, Coast Guard, and Navy. (NASM)

collective control in the main rotor was the cornerstone of the single-rotor concept.

In October yet another series of tail rotor experiments followed. After careful testing, Sikorsky decided to discard the horizontal tail rotor and support pylon, return full cyclic pitch control to the main rotor, and allow a single tail rotor to control torque. At this point, the complicated design evolution reached its mature stage. A workable single-rotor helicopter had been produced. Immediately, construction of the XR-4 was interrupted to incorporate the new changes. The VS-300 in this final configuration made its first flight on December 8, 1941, the day after

Pearl Harbor. On January 14, 1942, the XR-4 made its first test flight and three months later it was flown in a public demonstration flight.

A grand total of 102 hours and 35 minutes of flight time was logged by pilots flying all configurations of the VS-300.[9] The aircraft was flown by Sikorsky and other pilots including Serge Gluhareff, Dimitri "Jimmy" Viner, Les Morris, "Connie" Moeller, and H. Franklin Gregory. Even Sikorsky's old friend, Charles Lindbergh, took the controls of the historic helicopter.

For vertical flight, the VS-300 occupies a special place, a position of prominence not unlike

Igor Sikorsky hangs from one of the first experimental air rescue hoists during tests to develop life-saving techniques. The hoist is fitted to an HNS-1, the navy version of the R-4. One of Sikorsky's strongest beliefs was that the helicopter was destined to be a rescue vehicle. (UTC AS-346)

that enjoyed by the Wright flyer in the history of the airplane. The VS-300 marked the beginning of practical and efficient, single-rotor vertical flight. As a prototype helicopter, it met the requirements of full control and the ability to hover, using the simplest and most reliable technology. Sikorsky's VS-300 was the first of thousands of successful single-rotor helicopters to be manufactured during and after World War II.

The full magnitude of the leap in helicopter technology demonstrated in the VS-300 and incorporated in the XR-4, became apparent in May 1942, when the XR-4 made a five-day, 761-mile cross country flight to Wright Field, Dayton, Ohio. During a single flight, this helicopter piloted by Les Morris broke nearly all existing helicopter records and demonstrated the lead then enjoyed by the United States in the field of vertical flight. Sikorsky witnessed this flight firsthand and accompanied the flight on its last leg.

The U.S. Army Air Forces (USAAF) formally accepted the XR-4 on May 30, 1942, and began evaluation trials. Army helicopter pilots began training under the steady hand of Les Morris. Morris produced a training curriculum and flight manual to allow army trainees

Colonel H. F. Gregory conducts landing trials aboard the USS *Bunker Hill* on May 7, 1943, as Sikorsky and a throng of dignitaries look on. (NASM)

After World War II, a commercial version of the R-5 was ▶ built and designated S-51. It was the first civilianized Sikorsky helicopter. This well-kept example is fitted out, in keeping with most S-51s operated in the United States, to carry three passengers seated abreast behind the pilot. The English firm of Westland built the R-5 under license from Sikorsky and named it Dragonfly. An RAF squadron of Dragonflys served with distinction during the terrorist war in Malaya, 1950–56. (NASM)

to acquaint themselves with the utterly foreign flight characteristics of the helicopter. Morris discovered that the transition to vertical flight required the patience and skill of a good flight instructor, and a two-seat trainer with dual controls.

Sikorsky manufactured a total of 131 R-4s of all variants (XR-4, YR-4A, YR-4B) during the war years. The R-4 provided the army with an effective aircraft for reconnaissance and rescue. In April 1944, an army operational version of the XR-4, designated YR-4A, made the first aerial rescue under combat conditions in Burma.

While the helicopter quickly acquired important functions, Sikorsky himself hoped to see his invention assume a greater humanitarian role. Sikorsky saw this hope realized even in the context of the war years. Flying an R-4 Sikorsky helicopter, Commander Frank A. Erickson of the U.S. Coast Guard transferred urgently needed blood plasma from New York City to Sandy Hook, New Jersey, in January 1944. The occasion for the emergency was the explosion on a destroyer. Commander Erickson made the flight in a snowstorm that had grounded all other fixed-wing aircraft.[10] The event demonstrated the usefulness of the helicopter for mercy and rescue missions. This

◄ Sikorsky's interest in volcanos was fortuitously rewarded when a puff of smoke in a Mexican farmer's field grew into an active volcano named Paricutin. The Sikorsky R-6A helicopter carried members of a research expedition down into the crater, between eruptions. Photographed on August 14, 1945 (left to right), an army mechanic; Dr. Louis Graton, Harvard geologist; Igor Sikorsky, project manager; Capt. George Colchagoff, consultant; Ralph Alex, Sikorsky engineer and pilot; Roy Beer, flight officer; army mechanic; army photographer; A. Bertram, army photographer; Verne Short, Sikorsky photographer. (NASM)

To realize the dream of a helicopter in every backyard, Morris used his own as a proving ground. A swing set is under the trees behind the VS-300A, and the family garden is at lower right. (NASM)

Helmeted and goggled dancers perform next to this Sikorsky S-52 commercial helicopter on the stage of Radio City Music Hall in New York, just after World War II. The notion that the helicopter would complement or even replace the automobile in everyman's life was a popular postwar fantasy. Sikorsky was confident in the early 1940s that hundreds of thousands of helicopters would be flying in the near future. (NASM)

unique aircraft was no longer the product of maverick eccentrics who often labored years to construct machines of passing interest but no practical value.

The Sikorsky division mass-produced two other helicopter models during World War II. The USAAF ordered the Sikorsky R-5 early in 1943. The basic layout of the R-5 was similar to the R-4 except that seating was in tandem, and a Pratt & Whitney radial engine of 450 horsepower was used. Production continued until after the war, and the aircraft served again with distinction during the Korean War. The British built the R-5 under license from Sikorsky and redesignated it the Dragonfly. Another version, the S-51, became the first civil helicopter built by Sikorsky.

Using the rotor system and transmission from the R-4, Sikorsky built a refined model called the R-6. Over two hundred of these helicopters were constructed before August 1945. Sikorsky himself, with a team of scientists and explorers, used an R-6 to observe Paricutin, a Mexican volcano, between eruptions in August 1945.[11] The scientific usefulness of the helicopter had been demonstrated.

Sikorsky popularized the helicopter by making it available on a large scale, first to military

pilots who experienced firsthand the unique and practical uses of the new technology, later to civilian and commercial users. There was a period of economic readjustment for the aviation industry at the conclusion of World War II. Sikorsky shared with others the dream of a postwar aviation boom with returning military pilots seeking inexpensive ways to continue flying. Sikorsky anticipated that helicopters would secure a logical place in this civilian market. The dream did not materialize. Military interest in the helicopter was well established and would expand; commercial users of the helicopter soon became apparent as well. Sikorsky Aircraft would continue to supply advanced helicopter designs for military and commercial purposes, although on a smaller scale than hoped.

The military applications of the helicopter ran parallel to commercial. The Korean War (1950–53) saw the military expand the helicopter's operational scope to include air rescue and transport. In the 1960s, during the Vietnam War, the helicopter acquired a new combat role. The emergence of the attack helicopter was crucial to the evolution of modern land warfare. Sikorsky designs and those of other helicopter manufacturers such as Bell, Hughes, and Lockheed made contributions to

The first Sikorsky helicopter equipped with a turbine engine was the XH-39. In August 1954, pilot Warrant Officer Billy Wester established a world helicopter speed record of 156 miles per hour, and in October, a world altitude record of 24,521 feet. Both records were set flying the XH-39. (NASM)

Igor Sikorsky originated the concept embodied in the Sikorsky S-64, or flying crane, attempting to greatly expand the versatility of cargo helicopters. He conceived a number of unique uses for the enormous machine including transport of finished dwellings to remote sites. (NASM)

Previous Page
An L.A. Airways Sikorsky S-61L being prepared for flight. The airstair door on the starboard side of the aircraft is down and ready for boarding. (NASM)

this new technology. The Soviet Union, along with other nations, adapted the helicopter to modern ground combat operations. Soviet military operations in Afghanistan in the 1980s saw close integration of the helicopter with combat forces. Rotorcraft were employed as gun platforms, transports, rescue vehicles, and liaison aircraft.

While fully integrated into modern military operations, the helicopter has not fulfilled every civilian purpose Sikorsky originally outlined for it. Short-haul helicopter airlines have not emerged as a viable component of the modern commercial air transport system. However, other specialized roles have been established for the helicopter: from crop dusting to police work. For business and travel in urban areas the helicopter possesses unrivaled speed and accessibility.

The helicopter has emerged as an important means to transport medical supplies, rescue the stranded in emergency situations, and speedily evacuate the injured from accidents. One of the most dramatic demonstrations of the rescue capability of the helicopter came in the fall of 1967, when helicopters assisted in the evacuation of 144 men, women, and children from the *Skagerak*, an auto ferry that be-

gan sinking in rough weather in the strait between Norway and Denmark.[12]

After World War II, Igor Sikorsky remained active in helicopter design. He argued for the design of helicopters with enhanced load-carrying capacity. The first Sikorsky machine to benefit from this innovative philosophy was the S-55. This helicopter served with distinction in the Korean War, excelling in the roles of aerial ambulance and troop transport.

By the 1950s, Sikorsky was working to speed the transition to jet-turbine engines. In 1954, the first turbine-powered Sikorsky helicopter, the XH-39, set rotor-wing world records for speed and altitude.

Sikorsky's personal dream of a "flying crane" became a practical reality in 1962, when he was seventy-three. That year, the Sikorsky S-64 made its first flight and ushered in a bold new idea. The concept focused on removing a helicopter's traditional enclosed cargo bay, freeing it to lift cargos of almost any size and shape. Sikorsky envisioned factory-built houses lifted to any site, then lowered into place by the flying crane. Commuters would board special pods, then be whisked away to their destinations by the flying crane. Detaching the pod upon landing, the flying crane could return unencumbered by an empty pod, ready to pick up another load of commuters. The idea had merit but logistical consideration limited its use. A total of ninety-eight examples—ten of them commercial, the remainder for the military—were constructed. Called the CH-54 by the army, the flying crane was still in service in the late 1980s.

By 1957, Igor Sikorsky had retired from Sikorsky Aircraft Division of United Technologies Corporation. He died on October 26, 1972, closing a legacy of enduring contributions to the development of aviation in the Soviet Union and the United States over more than six decades.

Notes

1. Sergei Sikorsky, "The Development of the VS-300," in *Vertical Flight: The Age of the Helicopter*, ed. Walter J. Boyne and Donald S. Lopez (Washington, D.C.: Smithsonian Institution Press, 1984), p. 47.

2. Sergei Sikorsky, "A Brief Review of Sikorsky Aircraft Designs, 1909 through 1917" (East Hartford, CT: Sikorsky Aircraft, 1987), p. 1.

3. *Flight*, vol. 67 (April 29, 1955), p. 540.

4. Sikorsky, *The Story of the Winged-S* (New York: Dodd, Mead and Company, 1958), p. 242.

5. Frank J. Delear, *Igor Sikorsky: His Three Careers in Aviation* (New York: Dodd, Mead and Company, 1969), p. 186.

6. "General Dimensions of the VS-300 'Flight Model' Helicopter" (East Hartford, CT: Corporate Archives, United Technologies, May 20, 1940), p. 1, photocopied.

7. S. Sikorsky, "The Development of the VS-300," p. 50.

8. Charles L. Morris, *Pioneering the Helicopter* (Alexandria, VA: Helicopter Association International, reprint edition, 1985), p. 69.

9. S. Sikorsky, "The Development of the VS-300," p. 55.

10. Morris, *Pioneering the Helicopter*, pp. 150–51.

11. Ralph Alex, "How Are You Fixed for Blades? The Saga of the Helicopter, Circa 1940–1960," in *Vertical Flight*, ed. Boyne and Lopez, p. 26.

12. Delear, *Igor Sikorsky*, p. 201.

IV. IGOR SIKORSKY, ENGINEER AND PUBLIC MAN

Igor Sikorsky's enormous contributions to aviation were fueled in part by his lifelong confidence in technological progress. His faith in technology and material progress remained central to his personal philosophy. He viewed his own great strides in aircraft and helicopter design in this framework of optimism about the social benefits of technology.

Living in the twentieth century, however, brought this deeply rooted idealism into conflict with the darker realities of war and revolution. Many of his own designs became weapons of war, for Sikorsky a cruel necessity. But he retained a profound attachment to the idea that his designs would ultimately make a greater impact on commercial, scientific, and humanitarian work. This conflict weighed most heavily on Sikorsky during and after World War II. The rise of totalitarianism, the enormous destruction of two world wars, and the advent of the nuclear age prompted him to turn to religious and philosophical ideas to comprehend more fully the human predicament. In his *Message of the Lord's Prayer*, Sikorsky articulated a number of universal ideas, as he defined them from his own Christian heritage.

Igor Sikorsky was the "intuitive engineer," who could combine mechanical genius with visionary imagination to further the progress of aviation. (NASM)

In 1947, he published his most ambitious philosophical statement, *The Invisible Encounter*, in which he endeavored to define certain spiritual resources, sadly neglected in the twentieth century, that could bring stability to civilization. Sikorsky's writing of *The Invisible Encounter* was linked to his lifelong opposition to totalitarianism. Communism, of course, had survived World War II and, in many respects, possessed new vitality as a threat to democratic values. By exposing the materialistic basis of totalitarian dictatorships, Sikorsky hoped to challenge Western Civilization to rediscover its spiritual heritage and values.

When Igor Sikorsky revised his autobiography, *The Story of the Winged-S*, in 1958, he took the opportunity to speculate about the dynamic behind invention, the "mysterious faculty," as he called it. This was an exercise in self-understanding for Sikorsky. His own career possessed fortuitous elements and fateful choices. He was intrigued with his own personal motives, the determination at critical junctures in his life to ignore the sceptics and boldly design an aircraft that became in time a recognized breakthrough in technology. Successful pioneering in art, science, engineering, and all branches of human activity, according to Sikorsky, involved the "process of intuitive discovery," the capacity to comprehend or foresee beyond the limits of existing evidence. Such intuitive apprehension, Sikorsky acknowledged, would not be accepted as a reality by many people, but for him this phenomenon helped to explain his own engineering breakthroughs as well as great achievements in other fields. For Sikorsky it was important to understand, or, more properly, attempt to understand, the nature of human creativity; intuition provided one avenue.

Igor Sikorsky's life achievement was recognized in 1951 when he received the Collier Trophy, on behalf of the American helicopter industry, at a ceremony presided over by President Truman. This prestigious award, along with Sikorsky's many other awards, offered one measure of his public esteem. Belatedly, the Soviet Union recognized Sikorsky's enormous contribution to the Soviet and American aviation traditions. Full acknowledgment of Sikorsky, however, did not come until the 1980s. Things had come full circle; Sikorsky was now given his logical place in Russian/Soviet aeronautical history after many decades of silence.

APPENDIX 1.
DESIGN DRAWINGS

This compilation of drawings represents the majority of designs by Igor I. Sikorsky. The three-views of the American-built aircraft are all factory drawings. There are only a few drawings of the Russian-period aircraft that were generated in Russia and these are only preliminary or concept-type illustrations. The three-views depicting the early "S" series, as well as the Il'ya Muromets, are the most accurate renderings available for these historic aircraft. They have been drawn to scale using all available data.

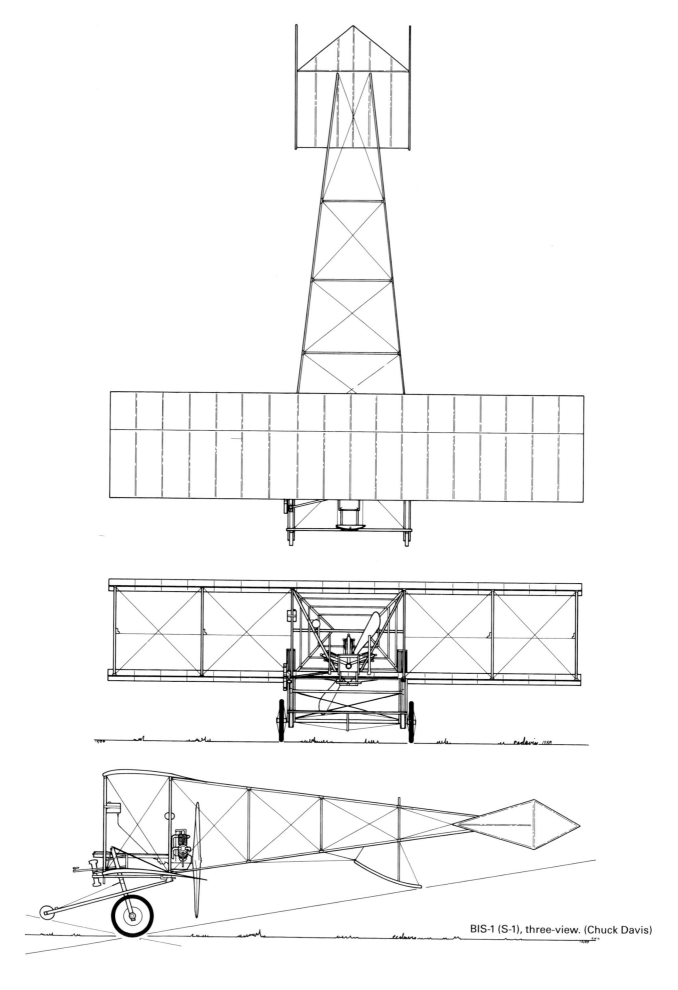

BIS-1 (S-1), three-view. (Chuck Davis)

THE AVIATION CAREERS OF IGOR SIKORSKY

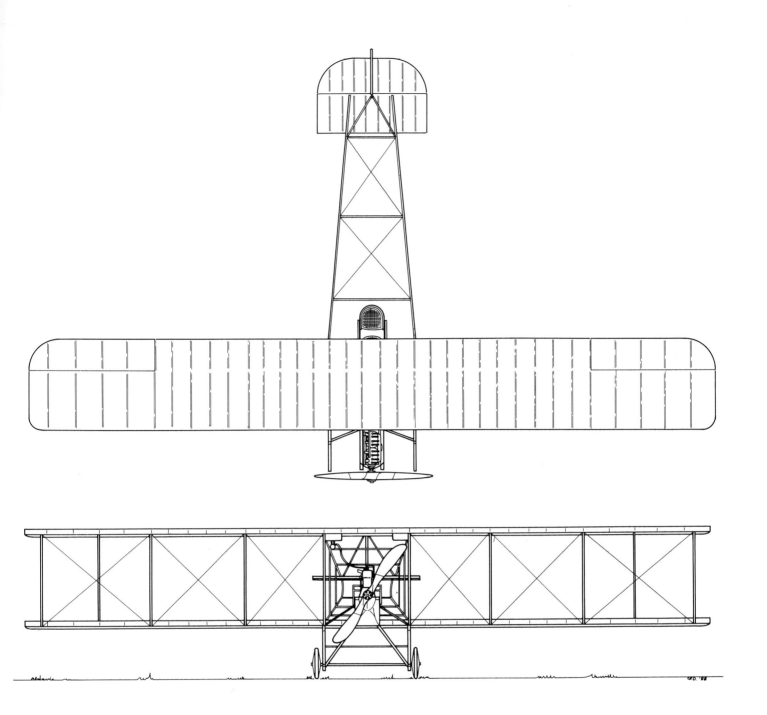

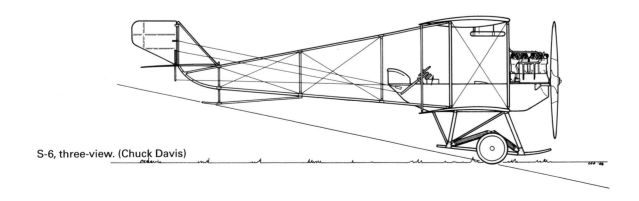

S-6, three-view. (Chuck Davis)

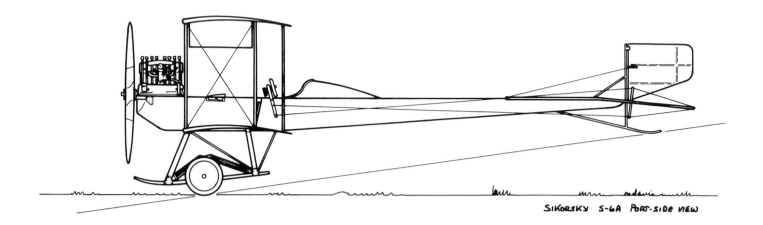

SIKORSKY S-6A PORT-SIDE VIEW

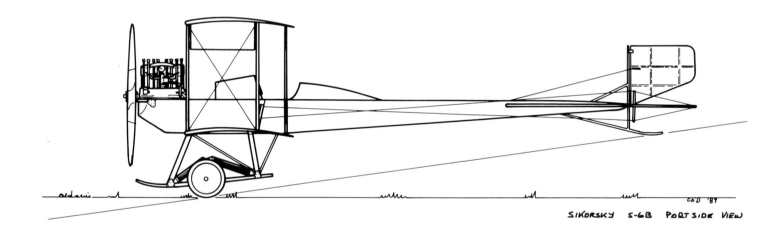

SIKORSKY S-6B PORTSIDE VIEW

S-6A and S-6B, side view. (Chuck Davis)

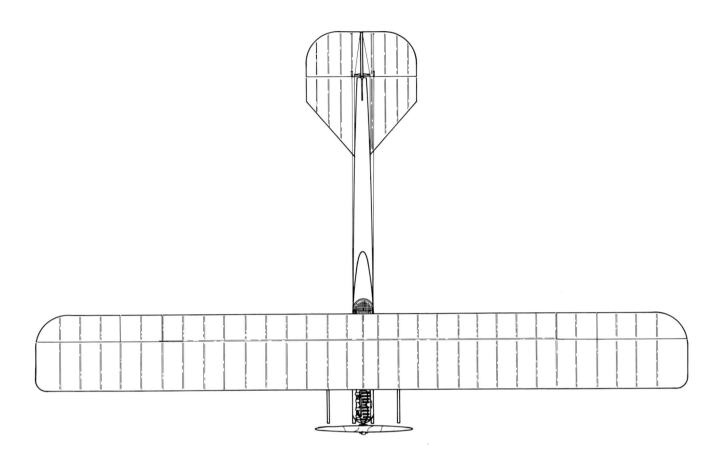

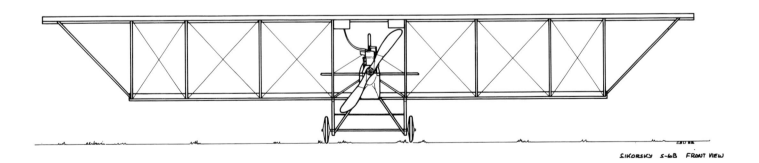

SIKORSKY S-6B FRONT VIEW

S-6B, top and front view. (Chuck Davis)

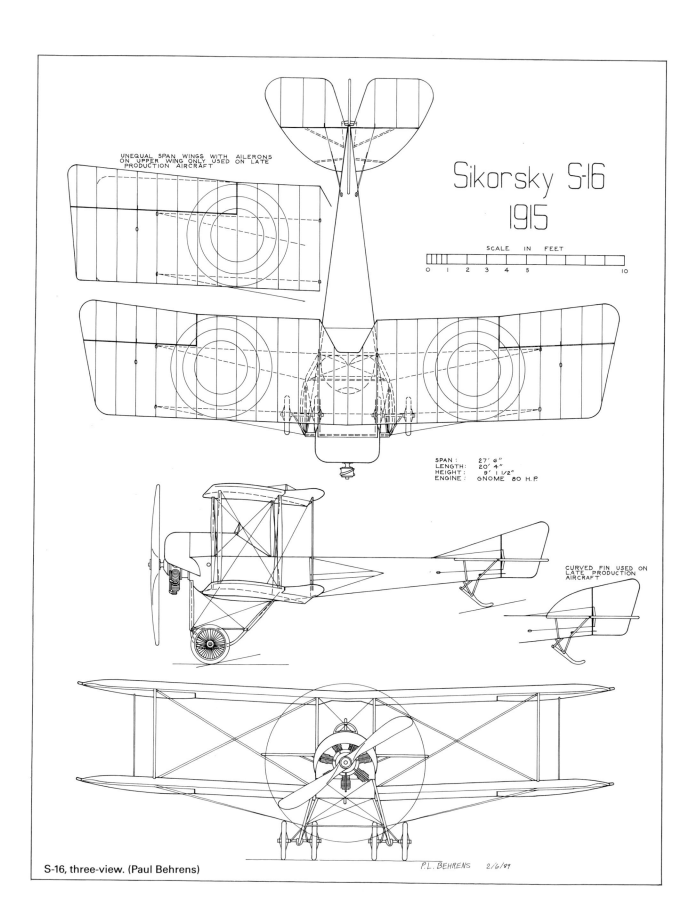

UNEQUAL SPAN WINGS WITH AILERONS
ON UPPER WING ONLY USED ON LATE
PRODUCTION AIRCRAFT

Sikorsky S-16
1915

SCALE IN FEET

0   1   2   3   4   5   10

SPAN: 27' 6"
LENGTH: 20' 4"
HEIGHT: 9' 1 1/2"
ENGINE: GNOME 80 H.P.

CURVED FIN USED ON
LATE PRODUCTION
AIRCRAFT

P.L. BEHRENS 2/6/89

S-16, three-view. (Paul Behrens)

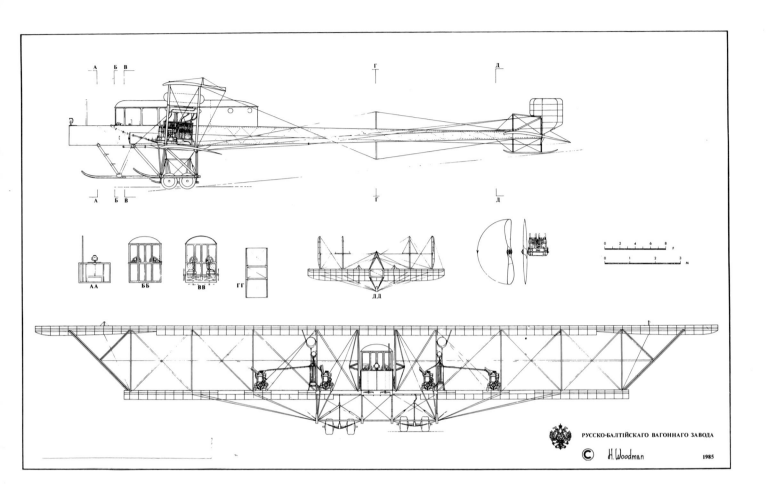

РУССКО-БАЛТІЙСКАГО ВАГОННАГО ЗАВОДА

© H. Woodman   1985

Grand—side and front view. (Harry Woodman)

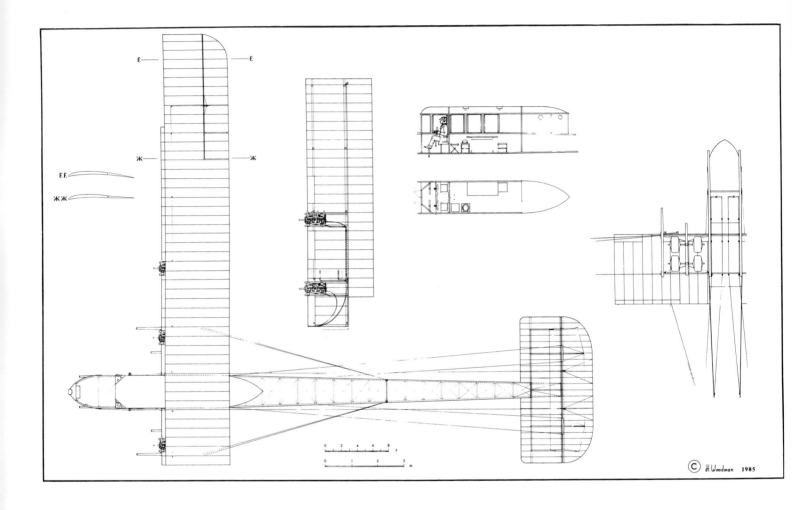

Grand—top and bottom view with interior details.
(Harry Woodman)

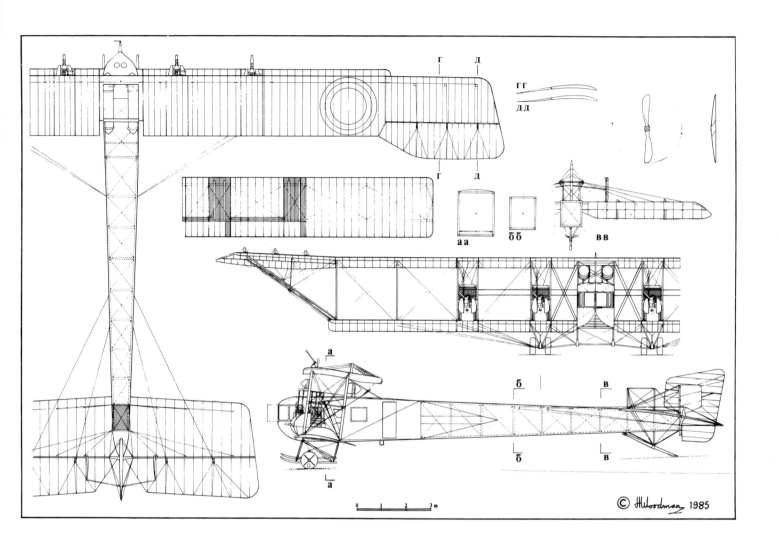

Il'ya Muromets Kievskiy, top, front, and side view.
(Harry Woodman)

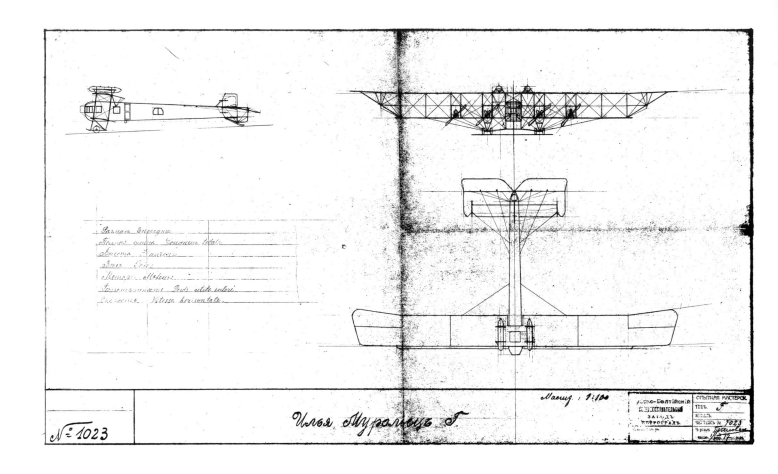

Il'ya Muromets Type G (original Russian drawing), side, front, and top view. (UTC Archives)

Il'ya Muromets Type G-3, sheet 1, side view, interior and ► construction details. (Harry Woodman)

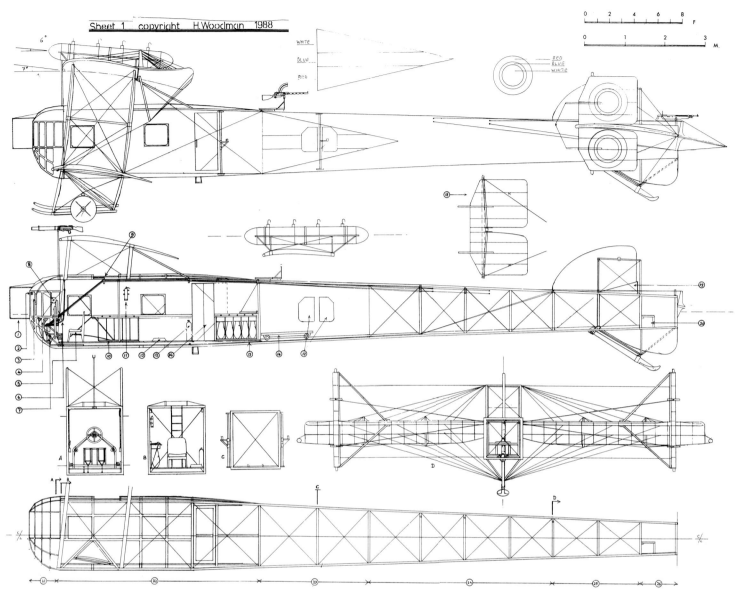

Key to Sheet 1

1. Sikorsky ''artificial horizon,'' reference point device for climbs, descents, and turns.
2. Electric lamp (tubular).
3. Fuel level indicators, one each side.
4. Tachometers, two each side.
5. Pilot's seat.
6. Switches, four on base board.
7. Rudder pedal assembly, welded tubular steel framework.
8. Barometric altitude indicator.
9. Firing step for upper gunner (board rests on stringers).
10. Forward bomb rack, shown empty.
11. Fire extinguisher.
12. Bomb sight.
13. Compressed air bottle (port side only).
14. Sliding door (port and starboard).
15. Rear bomb rack, loaded. Note that racks slide along side rail to pass over bomb bay.

16. Trolley on rails to enable rear gunner to reach tail position (details speculative).
17. Midships gun positions; panels removable.
18. Inboard view of starboard rudder. Note that oblique external support struts are fixed to side of rudder, inboard only.
19. Plywood windscreen for rear gunner.
20. Rear gunner's seat.
21. Nose section; light metal framework supporting triplex glass windows.
22. Main crew area; inner and outer plywood walls and decking, fabric-covered roof over light wooden stringers.
23. Fuselage forward; plywood floor with external fabric, double plywood fabric-covered sides.
24. Wood-braced fuselage center; fabric top, bottom, and sides.
25. Fuselage aft; plywood decking on top.
26. Tail gunner compartment; plywood bottom, floor, and sides with no bracing wires.

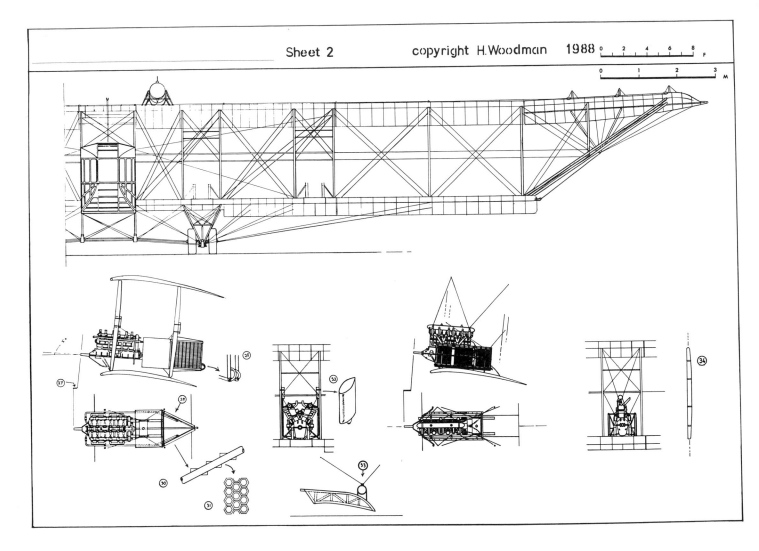

Key to Sheet 2

27. Note transition from side view of Renault engine to frontview.

28. Rear detail of radiators shows water outlet pipes passing back to water pump at rear of engine.

29. Top view with aluminum top cover plate removed to show water outlet pipes passing from engine to top of radiators, water reservoir tank between engine and radiators.

30. Detail top view of "Hazet"-type radiators showing angled cellules.

31. Cross-section of cellules (outer radiators same).

32. Detail view of water expansion tanks, four to each Renault engine; two tanks drain water pipes from cylinders, two from radiator banks.

33. Skeletal view of engine bearers; wooden framework with plywood covering, water reservoir tank on aft end of upperbeam. Top front beams built with extra length and sawn to fit various engines. Note that inboard Renault engines are placed slightly ahead of outboard R-BVZ-6 engines.

34. View of main interplane struts. Note cord binding at four points, same for all interplane struts and diagonal outer struts. On rear pair of struts around inboard Renault engines, center portion of each strut is sheathed in aluminum. On left-hand pair of struts (front and rear, exhaust side) of outboard R-BVZ-6 engines, aluminum sheathing also covers middle section.

Il'ya Muromets Type G-3, sheet 2, front view, engine details. (Harry Woodman)

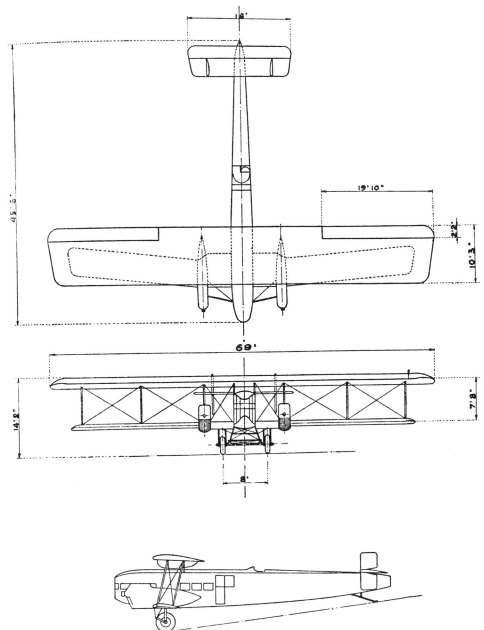

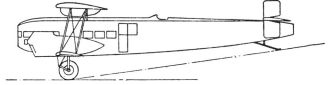

SIKORSKY AERO ENGINEERING CORPORATION

NEW YORK, N.Y.

SIKORSKY TWIN ENGINED TRANSPORT PLANE S-29-A.
ENGINES-LIBERTY "12"; SPEED 116 M.P.H., ON ONE MOTOR 75 M.P.H.
SERVICE CEILING 12500 FEET; CLIMB 5000 FEET IN 7 MIN 10 SEC

S-29-A, three-view. (UTC Archives, Aerospace Industries Association)

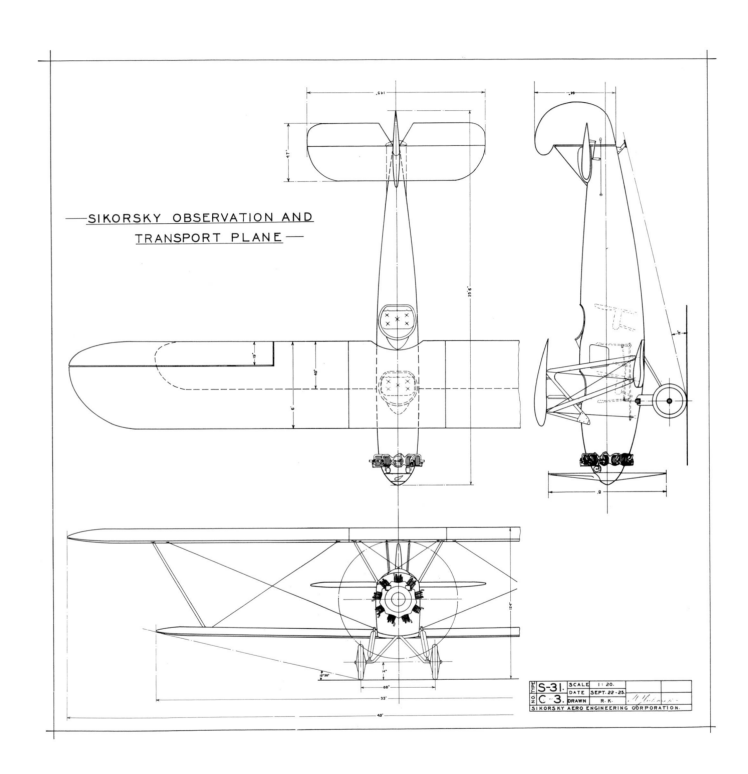

—SIKORSKY OBSERVATION AND
TRANSPORT PLANE—

S-31, three-view. (UTC Archives)

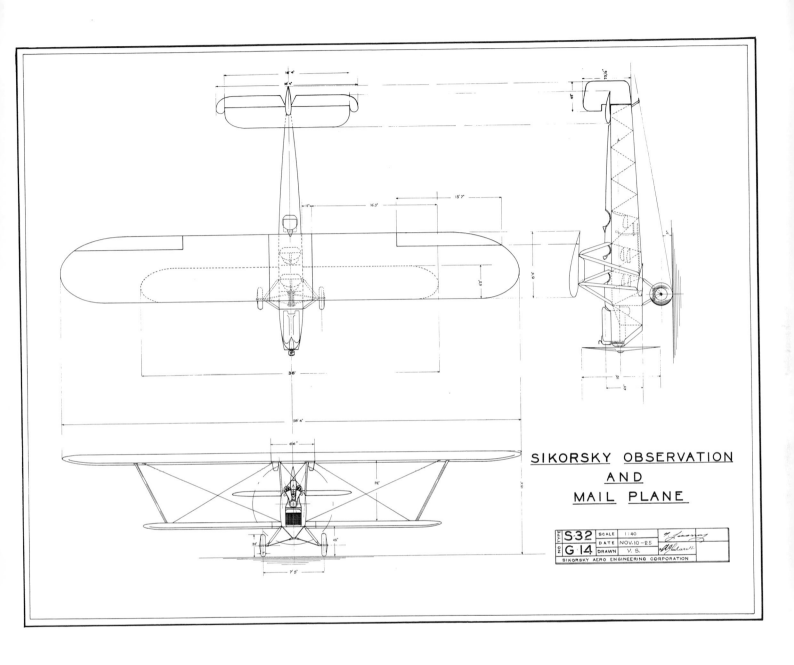

SIKORSKY OBSERVATION
AND
MAIL PLANE

S-32	SCALE	1:40	
NO. TYPE	DATE	NOV. 10-25	
G·14	DRAWN	V. S.	
SIKORSKY AERO ENGINEERING CORPORATION			

S-32, three-view. (UTC Archives)

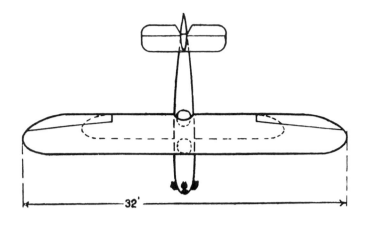

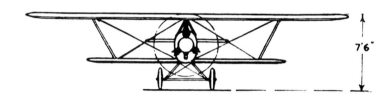

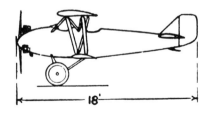

SIKORSKY MANUFACTURING CORPORATION
N. Y.

TWO SEATER MESSENGER S-33
MOTOR: WRIGHT 60 H.P.   SPEED 103 M.P.H.
USEFUL LOAD 500 LBS.   LOAD FACTOR 8.5

S-33, three-view. (UTC Archives, Aerospace Industries Association)

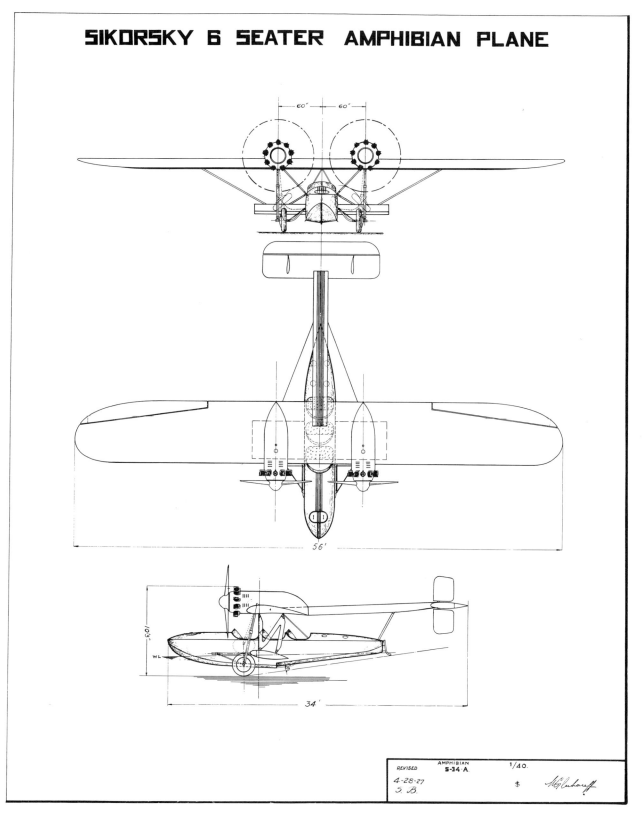

SIKORSKY 6 SEATER AMPHIBIAN PLANE

REVISED	AMPHIBIAN S-34-A	1/40.
4-28-27 S. B.		$

S-34-A, three-view. (UTC Archives)

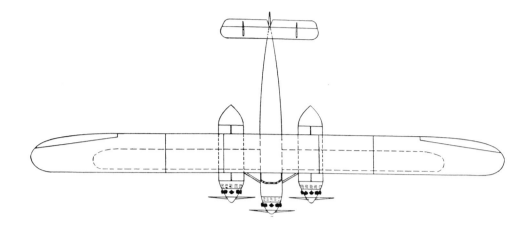

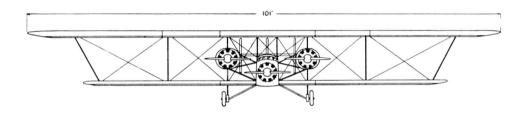

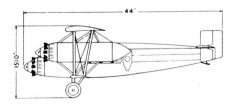

S-35, three-view. (UTC Archives, Aerospace Industries Association)

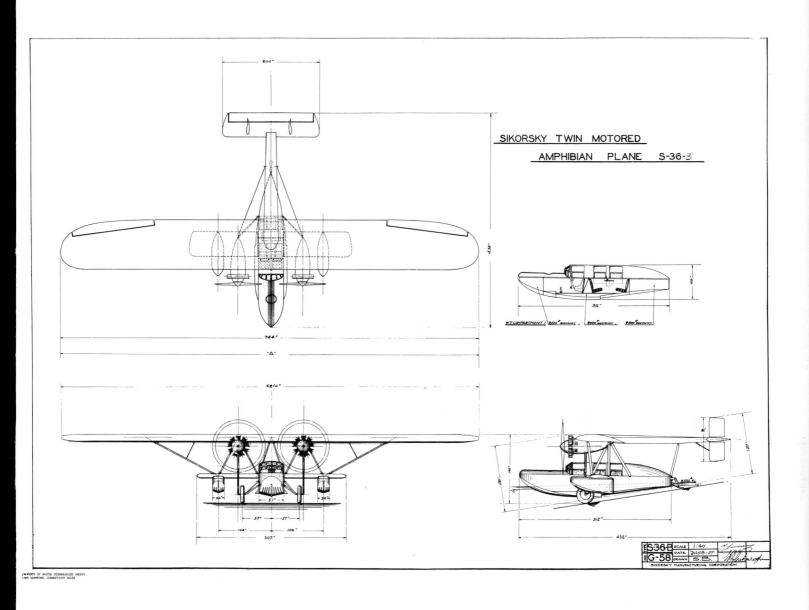

SIKORSKY TWIN MOTORED
AMPHIBIAN PLANE S-36-B

S-36-B, three-view with interior details. (UTC Archives)

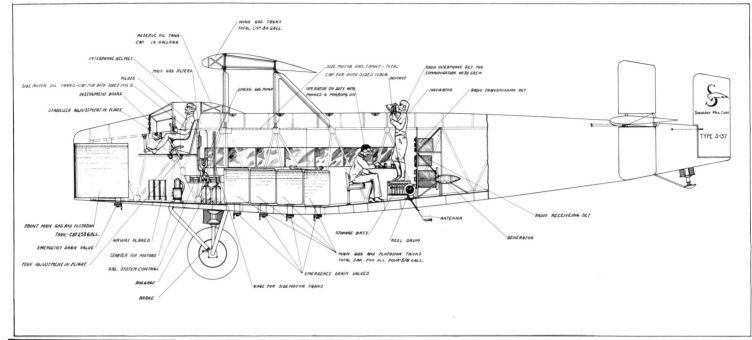

SIKORSKY TWIN ENGINE PLANE
EQUIPPED FOR LONG DISTANCE FLIGHT

S-37, side view with interior details. (UTC Archives)

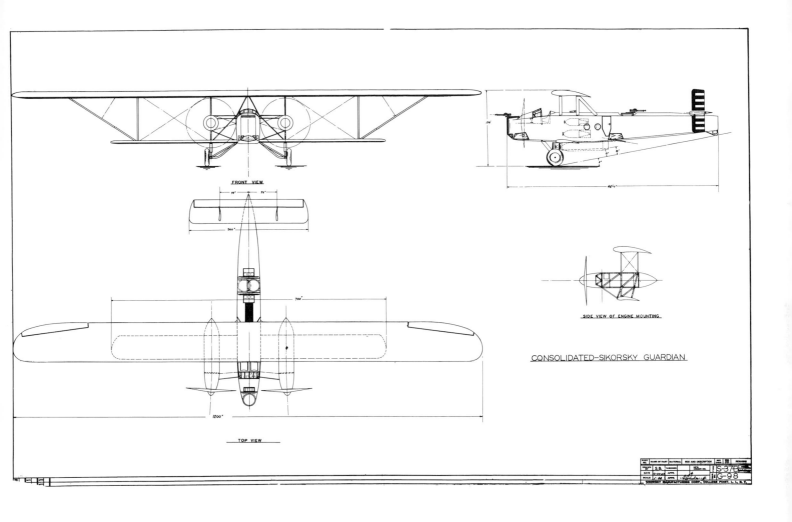

FRONT VIEW

TOP VIEW

SIDE VIEW OF ENGINE MOUNTING

CONSOLIDATED-SIKORSKY GUARDIAN

Consolidated-Sikorsky Guardian S-37-B, three-view.
(UTC Archives)

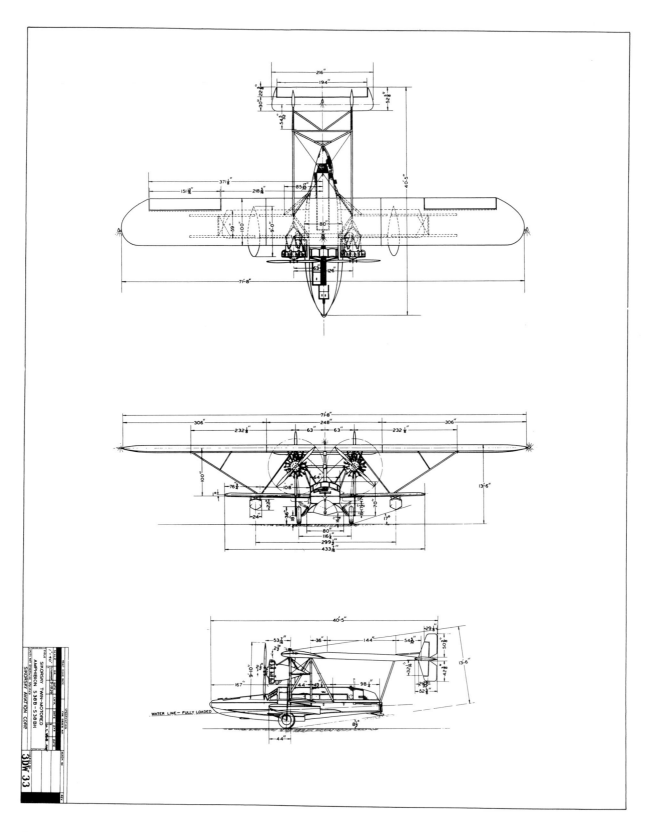

S-38-B, three-view. (UTC Archives)

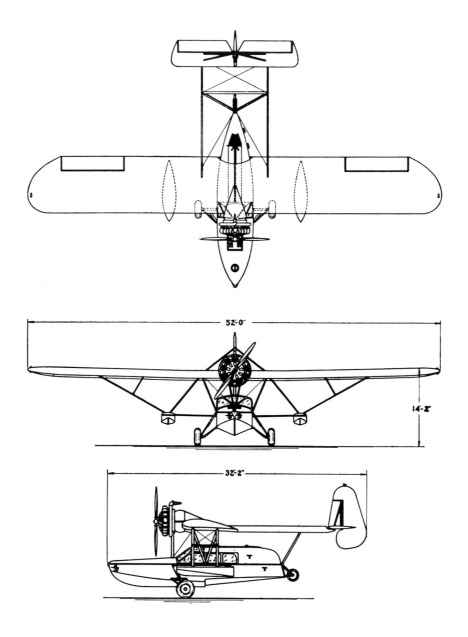

SIKORSKY AVIATION CORPORATION
Bridgeport, Conn.
AMPHIBION S–39 —— 5 PLACE
ENGINE: PRATT & WHITNEY WASP, JR.

S-39, three-view. (UTC Archives, Aerospace Industries Association)

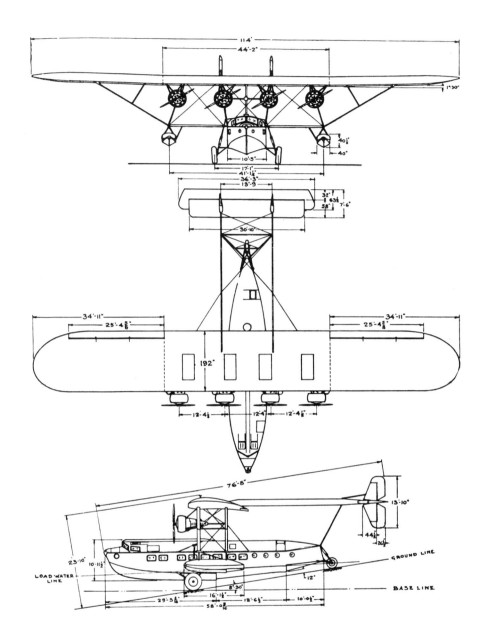

SIKORSKY AVIATION CORPORATION
Bridgeport, Conn.
AMPHIBION S-40 —— 38 PLACE
ENGINE: FOUR PRATT & WHITNEY HORNETS

S-40, three-view. (UTC Archives, Aerospace Industries Association)

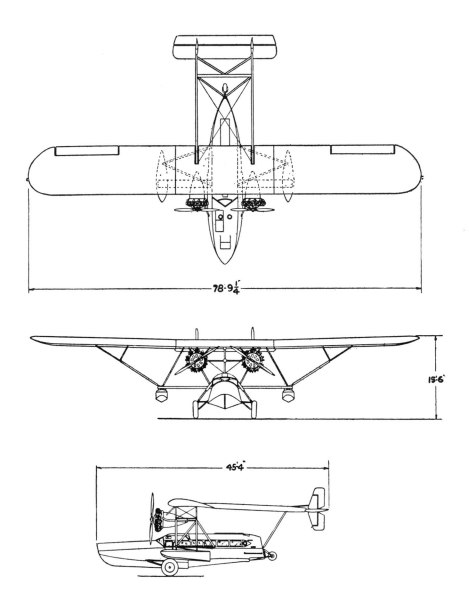

SIKORSKY AVIATION CORPORATION
Bridgeport, Conn.
AMPHIBION S–41 —— 16 PLACE
ENGINE: TWO PRATT & WHITNEY HORNETS

S-41, three-view. (UTC Archives, Aerospace Industries Association)

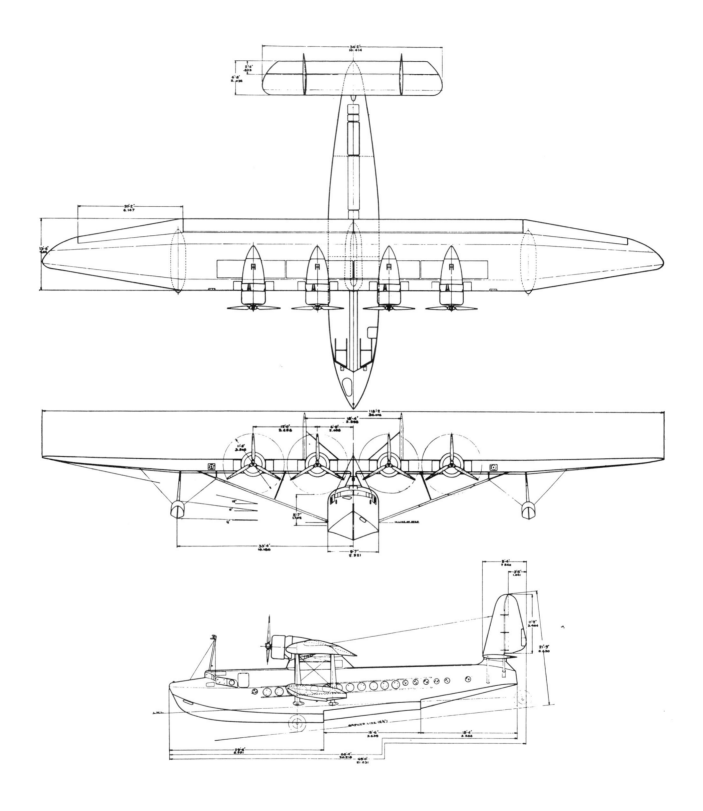

S-42, three-view. (UTC Archives)

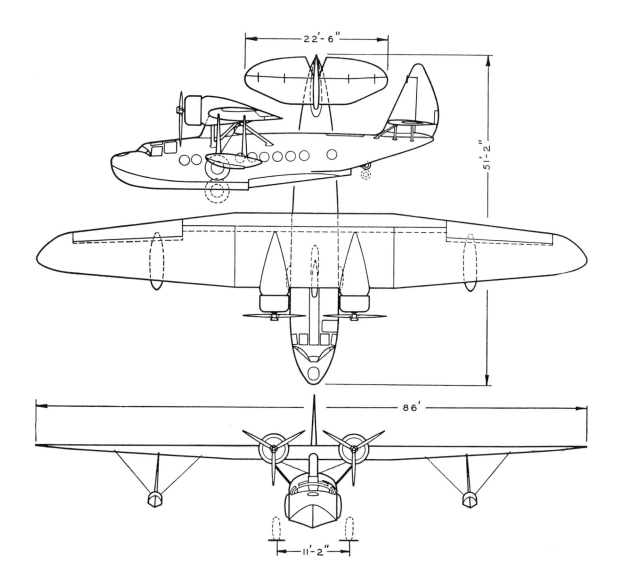

SIKORSKY S-43

A 15-25 place amphibion, powered with two Pratt & Whitney **Hornets.**

S-43, three-view. (UTC Archives, Aerospace Industries Association)

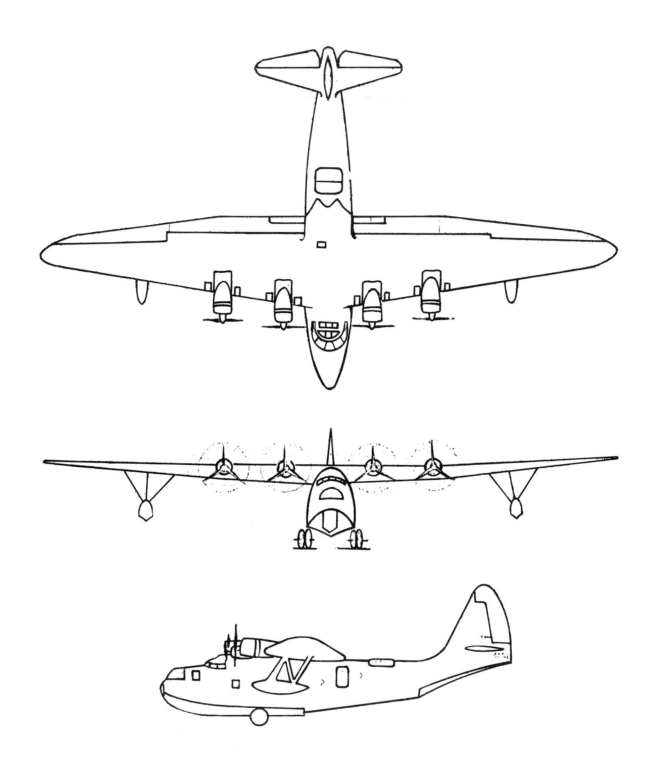

XPBS-1, three-view. (UTC Archives)

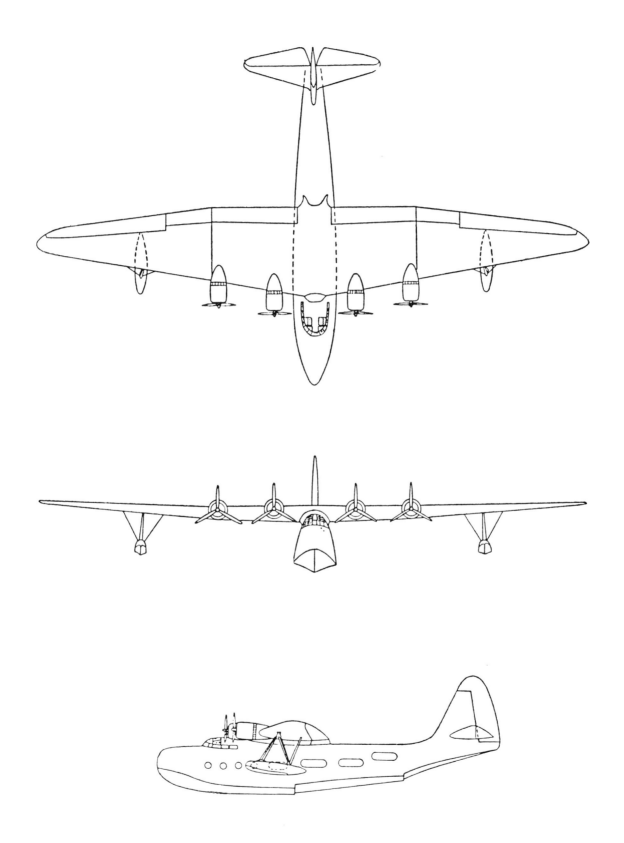

VS-44A, three-view. (UTC Archives)

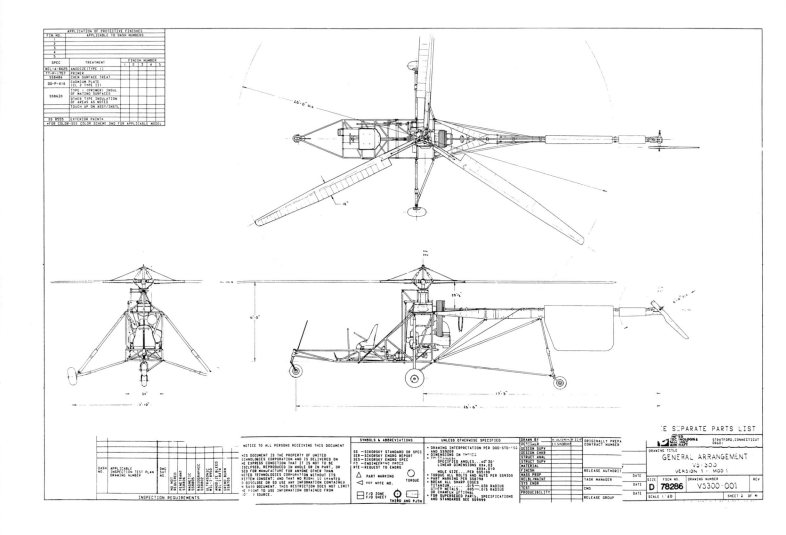

VS-300, Version 1-Mod 1, three-view. (UTC Archives)

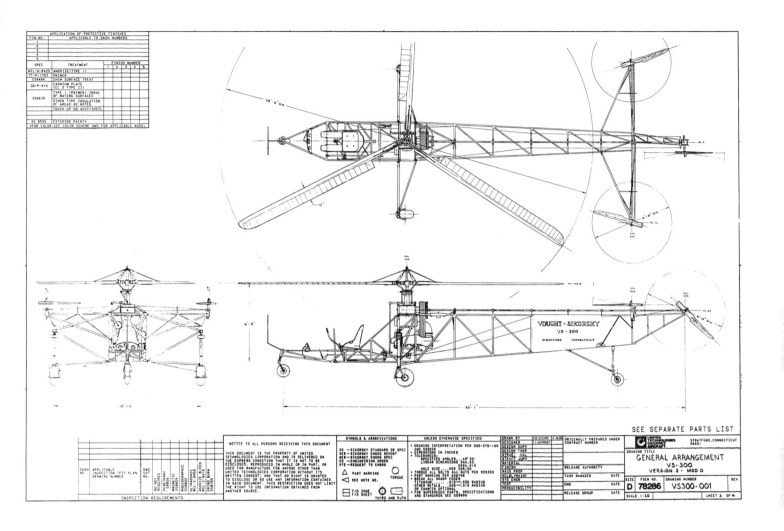

VS-300, Version 2-Mod 0, three-view. (UTC Archives)

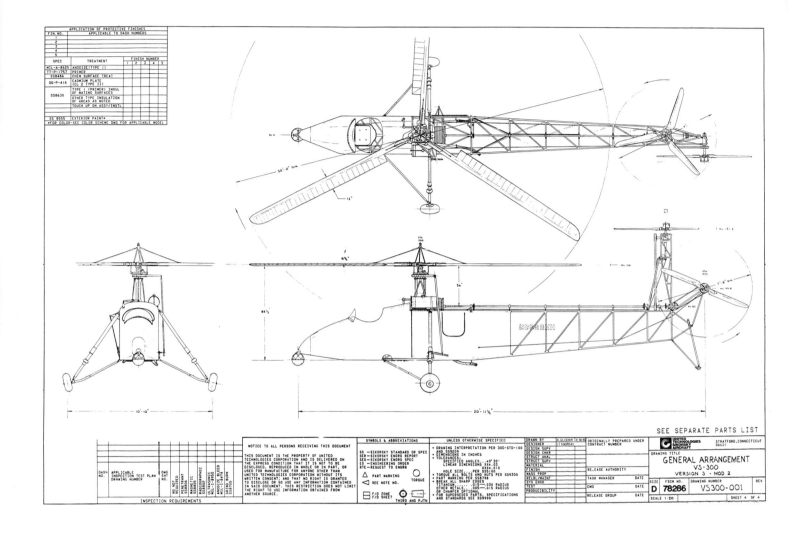

VS-300, Version 3-Mod 2, three-view. (UTC Archives)

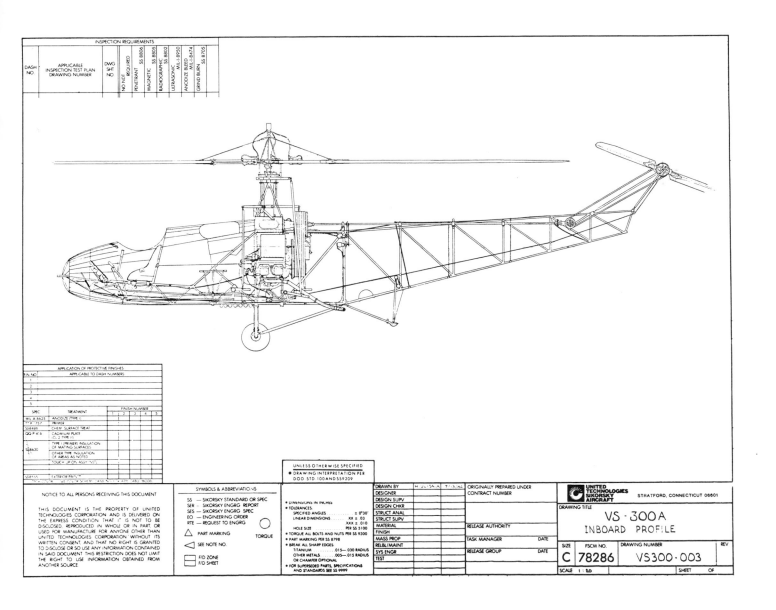

VS-300A, inboard profile, side view with interior details.
(UTC Archives)

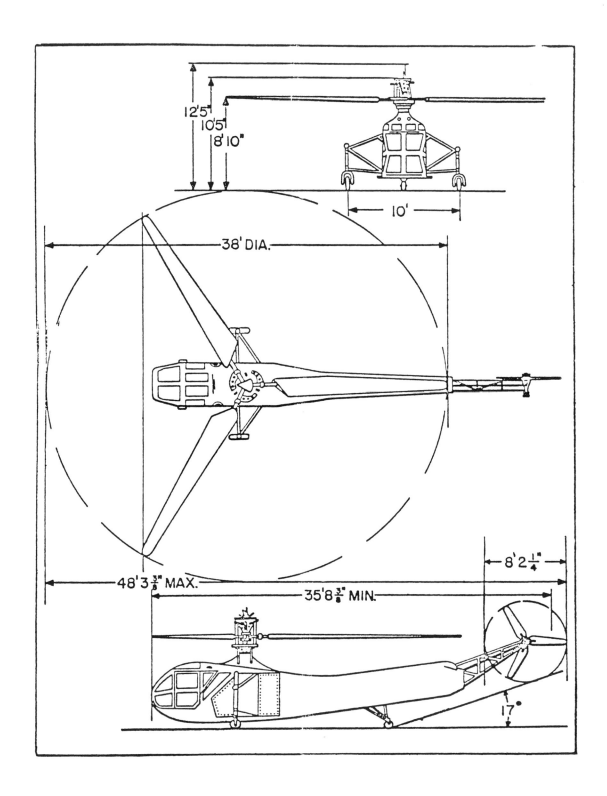

R-4, three-view. (UTC Archives)

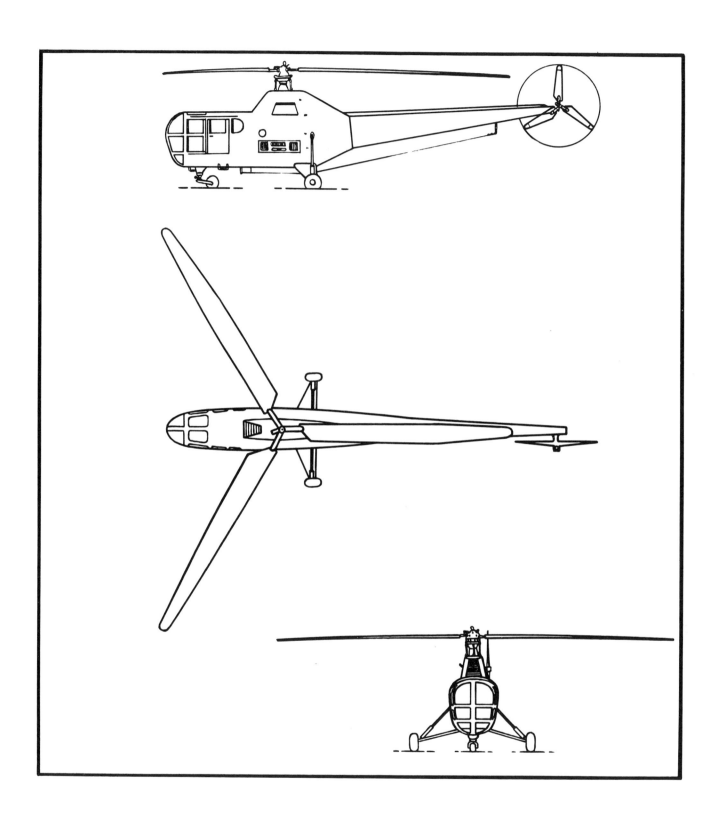

R-5, three-view. (NASM)

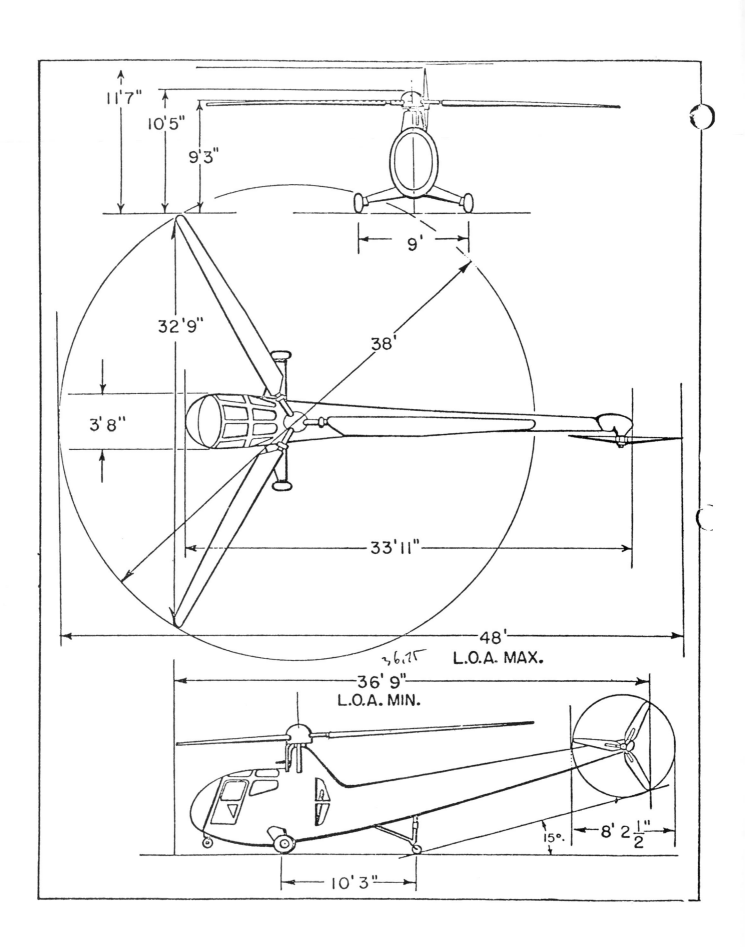

11'7"

10'5"

9'3"

9'

32'9"

38'

3'8"

33'11"

48'
L.O.A. MAX.

36.75

36' 9"
L.O.A. MIN.

15°.

8' 2 ½"

10' 3"

APPENDIX 2.
TECHNICAL SPECIFICATIONS

The technical specifications for all major Sikorsky aircraft and helicopters are included here. The data for his designs from the Russian period have been compiled from several sources, with special reference to V. B. Shavrov's *Istoriya konstruktsii samoletov v SSSR do 1938 q.* [A History of aircraft design in the USSR for the period before 1938] (Moscow, 1985). This reference work contains detailed information on the various types of Il'ya Muromets aircraft and some of Sikorsky's earlier work on the "S" series. P. D. Duz's book, *Istoriya vozdukhoplavaniya i aviatsii v SSSR, Period 1914-1918* [A History of aeronautics and aviation in the USSR for the period 1914-1918] (Moscow, 1979), provided additional detail. The specifications for the "Golden Age" and "Vertical Flight" sections were obtained from Professor I. A. Sikorsky's unpublished manuscript, "The Technical History of Sikorsky Aircraft and Its Predecessors (since 1909)," from the United Technologies Corporation Archives. The data contained in his work were derived from Sikorsky company records.

Each successive type of Il'ya Muromets manufactured during World War I (1914–17) was designated by a different letter according to the Russian alphabet. Since this alphabet does not follow the order of the English alphabet, confusion has arisen. For example, the Russian letter "B" is the English letter "V" and is pronounced "veh." This list preserves the Russian alphabetical order.

Note that the difference between an airplane's gross weight and its takeoff weight can be significant, as in the case of the S-35. Sikorsky initially built the S-35 for a gross weight (aircraft weight and payload) of 20,000 pounds. The modified transatlantic S-35 was expected to weigh about 24,000 pounds when fully fueled. The actual takeoff weight, however, was 28,000 pounds.

RUSSIAN PERIOD

Model: **Helicopter-1**
Type: Helicopter with two two-bladed rotors
Year: 1909
Manufacturer: Sikorsky
Engine(s) type: Anzani
H.P.: 25
Length: n/a
Rotor span(s): 4.6 m./5 m. (15 ft. 1 in./16 ft. 5 in.)
Rotor area: 2 sq.m. (22.5 sq. ft.)
Weight empty: 162 kg. (357 lbs.)
Weight fuel/oil: 15 kg. (33 lbs.)
Weight full load: +/− 90 kg. (198 lbs.)
Weight flying: 250 kg. (551 lbs.)
Wing load: n/a
Power load: 10 kg./hp. (22 lbs./hp.)
Max. speed: n/a

Model: **Helicopter-2**
Type: Helicopter with two three-bladed rotors
Year: 1910
Manufacturer: Sikorsky
Engine(s) type: Anzani
H.P.: 25
Length: n/a
Rotor span(s): n/a
Rotor area: n/a
Weight empty: 182 kg. (401 lbs.)
Weight fuel/oil: 15 kg. (33 lbs.)
Weight full load: +/− 90 kg. (198 lbs.)
Weight flying: 270 kg. (595 lbs.)
Wing load: n/a
Power load: 10.8 kg./hp. (23.8 lbs./hp.)
Max. speed: n/a

Model: **BIS-1 (S-1)**
Type: Biplane single-place with one pusher propeller
Year: 1910
Manufacturer: Sikorsky, Bylinkin, Iordan
Engine(s) type: Anzani
H.P.: 15
Length: 8 m. (26 ft. 3 in.)
Wing span(s) upper/lower: 8 m. (26 ft. 3 in.)
Wing area: 24 sq.m. (258.3 sq.ft.)
Weight empty: 180 kg. (397 lbs.)
Weight fuel/oil: 10 kg. (22 lbs.)
Weight full load: 70 kg. (154 lbs.)
Weight flying: 250 kg. (551 lbs.)
Wing load: 10.4 kg./sq.m. (2.1 lbs./sq.ft.)
Power load: 16 kg./hp. (36.7 lbs./hp.)
Max. speed: n/a

Model: **BIS-2 (S-2)**
Type: Biplane single-place with one tractor propeller
Year: 1910
Manufacturer: Sikorsky, Bylinkin, Iordan
Engine(s) type: Anzani
H.P.: 25
Length: 8 m. (26 ft. 3 in.)
Wing span(s) upper/lower: 8 m. (26 ft. 3 in.)
Wing area: 24 sq.m. (258.3 sq.ft.)
Weight empty: 190 kg. (419 lbs.)
Weight fuel/oil: 10 kg. (22 lbs.)
Weight full load: 70 kg. (154 lbs.)

Weight flying: 260 kg. (573 lbs.)
Wing load: 10.8 kg./sq.m. (2.2 lbs./sq.ft.)
Power load: 10.2 kg./hp. (23 lbs./hp.)
Max. speed: n/a

Model: **S-3**
Type: Biplane single-place with one tractor propeller
Year: 1910
Manufacturer: Sikorsky
Engine(s) type: Anzani
H.P.: 35
Length: 8 m. (26 ft. 3 in.)
Wing span(s) upper/lower: 8 m. (26 ft. 3 in.)
Wing area: 24 sq.m. (258.3 sq.ft.)
Weight empty: 220 kg. (485 lbs.)
Weight fuel/oil: 20 kg. (44 lbs.)
Weight full load: 90 kg. (198 lbs.)
Weight flying: 310 kg. (683 lbs.)
Wing load: 13 kg./sq.m. (2.6 lbs./sq.ft.)
Power load: 8.9 kg./hp. (19.5 lbs./hp.)
Max. speed: n/a

Model: **S-4**
Type: Biplane single-place with one tractor propeller
Year: 1910
Manufacturer: Sikorsky
Engine(s) type: Anzani
H.P.: 50
Length: 8 m. (26 ft. 3 in.)
Wing span(s) upper/lower: 9 m. (29 ft. 6 in.)
Wing area: 28 sq.m. (301.4 sq.ft.)
Weight empty: 260 kg. (573 lbs.)
Weight fuel/oil: 30 kg. (66 lbs.)
Weight full load: 100 kg. (220 lbs.)
Weight flying: 360 kg. (794 lbs.)
Wing load: 12.9 kg./sq.m. (2.6 lbs./sq.ft.)
Power load: 7.2 kg./hp. (15.9 lbs./hp.)
Max. speed: n/a

Model: **S-5**
Type: Biplane single-place with one tractor propeller
Year: 1911
Manufacturer: Sikorsky
Engine(s) type: Argus
H.P.: 50
Length: 8.5 m. (27 ft. 11 in.)
Wing span(s) upper/lower: 12 m./9 m. (39 ft. 4 in./29 ft. 6 in.)
Wing area: 33 sq.m. (355.2 sq.ft.)
Weight empty: 320 kg. (705 lbs.)
Weight fuel/oil: 40 kg. (88 lbs.)
Weight full load: 120 kg. (265 lbs.)
Weight flying: 440 kg. (970 lbs.)
Wing load: 13.3 kg./sq.m. (2.7 lbs./sq.ft.)
Power load: 8.8 kg./hp. (19.4 lbs./hp.)
Max. speed: n/a

Model: **S-6**
Type: Biplane three-place with one tractor propeller
Year: 1911
Manufacturer: Sikorsky
Engine(s) type: Argus
H.P.: 100
Length: 8.8 m. (28 ft. 10 in.)
Wing span(s) upper/lower: 11.8 m. (38 ft. 9 in.)

Wing area: 35.4 sq.m. (381 sq.ft.)
Weight empty: 650 kg. (1433 lbs.)
Weight fuel/oil: 60 kg. (132 lbs.)
Weight full load: 200/340 kg. (441/750 lbs.)
Weight flying: 850/990 kg. (1874/2183 lbs.)
Wing load: 24 sq./sq.m. (4.9 lbs./sq.ft.)
Power load: 8.5 kg./hp. (18.7 lbs./hp.)
Max. speed: n/a

Model: **S-5A**
Type: Biplane/seaplane with one tractor propeller
Year: 1912
Manufacturer: Russo-Baltic Wagon Company (R-BVZ)
Engine(s) type: Gnome/Gnome
H.P.: 60/80
Length: 8 m. (26 ft. 3 in.)
Wing span(s) upper/lower: 12 m./8.5 m. (39 ft. 4 in./27 ft. 11 in.)
Wing area: 30 sq.m. (323 sq.ft.)
Weight empty: n/a
Weight fuel/oil: n/a
Weight full load: n/a
Weight flying: n/a
Wing load: n/a
Power load: n/a
Max. speed: n/a

Model: **S-6A**
Type: Biplane three-place with one tractor propeller
Year: 1912
Manufacturer: Sikorsky
Engine(s) type: Argus
H.P.: 100
Length: 9.2 m. (30 ft. 2 in.)
Wing span(s) upper/lower: 14.5 m./11.7 m. (47 ft. 7 in./38 ft. 5 in.)
Wing area: 39 sq.m. (419.8 sq.ft.)
Weight empty: 650 kg. (1433 lbs.)
Weight fuel/oil: 60 kg. (132 lbs.)
Weight full load: 250/450 kg. (551/992 lbs.)
Weight flying: 900/1100 kg. (1984/2425 lbs.)
Wing load: 23 sq./sq.m. (4.7 lbs./sq.ft.)
Power load: 9 kg./hp. (19.8 lbs./hp.)
Max. speed: n/a

Model: **S-6B**
Type: Biplane three-place with one tractor propeller
Year: 1912
Manufacturer: Russo-Baltic Wagon Company (R-BVZ)
Engine(s) type: Argus
H.P.: 100
Length: 8.5 m. (27 ft. 11 in.)
Wing span(s) upper/lower: 14.9 m./10.9 m. (48 ft. 11 in./35 ft. 9 in.)
Wing area: 37.5 sq.m. (403.6 sq.ft.)
Weight empty: 590 kg. (1301 lbs.)
Weight fuel/oil: n/a
Weight full load: 327 kg. (721 lbs.)
Weight flying: 917 kg. (2022 lbs.)
Wing load: 24.4 sq./sq.m. (5 lbs./sq.ft.)
Power load: 9.2 kg./hp. (20.2 lbs./hp.)
Max. speed: 113 km./hr. (70 mi./hr.)

Model: **S-7**
Type: Monoplane two-place with one tractor propeller
Year: 1912

Manufacturer: Russo-Baltic Wagon Company (R-BVZ)
Engine(s) type: Gnome
H.P.: 70
Length: 8.2 m. (26 ft. 11 in.)
Wing span(s) upper/lower: 10 m. (32 ft. 10 in.)
Wing area: 20 sq.m. (215.3 sq.ft.)
Weight empty: 449 kg. (990 lbs.)
Weight fuel/oil: n/a
Weight full load: 327 kg. (721 lbs.)
Weight flying: 776 kg. (1711 lbs.)
Wing load: 39 sq./sq.m. (8 lbs./sq.ft.)
Power load: 11 kg./hp. (24.4 lbs./hp.)
Max. speed: 108 km./hr. (67 mi./hr.)

Model: **S-8 Malyutka (Baby)**
Type: Biplane two-place with one tractor propeller
Year: 1912
Manufacturer: Russo-Baltic Wagon Company (R-BVZ)
Engine(s) type: Gnome
H.P.: 50
Length: 7.5 m. (24 ft. 7 in.)
Wing span(s) upper/lower: 12 m./8 m. (39 ft. 4 in./26 ft. 3 in.)
Wing area: 27 sq.m. (290.6 sq.ft.)
Weight empty: n/a
Weight fuel/oil: n/a
Weight full load: n/a
Weight flying: n/a
Wing load: n/a
Power load: n/a
Max. speed: 80 km./hr. (50 mi./hr.)

Model: **S-9 Kruglyi (Round)**
Type: Monoplane three-place with one tractor propeller
Year: 1913
Manufacturer: Russo-Baltic Wagon Company (R-BVZ)
Engine(s) type: Gnome Monosoupape
H.P.: 100
Length: n/a
Wing span(s) upper/lower: 12 m. (39 ft. 4 in.)
Wing area: 30 sq.m. (323 sq.ft.)
Weight empty: 690 kg. (1521 lbs.)
Weight fuel/oil: n/a
Weight full load: 300 kg. (661 lbs.)
Weight flying: 990 kg. (2183 lbs.)
Wing load: 33 sq./sq.m. (6.8 lbs./sq.ft.)
Power load: 10 kg./hp. (21.8 lbs./hp.)
Max. speed: 80 km./hr. (50 mi./hr.)

Model: **S-10**
Type: Biplane two-place with one tractor propeller
Year: 1913
Manufacturer: Russo-Baltic Wagon Company (R-BVZ)
Engine(s) type: Argus
H.P.: 100
Length: n/a
Wing span(s) upper/lower: 13.7 m./8.8 m. (44 ft. 11 in./28 ft. 11 in.)
Wing area: 35.5 sq.m. (382.1 sq.ft.)
Weight empty: 550 kg. (1213 lbs.)
Weight fuel/oil: n/a
Weight full load: 300 kg. (661 lbs.)
Weight flying: 850 kg. (1874 lbs.)

Wing load: 24.3 kg./sq.m. (4.9 lbs./sq.ft.)
Power load: 8.5 kg./hp. (18.7 lbs./hp.)
Max. speed: n/a

Model: **S-10 competition**
Type: Biplane two-place with one tractor propeller
Year: 1913
Manufacturer: Russo-Baltic Wagon Company (R-BVZ)
Engine(s) type: Gnome
H.P.: 80
Length: 8 m. (26 ft. 3 in.)
Wing span(s) upper/lower: 16.9 m./12 m. (55 ft. 5 in./39 ft. 4 in.)
Wing area: 46 sq.m. (495.1 sq.ft.)
Weight empty: 567 kg. (1250 lbs.)
Weight fuel/oil: n/a
Weight full load: 444 kg. (979 lbs.)
Weight flying: 1011 kg. (2229 lbs.)
Wing load: 22 kg./sq.m. (4.5 lbs./sq.ft.)
Power load: 12.7 kg./hp. (27.9 lbs./hp.)
Max. speed: 99 km./hr. (61 mi./hr.)

Model: **S-10 Gidro (Hydro)**
Type: Biplane/seaplane two-place with one tractor propeller
Year: 1913
Manufacturer: Russo-Baltic Wagon Company (R-BVZ)
Engine(s) type: Argus
H.P.: 100
Length: n/a
Wing span(s) upper/lower: 13.7 m./8.8 m. (44 ft. 11 in./28 ft. 10 in.)
Wing area: 35.5 sq.m. (382.1 sq.ft.)
Weight empty: 700 kg. (1543 lbs.)
Weight fuel/oil: n/a
Weight full load: 380 kg. (838 lbs.)
Weight flying: 1080 kg. (2381 lbs.)
Wing load: 31 kg./sq.m. (6.2 lbs./sq.ft.)
Power load: 10.8 kg./hp. (23.8 lbs./hp.)
Max. speed: n/a

Model: **S-10A**
Type: Biplane two-place with one tractor propeller
Year: 1913
Manufacturer: Russo-Baltic Wagon Company (R-BVZ)
Engine(s) type: Anzani
H.P.: 125
Length: n/a
Wing span(s) upper/lower: 13.7 m./8.8 m. (44 ft. 11 in./28 ft. 10 in.)
Wing area: 35.5 sq.m. (382.1 sq.ft.)
Weight empty: n/a
Weight fuel/oil: 120/20 kg. (265/44 lbs.)
Weight full load: n/a
Weight flying: n/a
Wing load: n/a
Power load: n/a
Max. speed: n/a

Model: **S-10A Gidro (Hydro)**
Type: Biplane/seaplane two-place with one tractor propeller
Year: 1914
Manufacturer: Russo-Baltic Wagon Company (R-BVZ)
Engine(s) type: Gnome Monosoupape
H.P.: 100

Length: n/a
Wing span(s) upper/lower: 13.7 m./8.8 m. (44 ft. 11 in./28 ft. 10 in.)
Wing area: 35.5 sq.m. (382.1 sq.ft.)
Weight empty: 565 kg. (1246 lbs.)
Weight fuel/oil: 160 kg. (353 lbs.)
Weight full load: 310 kg. (683 lbs.)
Weight flying: 875 kg. (1929 lbs.)
Wing load: 24.7 kg./sq.m. (5 lbs./sq.ft.)
Power load: 8.7 kg./hp. (19.3 lbs./hp.)
Max. speed: n/a

Model: **S-11**
Type: Monoplane two-place with one tractor propeller
Year: 1913
Manufacturer: Russo-Baltic Wagon Company (R-BVZ)
Engine(s) type: Gnome Monosoupape
H.P.: 100
Length: 7.6 m. (24 ft. 11 in.)
Wing span(s) upper/lower: 11.6 m. (38 ft. 1 in.)
Wing area: 26 sq.m. (280 sq.ft.)
Weight empty: 578 kg. (1274 lbs.)
Weight fuel/oil: n/a
Weight full load: 427 kg. (941 lbs.)
Weight flying: 1005 kg. (2216 lbs.)
Wing load: 38.6 kg./sq.m. (8 lbs./sq.ft.)
Power load: 10 kg./hp. (22.2 lbs./hp.)
Max. speed: 102 km./hr. (63 mi./hr.)

Model: **S-12**
Type: Monoplane with one tractor propeller
Year: 1913
Manufacturer: Russo-Baltic Wagon Company (R-BVZ)
Engine(s) type: Gnome
H.P.: 80
Length: n/a
Wing span(s) upper/lower: n/a
Wing area: 19.7 sq.m. (212 sq.ft.)
Weight empty: 419 kg. (924 lbs.)
Weight fuel/oil: 72/24 kg. (159/53 lbs.)
Weight full load: 262 kg. (578 lbs.)
Weight flying: 681 kg. (1501 lbs.)
Wing load: 34.5 kg./sq.m. (7 lbs./sq.ft.)
Power load: 8.5 kg./hp. (18.8 lbs./hp.)
Max. speed: n/a

Model: **S-15**
Type: Biplane/seaplane with one tractor propeller
Year: 1913
Manufacturer: Russo-Baltic Wagon Company (R-BVZ)
Engine(s) type: Argus
H.P.: 125
Length: n/a
Wing span(s) upper/lower: n/a
Wing area: n/a
Weight empty: n/a
Weight fuel/oil: n/a
Weight full load: n/a
Weight flying: n/a
Wing load: n/a
Power load: n/a
Max. speed: n/a

Model: **S-16**
Type: Biplane two-place with one tractor propeller
Year: 1915
Manufacturer: Russo-Baltic Wagon Company (R-BVZ)
Engine(s) type: Gnome/Kalep
H.P.: 80/60
Length: 5.9 m. (19 ft. 4 in.)
Wing span(s) upper/lower: 8 m. (26 ft. 3 in.)
Wing area: 25.3 sq.m. (272.3 sq.ft.)
Weight empty: 407 kg. (897 lbs.)
Weight fuel/oil: 96 kg. (212 lbs.)
Weight full load: 270 kg. (594 lbs.)
Weight flying: 676 kg. (1490 lbs.)
Wing load: 26.7 kg./sq.m. (5.5 lbs./sq.ft.)
Power load: 8.5 kg./hp. 11.3 kg./hp. (18.6 lbs./hp. 24.8 lbs./hp.)
Max. speed: 120 km./hr. (74 mi./hr.)

Model: **S-17**
Type: Biplane two-place with one tractor propeller
Year: 1916
Manufacturer: Russo-Baltic Wagon Company (R-BVZ)
Engine(s) type: Sunbeam
H.P.: 150
Length: n/a
Wing span(s) upper/lower: 13.8 m./12.5 m. (45 ft. 3 in./41 ft.)
Wing area: 43.5 sq.m. (468.2 sq.ft.)
Weight empty: 845 kg. (1863 lbs.)
Weight fuel/oil: 160/32 kg. (353/71 lbs.)
Weight full load: 342 kg. (754 lbs.)
Weight flying: 1190 kg. (2624 lbs.)
Wing load: 27.4 kg./sq.m. (5.6 lbs./sq.ft.)
Power load: 7.9 kg./hp. (17.5 lbs./hp.)
Max. speed: n/a

Model: **S-18**
Type: Biplane two-place with two pusher propellers
Year: 1916
Manufacturer: Russo-Baltic Wagon Company (R-BVZ)
Engine(s) type: Sunbeam x 2
H.P.: 150
Length: 9.7 m. (31 ft. 10 in.)
Wing span(s) upper/lower: 16.5 m./15.3 m. (54 ft. 2 in./50 ft. 2 in.)
Wing area: 58 sq.m. (624.3 sq.ft.)
Weight empty: 1485 kg. (3274 lbs.)
Weight fuel/oil: 380 kg. (838 lbs.)
Weight full load: 600 kg. (1323 lbs.)
Weight flying: 2100 kg. (4630 lbs.)
Wing load: 36.2 kg./sq.m. (7.4 lbs./sq.ft.)
Power load: 7 kg./hp. (15.4 lbs./hp.)
Max. speed: n/a

Model: **S-19**
Type: Biplane two-place with one tractor propeller and one pusher propeller
Year: 1916
Manufacturer: Russo-Baltic Wagon Company (R-BVZ)
Engine(s) type: Sunbeam x 2
H.P.: 150
Length: 17.1 m. (56 ft. 1 in.)
Wing span(s) upper/lower: 28 m. (98 ft. 10 in.)
Wing area: n/a

Weight empty: n/a
Weight fuel/oil: n/a
Weight full load: n/a
Weight flying: n/a
Wing load: n/a
Power load: n/a
Max. speed: 115 km./hr. (71 mi./hr.)

Model: **S-20**
Type: Biplane single-place with one tractor propeller
Year: 1916
Manufacturer: Russo-Baltic Wagon Company (R-BVZ)
Engine(s) type: Le Rhone
H.P.: 120
Length: 6.5 m. (21 ft. 4 in.)
Wing span(s) upper/lower: 8.2 m. (26 ft. 11 in.)
Wing area: 17 sq.m. (183 sq.ft.)
Weight empty: 395 kg. (871 lbs.)
Weight fuel/oil: 65 kg. (143 lbs.)
Weight full load: 175 kg. (386 lbs.)
Weight flying: 570 kg. (1254 lbs.)
Wing load: 33.5 kg./sq.m. (6.9 lbs./sq.ft.)
Power load: 4.7 kg./hp. (10.5 lbs./hp.)
Max. speed: 190 km./hr. (117 mi./hr.)

Model: **Grand: Bolshoi Baltiskiy, Great Baltic (S-21)**
Type: Biplane with two tractor propellers
Year: 1913
Manufacturer: Russo-Baltic Wagon Company (R-BVZ)
Engine(s) type: Argus x 2
H.P.: 100
Length: 20 m. (65 ft. 7 in.)
Wing span(s) upper/lower: 27/20 m. (88 ft. 7 in./65 ft. 7 in.)
Wing area: 120 sq.m. (1291.7 sq.ft.)
Weight empty: 3000 kg. (6614 lbs.)
Weight fuel/oil: 150 kg. (331 lbs.)
Weight full load: 400 kg. (882 lbs.)
Weight flying: 3400 kg. (7496 lbs.)
Wing load: 28.5 kg./sq.m. (5.8 lbs./sq.ft.)
Power load: 18 kg./hp. (37.5 lbs./hp.)
Load ratio %: 12
Max. speed: 80 km./hr. (50 mi./hr.)
Landing speed: 65 km./hr. (40 mi./hr.)
Time to height: n/a
Practical ceiling: 100 m. (328 ft.)
Duration hrs.: 2
Range: 150 km. (90 mi.)
Take-off run: 650 m. (2133 ft.)
Landing run: 150 m. (492 ft.)

Model: **Grand: Bolshoi Baltiskiy, Great Baltic (S-21)**
Type: Biplane with two tractor propellers and two pusher propellers in tandem
Year: 1913
Manufacturer: Russo-Baltic Wagon Company (R-BVZ)
Engine(s) type: Argus x 4
H.P.: 100
Length: 20 m. (65 ft. 7 in.)
Wing span(s) upper/lower: 27/20 m. (88 ft. 7 in./65 ft. 7 in.)
Wing area: 120 sq.m. (1291.7 sq.ft.)
Weight empty: 3400kg. (7496 lbs.)
Weight fuel/oil: 250 kg. (551 lbs.)
Weight full load: 600 kg. (1323 lbs.)

Weight flying: 4000 kg. (8818 lbs.)
Wing load: 33 kg./sq.m. (6.8 lbs./sq.ft.)
Power load: 11 kg.hp. (22 lbs./hp.)
Load ratio %: 15
Max. speed: 90 km./hr. (56 mi./hr.)
Landing speed: 70 km./hr. (43 mi./hr.)
Time to height: n/a
Practical ceiling: 500 m. (1640 ft.)
Duration hrs.: 2
Range: 170 km. (106 mi.)
Take-off run: 400 m. (1312 ft.)
Landing run: 200 m. (656 ft.)

Model: **Grand Russkii vityaz, Russian knight (S-21)**
Type: Biplane with four tractor propellers
Year: 1913
Manufacturer: Russo-Baltic Wagon Company (R-BVZ)
Engine(s) type: Argus x 4
H.P.: 100
Length: 20 m. (65 ft. 7 in.)
Wing span(s) 27/20 m. (88 ft. 7 in./65 ft. 7 in.)
Wing area: 120 sq.m. (1291.7 sq.ft.)
Weight empty: 3500 kg. (7716 lbs.)
Weight fuel/oil: 250 kg. (551 lbs.)
Weight full load: 700 kg. (1543 lbs.)
Weight flying: 4200 kg. (9259 lbs.)
Wing load: 35 kg./sq.m. (7.2 lbs./sq.ft.)
Power load: 11.5 kg./hp. (23.1 lbs./hp.)
Load ratio %: 17
Max. speed: 90 km./hr. (56 mi./hr.)
Landing speed: 70 km./hr. (43 mi./hr.)
Time to height: n/a
Practical ceiling: 600 m. (1969 ft.)
Duration hrs.: 2
Range: 170 km. (106 mi.)
Take-off run: 350 m. (1148 ft.)
Landing run: 200 m. (656 ft.)

Model: **Il'ya Muromets #107 with additional wing (S-22 "A")**
Type: Biplane with four tractor propellers
Year: 1913
Manufacturer: Russo-Baltic Wagon Company (R-BVZ)
Engine(s) type: Argus x 4
H.P.: 100
Length: 22 m. (72 ft. 2 in.)
Wing span(s) upper/lower: 32/22 m. [add. wing 16 m.] (105 ft./72 ft. 2 in.) (add. wing 52 ft. 6 in.)
Wing area: 210 sq.m. (2260.4 sq.ft.)
Weight empty: 4000 kg. (8818 lbs.)
Weight fuel/oil: 384 kg. (847 lbs.)
Weight full load: 1500 kg. (3307 lbs.)
Weight flying: 5500 kg. (12125 lbs.)
Wing load: 26 kg./sq.m. (5.4 lbs./sq.ft.)
Power load: 14.8 kg./hp. (30.3 lbs./hp.)
Load ratio %: 27
Max. speed: 85 km./hr. (53 mi./hr.)
Landing speed: 70 km./hr. (43 mi./hr.)
Time to height: n/a
Practical ceiling: 500 m. (1640 ft.)
Duration hrs.: 3
Range: 250 km. (155 mi.)
Take-off run: 400 m. (1312 ft.)
Landing run: 200 m. (656 ft.)

Model: **Il'ya Muromets #107 (S-22 "A")**
Type: Biplane with four tractor propellers
Year: 1913
Manufacturer: Russo-Baltic Wagon Company (R-BVZ)
Engine(s) type: Argus x 4
H.P.: 100
Length: 22 m. (72 ft. 2 in.)
Wing span(s) upper/lower: 32/22 m. (105 ft./72 ft. 2 in.)
Wing area: 182 sq.m. (1959 sq.ft.)
Weight empty: 2800 kg. (6173 lbs.)
Weight fuel/oil: 384 kg. (847 lbs.)
Weight full load: 1300 kg. (2866 lbs.)
Weight flying: 5100 kg. (11244 lbs.)
Wing load: 28 kg./sq.m. (5.7 lbs./sq.ft.)
Power load: 13.8 kg./hp. (28.1 lbs./hp.)
Load ratio %: 25
Max. speed: 95 km./hr. (59 mi./hr.)
Landing speed: 75 km./hr. (47 mi./hr.)
Time to height: 1000 m./25 min. (3281 ft./25 min.)
Practical ceiling: 1500 m. (4921 ft.)
Duration hrs.: 3
Range: 270 km. (168 mi.)
Take-off run: 300 m. (984 ft.)
Landing run: 200 m. (656 ft.)

Model: **Il'ya Muromets #107 (S-22 "A")**
Type: Biplane/seaplane with four tractor propellers
Year: 1914
Manufacturer: Russo-Baltic Wagon Company (R-BVZ)
Engine(s) type: Argus x 2/Salmson x 2
H.P.: 115/200
Length: 23.5 m. (77 ft. 1 in.)
Wing span(s) upper/lower: 32/22 m. (105 ft./72 ft. 2 in.)
Wing area: 182 sq.m. (1959 sq.ft.)
Weight empty: 4800 kg. (10582 lbs.)
Weight fuel/oil: 900 kg. (1984 lbs.)
Weight full load: 1500 kg. (3307 lbs.)
Weight flying: 6300 kg. (13889 lbs.)
Wing load: 34.5 kg./sq.m. (7.1 lbs./sq.ft.)
Power load: 10 kg./hp. (22 lbs./hp.)
Load ratio %: 24
Max. speed: 90 km./hr. (56 mi./hr.)
Landing speed: 75 km./hr. (47 mi./hr.)
Time to height: 1000 m./20 min. 2000 m./60 min. (3281 ft./20 min.) (6562 ft./60 min.)
Practical ceiling: 2000 m. (6562 ft.)
Duration hrs.: 6
Range: 550 km. (342 mi.)
Take-off run: 500 m. (1640 ft.)
Landing run: 180 m. (591 ft.)

Model: **Il'ya Mourmets #128 "Kievskiy" 1st (S-22 "B")**
Type: Biplane with four tractor propellers
Year: 1914
Manufacturer: Russo-Baltic Wagon Company (R-BVZ)
Engine(s) type: Argus x 2/Argus x 2
H.P.: 140/125
Length: 19 m. (62 ft. 4 in.)
Wing span(s) upper/lower: 30.95/22.45 m. (101 ft. 7 in./73 ft. 8 in.)
Wing area: 150 sq.m. (1614.6 sq.ft.)
Weight empty: 3040 kg. (6702 lbs.)

Weight fuel/oil: 700 kg. (1543 lbs.)
Weight full load: 1610 kg. (3549 lbs.)
Weight flying: 4650 kg. (10251 lbs.)
Wing load: 31 kg./sq.m. (6.3 lbs./sq.ft.)
Power load: 8.6 kg./hp. (19.3 lbs./hp.)
Load ratio %: 34
Max. speed: 100 km./hr. (62 mi./hr.)
Landing speed: 75 km./hr. (47 mi./hr.)
Time to height: 1000 m./15 min. 2000 m./35 min. 3000 m./70 min. (3281 ft./15 min.) (6562 ft./35 min.) (9843 ft./70 min.)
Practical ceiling: 3000 m. (9843 ft.)
Duration hrs.: 5
Range: 500 km. (311 mi.)
Take-off run: n/a
Landing run: n/a

Model: **Il'ya Muromets B ("Beh") #135 (S-22 "B")**
Type: Biplane with four tractor propellers
Year: 1914
Manufacturer: Russo-Baltic Wagon Company (R-BVZ)
Engine(s) type: Argus x 4
H.P.: 130
Length: 19 m. (62 ft. 4 in.)
Wing span(s) upper/lower: 30.95/22.45 m. (101 ft. 7 in./73 ft. 8 in.)
Wing area: 150 sq.m. (1614.6 sq.ft.)
Weight empty: 3100 kg. (6834 lbs.)
Weight fuel/oil: 700 kg. (1543 lbs.)
Weight full load: 1500 kg. (3307 lbs.)
Weight flying: 4600 kg. (10141 lbs.)
Wing load: 30.7 kg./sq.m. (6.3 lbs./sq.ft.)
Power load: 8.3 kg./hp. (19.5 lbs./hp.)
Load ratio %: 33
Max. speed: 105 km./hr. (65 mi./hr.)
Landing speed: 75 km./hr. (47 mi./hr.)
Time to height: 1000 m./13 min. 2000 m./30 min. (3281 ft./13 min.) (6562 ft./30 min.)
Practical ceiling: 3000 m. (9843 ft.)
Duration hrs.: 5
Range: 520 km. (323 mi.)
Take-off run: n/a
Landing run: n/a

Model: **Il'ya Muromets B ("Beh") #136–139 (S-22 "B")**
Type: Biplane with four tractor propellers
Year: 1914
Manufacturer: Russo-Baltic Wagon Company (R-BVZ)
Engine(s) type: Salmson x 2/Salmson x 2
H.P.: 200/135
Length: 19 m. (62 ft. 4 in.)
Wing span(s) upper/lower: 30.95/22.45 m. (101 ft. 7 in./73 ft. 8 in.)
Wing area: 150 sq.m. (1614.6 sq.ft.)
Weight empty: 3600 kg. (7937 lbs.)
Weight fuel/oil: 700 kg. (1543 lbs.)
Weight full load: 1200 kg. (2646 lbs.)
Weight flying: 4800 kg. (10582 lbs.)
Wing load: 32 kg./sq.m. (6.5 lbs./sq.ft.)
Power load: 7.2 kg./hp. (15.8 lbs./hp.)
Load ratio %: 26
Max. speed: 96 km./hr. (60 mi./hr.)
Landing speed: 75 km./hr. (47 mi./hr.)
Time to height: 1000 m./20 min. 2000 m./70 min. (3281 ft./20 min.) (6562 ft./70 min.)
Practical ceiling: 2000 m. (6562 ft.)

Duration hrs.: 4
Range: 380 km. (236 mi.)
Take-off run: n/a
Landing run: n/a

Model: **Il'ya Muromets V ("Veh") #143 Kievskiy 2nd (S-23)**
Type: Biplane with four tractor propellers
Year: 1914
Manufacturer: Russo-Baltic Wagon Company (R-BVZ)
Engine(s) type: Argus x 2/Argus x 2
H.P.: 140/125
Length: 17.1 m. (56 ft. 1 in.)
Wing span(s) upper/lower: 29.8/21 m. (97 ft. 9 in./68 ft. 11 in.)
Wing area: 125 sq.m. (1345.5 sq.ft.)
Weight empty: 2900 kg. (6393 lbs.)
Weight fuel/oil: 550 kg. (1213 lbs.)
Weight full load: 1500 kg. (3307 lbs.)
Weight flying: 4400 kg. (9700 lbs.)
Wing load: 35.3 kg./sq.m. (7.2 lbs./sq.ft.)
Power load: 8.1 kg./hp. (18.3 lbs./hp.)
Load ratio %: 34
Max. speed: 125 km./hr. (78 mi./hr.)
Landing speed: 75 km./hr. (47 mi./hr.)
Time to height: 1000 m./11 min. 2000 m./25 min. (3281 ft./11 min.) (6562 ft./25 min.)
Practical ceiling: 3700 m. (12139 ft.)
Duration hrs.: 5.3
Range: 650 km. (404 mi.)
Take-off run: 220 m./17 sec. (722 ft./17 sec.)
Landing run: 200 m. (656 ft.)

Model: **Il'ya Muromets V ("Veh") #151 (S-23)**
Type: Biplane with four tractor propellers
Year: 1915
Manufacturer: Russo-Baltic Wagon Company (R-BVZ)
Engine(s) type: Argus x 4
H.P.: 140
Length: 17.1 m. (56 ft. 1 in.)
Wing span(s) upper/lower: 29.8/21 m. (97 ft. 9 in./68 ft. 11 in.)
Wing area: 125 sq.m. (1345.5 sq.ft.)
Weight empty: 2950 kg. (6504 lbs.)
Weight fuel/oil: 550 kg. (1213 lbs.)
Weight full load: 1500 kg. (3307 lbs.)
Weight flying: 4450 kg. (9811 lbs.)
Wing load: 35.5 kg./sq.m. (7.3 lbs./sq.ft.)
Power load: 8.3 kg./hp. (17.5 lbs./hp.)
Load ratio %: 34
Max. speed: 120 km./hr. (75 mi./hr.)
Landing speed: 75 km./hr. (47 mi./hr.)
Time to height: 1000 m./12 min. 2000 m./25 min. 3000 m./55 min. (3281 ft./12 min.) (6562 ft./25 min.) (9843 ft./55 min.)
Practical ceiling: 3500 m. (11483 ft.)
Duration hrs.: 5
Range: 630 km. (391 mi.)
Take-off run: 250 m./17 sec. (820 ft./17 sec.)
Landing run: 200 m. (656 ft.)

Model: **Il'ya Muromets V ("Veh") #150, 157 (S-23)**
Type: Biplane trainer with two tractor propellers
Year: 1915
Manufacturer: Russo-Baltic Wagon Company (R-BVZ)
Engine(s) type: Salmson x 2

H.P.: 200
Length: 17.1 m. (56 ft. 1 in.)
Wing span(s) upper/lower: 28/19.2 m.
(91 ft. 10 in./63 ft.)
Wing area: 120 sq.m. (1291.7 sq.ft.)
Weight empty: 2700 kg. (5952 lbs.)
Weight fuel/oil: 400 kg. (882 lbs.)
Weight full load: 800 kg. (1764 lbs.)
Weight flying: 3500 kg. (7716 lbs.)
Wing load: 29 kg./sq.m. (6 lbs./sq.ft.)
Power load: 8.8 kg./hp. (19.3 lbs./hp.)
Load ratio %: 23
Max. speed: 100 km./hr. (62 mi./hr.)
Landing speed: 70 km./hr. (43 mi./hr.)
Time to height: n/a
Practical ceiling: n/a
Duration hrs.: n/a
Range: n/a
Take-off run: n/a
Landing run: n/a

Model: **Il'ya Muromets V ("Veh") #159, #161 (S-23)**
Type: Biplane trainer with two tractor propellers
Year: 1915
Manufacturer: Russo-Baltic Wagon Company (R-BVZ)
Engine(s) type: Sunbeam x 2
H.P.: 225
Length: 17.1 m. (56 ft. 1 in.)
Wing span(s) upper/lower: 20/19.2 m.
(65 ft. 7 in./63 ft.)
Wing area: 120 sq.m. (1291.7 sq.ft.)
Weight empty: 2800 kg. (6173 lbs.)
Weight fuel/oil: 400 kg. (882 lbs.)
Weight full load: 800 kg. (1764 lbs.)
Weight flying: 3600 kg. (7937 lbs.)
Wing load: 30 kg./sq.m. (6.1 lbs./sq.ft.)
Power load: 8 kg./hp. (17.6 lbs./hp.)
Load ratio %: 22
Max. speed: 105 km./hr. (65 mi./hr.)
Landing speed: 70 km./hr. (43 mi./hr.)
Time to height: n/a
Practical ceiling: n/a
Duration hrs.: n/a
Range: n/a
Take-off run: n/a
Landing run: n/a

Model: **Il'ya Muromets V ("Veh") (S-23)**
Type: Biplane with four tractor propellers
Year: 1915
Manufacturer: Russo-Baltic Wagon Company (R-BVZ)
Engine(s) type: Sunbeam x 4
H.P.: 150
Length: 17.5 m. (57 ft. 5 in.)
Wing span(s) upper/lower: 29.8/21 m.
(97 ft. 9 in./68 ft. 11 in.)
Wing area: 125 sq.m. (1345.5 sq.ft.)
Weight empty: 3150 kg. (6945 lbs.)
Weight fuel/oil: 600 kg. (1323 lbs.)
Weight full load: 1450 kg. (3197 lbs.)
Weight flying: 4600 kg. (10141 lbs.)
Wing load: 36.8 kg./sq.m. (7.5 lbs./sq.ft.)
Power load: 7.7 kg./hp. (17 lbs./hp.)
Load ratio %: n/a
Max. speed: 110 km./hr. (68 mi./hr.)
Landing speed: 73 km./hr. (45 mi./hr.)

Time to height: 1000 m./16 min. 2000 m./
40 min. (3281 ft./16 min.) (6562 ft./40 min.)
Practical ceiling: 2900 m. (9514 ft.)
Duration hrs.: 4
Range: 440 km. (273 mi.)
Take-off run: 400 m. (1312 ft.)
Landing run: 220 m. (722 ft.)

Model: **Il'ya Muromets V ("Veh") (S-23)**
Type: Biplane trainer
Year: 1915
Manufacturer: Russo-Baltic Wagon Company (R-BVZ)
Engine(s) type: Sunbeam x 2
H.P.: 150
Length: 17.1 m. (56 ft. 1 in.)
Wing span(s) upper/lower: 28/19.2 m.
(91 ft. 10 in./63 ft.)
Wing area: 120 sq.m. (1291.7 sq.ft.)
Weight empty: 2500 kg. (5512 lbs.)
Weight fuel/oil: 300 kg. (661 lbs.)
Weight full load: 700 kg. (1543 lbs.)
Weight flying: 3200 kg. (7055 lbs.)
Wing load: 27 kg./sq.m. (5.5 lbs./sq.ft.)
Power load: 10.7 kg./hp. (23.5 lbs./hp.)
Load ratio %: 22
Max. speed: 90 km./hr. (56 mi./hr.)
Landing speed: 70 km./hr. (43 mi./hr.)
Time to height: n/a
Practical ceiling: n/a
Duration hrs.: n/a
Range: n/a
Take-off run: 400 m. (1312 ft.)
Landing run: 180 m. (591 ft.)

Model: **Il'ya Muromets V ("Veh") #167 (S-23)**
Type: Biplane with four tractor propellers
Year: 1915
Manufacturer: Russo-Baltic Wagon Company (R-BVZ)
Engine(s) type: R-BVZ x 4
H.P.: 150
Length: 17.5 m. (57 ft. 5 in.)
Wing span(s) upper/lower: 29.8/21 m.
(97 ft. 9 in./68 ft. 11 in.)
Wing area: 125 sq.m. (1345.5 sq.ft.)
Weight empty: 3500 kg. (7716 lbs.)
Weight fuel/oil: 600 kg. (1323 lbs.)
Weight full load: 1500 kg. (3307 lbs.)
Weight flying: 5000 kg. (11023 lbs.)
Wing load: 40 kg./sq.m. (8.2 lbs./sq.ft.)
Power load: 8.3 kg./hp. (18.4 lbs./hp.)
Load ratio %: 30
Max. speed: 120 km./hr. (75 mi./hr.)
Landing speed: 75 km./hr. (47 mi./hr.)
Time to height: 1000 m./9 min. 2000 m./
20 min. 3000 m./45 min. (3281 ft./9 min.)
(6562 ft./20 min.) (9843 ft./45 min.)
Practical ceiling: 2500 m. (8202 ft.)
Duration hrs.: 4.5
Range: n/a
Take-off run: n/a
Landing run: n/a

Model: **Il'ya Muromets V ("Veh") #179 (S-23)**
Type: Biplane with four tractor propellers
Year: 1915
Manufacturer: Russo-Baltic Wagon Company (R-BVZ)
Engine(s) type: Sunbeam x 4

H.P.: 150
Length: 17.1 m. (56 ft. 1 in.)
Wing span(s) upper/lower: 30.87/22 m.
(101 ft. 3 in./72 ft. 2 in.)
Wing area: 148 sq.m. (1593 sq.ft.)
Weight empty: 3800 kg. (8378 lbs.)
Weight fuel/oil: 600 kg. (1323 lbs.)
Weight full load: 1300 kg. (2866 lbs.)
Weight flying: 5100 kg. (11244 lbs.)
Wing load: 34.5 kg./sq.m. (7 lbs./sq.ft.)
Power load: 8.5 kg./hp. (18.7 lbs./hp.)
Load ratio %: 25
Max. speed: 110 km./hr. (68 mi./hr.)
Landing speed: 75 km./hr. (47 mi./hr.)
Time to height: n/a
Practical ceiling: n/a
Duration hrs.: n/a
Range: n/a
Take-off run: n/a
Landing run: n/a

Model: **Il'ya Muromets G-1 #183 (S-24)**
Type: Biplane with four tractor propellers
Year: 1915
Manufacturer: Russo-Baltic Wagon Company (R-BVZ)
Engine(s) type: Sunbeam x 4
H.P.: 150
Length: 17.1 m. (56 ft. 1 in.)
Wing span(s) upper/lower: 30.87/22 m.
(101 ft. 3 in./72 ft. 2 in.)
Wing area: 148 sq.m. (1593 sq.ft.)
Weight empty: 3800 kg. (8378 lbs.)
Weight fuel/oil: 600 kg. (1323 lbs.)
Weight full load: 1300 kg. (2866 lbs.)
Weight flying: 5100 kg. (11244 lbs.)
Wing load: 34.5 kg./sq.m. (7 lbs./sq.ft.)
Power load: 8.5 kg./hp. (18.7 lbs./hp.)
Load ratio %: 25
Max. speed: 110 km./hr. (68 mi./hr.)
Landing speed: 75 km./hr. (47 mi./hr.)
Time to height: n/a
Practical ceiling: n/a
Duration hrs.: 4
Range: 440 km. (273 mi.)
Take-off run: 450 m. (1476 ft.)
Landing run: 250 m. (820 ft.)

Model: **Il'ya Muromets G-1 #187 (S-24)**
Type: Biplane with four tractor propellers
Year: 1916
Manufacturer: Russo-Baltic Wagon Company (R-BVZ)
Engine(s) type: Argus x 4
H.P.: 125
Length: 17.1 m. (56 ft. 1 in.)
Wing span(s) upper/lower: 30.87/22 m.
(101 ft. 3 in./72 ft. 2 in.)
Wing area: 148 sq.m. (1593 sq.ft.)
Weight empty: 3700 kg. (8157 lbs.)
Weight fuel/oil: 500 kg. (1102 lbs.)
Weight full load: 1500 kg. (3307 lbs.)
Weight flying: 5200 kg. (11464 lbs.)
Wing load: 35.1 kg./sq.m. (7.2 lbs./sq.ft.)
Power load: 10.4 kg./hp. (23 lbs./hp.)
Load ratio %: 29
Max. speed: 120 km./hr. (75 mi./hr.)
Landing speed: 75 km./hr. (47 mi./hr.)
Time to height: n/a
Practical ceiling: n/a

Duration hrs.: n/a
Range: n/a
Take-off run: n/a
Landing run: 250 m. (820 ft.)

Model: **Il'ya Muromets G-1 #190/G-44 (S-24)**
Type: Biplane with four tractor propellers
Year: 1916
Manufacturer: Russo-Baltic Wagon Company (R-BVZ)
Engine(s) type: Argus x 4
H.P.: 140
Length: 17.1 m. (56. ft. 1 in.)
Wing span(s) upper/lower: 30.87/22 m.
(101 ft. 3 in./72 ft. 2 in.)
Wing area: 148 sq.m. (1593 sq.ft.)
Weight empty: 3750 kg. (8267 lbs.)
Weight fuel/oil: 500 kg. (1102 lbs.)
Weight full load: 1600 kg. (3527 lbs.)
Weight flying: 5350 kg. (11795 lbs.)
Wing load: 36.2 kg./sq.m. (7.4 lbs./sq.ft.)
Power load: 9.6 kg./hp. (21.1 lbs./hp.)
Load ratio %: 30
Max. speed: 125 km./hr. (78 mi./hr.)
Landing speed: 75 km./hr. (47 mi./hr.)
Time to height: n/a
Practical ceiling: n/a
Duration hrs.: n/a
Range: n/a
Take-off run: n/a
Landing run: n/a

Model: **Il'ya Muromets G-1 (S-24)**
Type: Biplane with four tractor propellers
Year: 1916
Manufacturer: Russo-Baltic Wagon Company (R-BVZ)
Engine(s) type: Sunbeam x 4
H.P.: 160
Length: 17.1 m. (56 ft. 1 in.)
Wing span(s) upper/lower: 30.87/22 m.
(101 ft. 3 in./72 ft. 2 in.)
Wing area: 148 sq.m. (1593 sq.ft.)
Weight empty: 3800 kg. (8378 lbs.)
Weight fuel/oil: 650 kg. (1433 lbs.)
Weight full load: 1560 kg. (3439 lbs.)
Weight flying: 5400 kg. (11905 lbs.)
Wing load: 36.5 kg./sq.m. (7.5 lbs./sq.ft.)
Power load: 8.4 kg./hp. (18.5 lbs./hp.)
Load ratio %: 28
Max. speed: 135 km./hr. (84 mi./hr.)
Landing speed: 75 km./hr. (47 mi./hr.)
Time to height: 1000 m./8 min. 2000 m./
18 min. 3000 m./35 min. (3281 ft./8 min.)
(6562 ft./18 min.) (9843 ft./35 min.)
Practical ceiling: 4000 m. (13123 ft.)
Duration hrs.: 4
Range: 500 km. (311 mi.)
Take-off run: n/a
Landing run: 300 m. (984 ft.)

Model: **Il'ya Muromets G-2 (S-24)**
Type: Biplane with four tractor propellers
Year: 1916
Manufacturer: Russo-Baltic Wagon Company (R-BVZ)
Engine(s) type: R-BVZ x 4
H.P.: 150
Length: 17.1 m. (56 ft. 1 in.)
Wing span(s) upper/lower: 30.87/22 m.
(101 ft. 3 in./72 ft. 2 in.)

Wing area: 159.6 sq.m. (1718 sq.ft.)
Weight empty: 3800 kg. (8378 lbs.)
Weight fuel/oil: 600 kg. (1323 lbs.)
Weight full load: 1500 kg. (3307 lbs.)
Weight flying: 5300 kg. (11684 lbs.)
Wing load: 33.2 kg./sq.m. (6.8 lbs./sq.ft.)
Power load: 8.8 kg./hp. (19.5 lbs./hp.)
Load ratio %: 28
Max. speed: 115 km./hr. (71 mi./hr.)
Landing speed: 75 km./hr. (47 mi./hr.)
Time to height: n/a
Practical ceiling: n/a
Duration hrs.: 4
Range: 460 km. (286 mi.)
Take-off run: n/a
Landing run: n/a

Model: **Il'ya Muromets G-2 (S-24)**

Type: Biplane with four tractor propellers
Year: 1916
Manufacturer: Russo-Baltic Wagon Company
(R-BVZ)
Engine(s) type: Renault x 2/R-BVZ x 2
H.P.: 220/150
Length: 17.1 m. (56 ft. 1 in.)
Wing span(s) upper/lower: 30.87/22 m.
(101 ft. 3 in./72 ft. 2 in.)
Wing area: 159.6 sq.m. (1718 sq.ft.)
Weight empty: 3800 kg. (8378 lbs.)
Weight fuel/oil: 740 kg. (1631 lbs.)
Weight full load: 1700 kg. (3748 lbs.)
Weight flying: 5500 kg. (12125 lbs.)
Wing load: 34.5 kg./sq.m. (7 lbs./sq.ft.)
Power load: 7.4 kg./hp. (16.4 lbs./hp.)
Load ratio %: 31
Max. speed: 120 km./hr. (75 mi./hr.)
Landing speed: 75 km./hr. (47 mi./hr.)
Time to height: 1000 m./9 min. 2000 m./
20 min. 3000 m./40 min. (3281 ft./9 min.)
(6562 ft./20 min.) (9843 ft./40 min.)
Practical ceiling: 3500 m. (11483 ft.)
Duration hrs.: 4
Range: 480 km. (298 mi.)
Take-off run: n/a
Landing run: n/a

Model: **Il'ya Muromets G-2 "Kievskiy" 3rd (S-24)**

Type: Biplane with four tractor propellers
Year: 1916
Manufacturer: Russo-Baltic Wagon Company
(R-BVZ)
Engine(s) type: Beardmore x 4
H.P.: 160
Length: 17.1 m. (56 ft. 1 in.)
Wing span(s) upper/lower: 30.87/22 m.
(101 ft. 3 in./72 ft. 2 in.)
Wing area: 159.6 sq.m. (1718 sq.ft.)
Weight empty: 3800 kg. (8378 lbs.)
Weight fuel/oil: 686/57 kg. (1512/126 lbs.)
Weight full load: 1700 kg. (3748 lbs.)
Weight flying: 5500 kg. (12125 lbs.)
Wing load: 34.5 kg./sq.m. (7 lbs./sq.ft.)
Power load: 8.6 kg./hp. (19 lbs./hp.)
Load ratio %: 31
Max. speed: 137 km./hr. (85 mi./hr.)
Landing speed: 78 km./hr. (48 mi./hr.)
Time to height: 1000 m./6 min. 2000 m./
14 min. 3000 m./35 min. (3281 ft./6 min.)
(6562 ft./14 min.) (9843 ft./35 min.)
Practical ceiling: 4600 m. (15092 ft.)

Duration hrs.: 4
Range: 540 km. (336 mi.)
Take-off run: 350 m. (1148 ft.)
Landing run: 250 m. (820 ft.)

Model: **Il'ya Muromets G-2 (S-24)**

Type: Biplane with four tractor propellers
Year: 1916
Manufacturer: Russo-Baltic Wagon Company
(R-BVZ)
Engine(s) type: Sunbeam x 2/R-BVZ x 2
H.P.: 150/150
Length: 17. 1m. (56 ft. 1 in.)
Wing span(s) upper/lower: 30.87/22 m.
(101 ft. 3 in./72 ft. 2 in.)
Wing area: 159.6 sq.m. (1718 sq.ft.)
Weight empty: 3800 kg. (8378 lbs.)
Weight fuel/oil: 600 kg. (1323 lbs.)
Weight full load: 1470 kg. (3241 lbs.)
Weight flying: 5300 kg. (11684 lbs.)
Wing load: 33 kg./sq.m. (6.8 lbs./sq.ft.)
Power load: 8.8 kg./hp (19.5 lbs./hp.)
Load ratio %: 27.5
Max. speed: 115 km./hr. (71 mi./hr.)
Landing speed: 78 km./hr. (48 mi./hr.)
Time to height: 1000 m./10 min. 2000 m./
22 min. 3000 m./48 min. (3281 ft./10 min.)
(6562 ft./22 min.) (9843 ft./48 min.)
Practical ceiling: 3200 m. (10499 ft.)
Duration hrs.: 4
Range: 460 km. (286 mi.)
Take-off run: n/a
Landing run: n/a

Model: **Il'ya Muromets G-2 (S-24)**

Type: Biplane with four tractor propellers
Year: 1917
Manufacturer: Russo-Baltic Wagon Company
(R-BVZ)
Engine(s) type: Renault x 2/R-BVZ x 2
H.P.: 220/150
Length: 17.1 m. (56 ft. 1 in.)
Wing span(s) upper/lower: 30.87/22 m.
(101 ft. 3 in./72 ft. 2 in.)
Wing area: 129.6 sq.m. (1395 sq.ft.)
Weight empty: 3800 kg. (8378 lbs.)
Weight fuel/oil: 656/57 kg. (1446/126 lbs.)
Weight full load: 1500 kg. (3307 lbs.)
Weight flying: 5300 kg. (11684 lbs.)
Wing load: 33.2 kg./sq.m. (8.4 lbs./sq.ft.)
Power load: 7.1 kg./hp. (15.8 lbs./hp.)
Load ratio %: 28.3
Max. speed: 120 km./hr. (75 mi./hr.)
Landing speed: 78 km./hr. (48 mi./hr.)
Time to height: 1000 m./9 min. 2000 m./
20 min. 3000 m./40 min. (3281 ft./9 min.)
(6562 ft./20 min.) (9843 ft./40 min.)
Practical ceiling: 3500 m. (11483 ft.)
Duration hrs.: 4
Range: 480 km. (298 mi.)
Take-off run: n/a
Landing run: n/a

Model: **Il'ya Muromets G-3 (S-25)**

Type: Biplane with four tractor propellers
Year: 1916
Manufacturer: Russo-Baltic Wagon Company
(R-BVZ)
Engine(s) type: Renault x 2/R-BVZ x 2
H.P.: 220/150

Length: 17.1 m. (56 ft. 1 in.)
Wing span(s) upper/lower: 30.87/22 m. (101 ft.
3 in./72 ft. 2 in.)
Wing area: 159.6 sq.m. (1718 sq.ft.)
Weight empty: 3800 kg. (8378 lbs.)
Weight fuel/oil: 880 kg. (1940 lbs.)
Weight full load: 1600 kg. (3527 lbs.)
Weight flying: 5400 kg. (11905 lbs.)
Wing load: 33.8 kg./sq.m. (7 lbs./sq.ft.)
Power load: 7.3 kg./hp. (16.1 lbs./hp.)
Load ratio %: 29.6
Max. speed: 115 km./hr. (71 mi./hr.)
Landing speed: 80 km./hr. (50 mi./hr.)
Time to height: 1000 m./7.3 min. 2000 m./
17 min. 3000 m./44 min. (3281 ft./7.3 min.)
(6562 ft./17 min.) (9843 ft./44 min.)
Practical ceiling: 3400 m. (11155 ft.)
Duration hrs.: 4.5
Range: 570 km. (354 mi.)
Take-off run: 220 m. (722 ft.)
Landing run: 250 m. (820 ft.)

Model: **Il'ya Muromets G-3 (S-25)**

Type: Biplane with four tractor propellers
Year: 1916
Manufacturer: Russo-Baltic Wagon Company
(R-BVZ)
Engine(s) type: Renault x 2/Sunbeam x 2
H.P.: 220/150
Length: 17.1 m. (56 ft. 1 in.)
Wing span(s) upper/lower: 30.87/22 m.
(101 ft. 3 in./72 ft. 2 in.)
Wing area: 159.6 sq.m. (1718 sq.ft.)
Weight empty: 3800 kg. (8378 lbs.)
Weight fuel/oil: 880 kg. (1940 lbs.)
Weight full load: 1500 kg. (3307 lbs.)
Weight flying: 5300 kg. (11684 lbs.)
Wing load: 33.1 kg./sq.m. (6.8 lbs./sq.ft.)
Power load: 7.2 kg./hp. (15.8 lbs./hp.)
Load ratio %: 28.3
Max. speed: 115 km./hr. (71 mi./hr.)
Landing speed: 78 km./hr. (48 mi./hr.)
Time to height: 1000 m./12 min. 2000 m./
29 min. (3281 ft./12 min.) (6562 ft./29 min.)
Practical ceiling: 2700 m. (8858 ft.)
Duration hrs.: 4
Range: 460 km. (286 mi.)
Take-off run: n/a
Landing run: n/a

Model: **Il'ya Muromets G-3 (S-25)**

Type: Biplane with four tractor propellers
Year: 1917
Manufacturer: Russo-Baltic Wagon Company
(R-BVZ)
Engine(s) type: Renault x 2/R-BVZ x 2
H.P.: 220/150
Length: 17.1 m. (56 ft. 1 in.)
Wing span(s) upper/lower: 30.87/22 m.
(101 ft. 3 in./72 ft. 2 in.)
Wing area: 159.6 sq.m. (1718 sq.ft.)
Weight empty: 4070 kg. (8973 lbs.)
Weight fuel/oil: 686/57 kg. (1512/126 lbs.)
Weight full load: 1530 kg. (3373 lbs.)
Weight flying: 5600 kg. (12346 lbs.)
Wing load: 35 kg./sq.m. (7.2 lbs./sq.ft.)
Power load: 7.6 kg./hp. (16.7 lbs./hp.)
Load ratio %: 27.3
Max. speed: 115 km./hr. (71 mi./hr.)
Landing speed: 80 km./hr. (50 mi./hr.)

Time to height: 1000 m./11 min. 2000 m./
27 min. (3281) ft./11 min.) (6562 ft./27 min.)
Practical ceiling: 2800 m. (9186 ft.)
Duration hrs.: 4
Range: 460 km. (286 mi.)
Take-off run: n/a
Landing run: n/a

Model: **Il'ya Muromets G-4 (S-25)**

Type: Biplane with four tractor propellers
Year: 1917
Manufacturer: Russo-Baltic Wagon Company
(R-BVZ)
Engine(s) type: Renault x 2/R-BVZ x 2
H.P.: 220/150
Length: 17.1 m. (56 ft. 1 in.)
Wing span(s) upper/lower: 30.87/22 m.
(101 ft. 3 in./72 ft. 2 in.)
Wing area: 159.6 sq.m. (1718 sq.ft.)
Weight empty: 3900 kg. (8598 lbs.)
Weight fuel/oil: 686/57 kg. (1512/126 lbs.)
Weight full load: 1500 kg. (3307 lbs.)
Weight flying: 5400 kg. (11905 lbs.)
Wing load: 33.8 kg./sq.m. (7 lbs./sq.ft.)
Power load: 7.3 kg./hp. (16.1 lbs./hp.)
Load ratio %: 28
Max. speed: 128 km./hr. (80 mi./hr.)
Landing speed: 78 km./hr. (48 mi./hr.)
Time to height: 1000 m./10 min. 2000 m./
25 min. 3000 m./78 min. (3281 ft./10 min.)
(6562 ft./25 min.) (9843 ft./78 min.)
Practical ceiling: 3300 m. (10827 ft.)
Duration hrs.: 4
Range: 500 km. (311 mi.)
Take-off run: n/a
Landing run: n/a

Model: **Il'ya Muromets D-1 (S-26)**

Type: Biplane with two tractor and two pusher
propellers in tandem
Year: 1916
Manufacturer: Russo-Baltic Wagon Company
(R-BVZ)
Engine(s) type: Sunbeam x 4
H.P.: 150
Length: 15.5 m. (50 ft. 10 in.)
Wing span(s) upper/lower: 24.9/17.6 m.
(81 ft. 8 in./57 ft. 9 in.)
Wing area: 132 sq.m. (1420.8 sq.ft.)
Weight empty: 3150 kg. (6945 lbs.)
Weight fuel/oil: 690 kg. (1522 lbs.)
Weight full load: 1250 kg. (2756 lbs.)
Weight flying: 4400 kg. (9700 lbs.)
Wing load: 33.2 kg./sq.m. (6.8 lbs./sq.ft.)
Power load: 7.3 kg./hp. (16.2 lbs./hp.)
Load ratio %: 28.4
Max. speed: 120 km./hr. (75 mi./hr.)
Landing speed: 80 km./hr. (50 mi./hr.)
Time to height: n/a
Practical ceiling: 200 m. (656 ft.)
Duration hrs.: 4
Range: 480 km. (298 mi.)
Take-off run: 700 m. (2297 ft.)
Landing run: 350 m. (1148 ft.)

Model: **Il'ya Muromets D-2 (S-26)**

Type: Biplane with four tractor propellers
Year: 1916
Manufacturer: Russo-Baltic Wagon Company
(R-BVZ)

Engine(s) type: Sunbeam x 4
H.P.: 150
Length: 17 m. (55 ft. 9 in.)
Wing span(s) upper/lower: 29.7/29.7 m.
  (97 ft. 5 in./97 ft. 5 in.)
Wing area: 148 sq.m. (1593 sq.ft.)
Weight empty: 3800 kg. (8378 lbs.)
Weight fuel/oil: 540/160 kg. (1190/353 lbs.)
Weight full load: 1400 kg. (3086 lbs.)
Weight flying: 5200 kg. (11464 lbs.)
Wing load: 35.5 kg./sq.m. (7.2 lbs./sq.ft.)
Power load: 8.5 kb./hp. (19.1 lbs./hp.)
Load ratio %: 27
Max. speed: 110 km./hr. (68 mi./hr.)
Landing speed: 75 km./hr (47 mi./hr.)
Time to height: 1000 m./16 min. 2000 m./
  40 min. (3281 ft./16 min.) (6562 ft./40 min.)
Practical ceiling: 2900 m. (9514 ft.)
Duration hrs.: 4.8
Range: 520 km. (323 mi.)
Take-off run: n/a
Landing run: n/a

Model: Il'ya Muromets E ("Yeh") (S-27)
Type: Biplane with four tractor propellers
Year: 1916
Manufacturer: Russo-Baltic Wagon Company
  (R-BVZ)
Engine(s) type: Renault x 4
H.P.: 220
Length: 17.1 m. (56 ft. 1 in.)
Wing span(s) upper/lower: 33/27 m.
  (108 ft. 3 in./88 ft. 7 in.)
Wing area: 190 sq.m. (2045.1 sq.ft.)
Weight empty: 4620 kg. (10185 lbs.)
Weight fuel/oil: 540/160 kg. (1190/353 lbs.)
Weight full load: 2000 kg. (4409 lbs.)
Weight flying: 6620 kg. (14595 lbs.)
Wing load: 34.8 kg./sq.m. (7.1 lbs./sq.ft.)
Power load: 7 kg./hp. (16.5 lbs./hp.)
Load ratio %: 32.2
Max. speed: 130 km./hr. (81 mi./hr.)
Landing speed: 80 km./hr (50 mi./hr.)
Time to height: 1000 m./10.1 min. 2000 m./
  25 min. 3000 m./75 min. (3281 ft./10.1 min.)
  (6562 ft./25 min.) (9843 ft./75 min.)
Practical ceiling: 3000 m. (9843 ft.)
Duration hrs.: 4.8
Range: 620 km. (385 mi.)
Take-off run: 350 m. (1148 ft.)
Landing run: n/a

Model: Il'ya Muromets E-1 ("Yeh") (S-27)
Type: Biplane with four tractor propellers
Year: 1916
Manufacturer: Russo-Baltic Wagon Company
  (R-BVZ)
Engine(s) type: Renault x 4
H.P.: 220
Length: 18.2 m. (59 ft. 9 in.)
Wing span(s) upper/lower: 31.35/24 m.
  (102 ft. 10 in./78 ft. 9 in.)
Wing area: 200 sq.m. (2152.8 sq.ft.)
Weight empty: 4800 kg. (10582 lbs.)
Weight fuel/oil: 920/130 kg. (2028/287 lbs.)
Weight full load: 2200 kg. (4850 lbs.)
Weight flying: 7000 kg. (15432 lbs.)
Wing load: 35 kg./sq.m. (7.2 lbs./sq.ft.)
Power load: 8 kg./hp. (17.5 lbs./hp.)
Load ratio %: 29
Max. speed: 130 km./hr. (81 mi./hr.)

Landing speed: 80 km./hr. (50 mi./hr.)
Time to height: 1000 m./9 min. 2000 m./
  25 min. 3000 m./74 min. (3281 ft./9 min.)
  (6562 ft./25 min.) (9843 ft./74 min.)
Practical ceiling: 3000 m. (9843 ft.)
Duration hrs.: 4.4
Range: 560 km. (348 mi.)
Take-off run: 400 m. (1312 ft.)
Landing run: 300 m. (984 ft.)

Model: Il'ya Muromets E-2 ("Yeh") (S-27)
Type: Biplane with four tractor propellers
Year: 1917
Manufacturer: Russo-Baltic Wagon Company
  (R-BVZ)
Engine(s) type: Renault x 4
H.P.: 220
Length: 18.8 m. (61 ft. 8 in.)
Wing span(s) upper/lower: 34.5/26.6 m.
  (113 ft. 2 in./87 ft. 3 in.)
Wing area: 220 sq.m. (2368 sq.ft.)
Weight empty: 5000 kg. (11023 lbs.)
Weight fuel/oil: 920/130 kg. (2028/287 lbs.)
Weight full load: 2460 kg. (5423 lbs.)
Weight flying: 7460 kg. (16446 lbs.)
Wing load: 34.2 kg./sq.m. (7 lbs./sq.ft.)
Power load: 8.5 kg./hp. (18.7 lbs./hp.)
Load ratio %: 33
Max. speed: 130 km./hr. (81 mi./hr.)
Landing speed: 80 km./hr. (50 mi./hr.)
Time to height: 1000 m./9.4 min. 2000 m./
  26 min. 3000 m./68 min. (3281 ft./9.4 min.)
  (6562 ft./26 min.) (9843 ft./68 min.)
Practical ceiling: 3200 m. (10499 ft.)
Duration hrs.: 4.4
Range: 560 km. (348 mi.)
Take-off run: 450 m. (1476 ft.)
Landing run: 300 m. (984 ft.)

Model: Il'ya Muromets E ("Yeh") (S-27)
Type: Biplane with four tractor propellers
Year: 1918
Manufacturer: Russo-Baltic Wagon Company
  (R-BVZ)
Engine(s) type: Renault x 4
H.P.: 220
Length: 18.5 m. (60 ft. 8 in.)
Wing span(s) upper/lower: 30.4/24.4 m.
  (99 ft. 9 in./80 ft.)
Wing area: 190 sq.m. (2045.1 sq.ft.)
Weight empty: 4200 kg. (9259 lbs.)
Weight fuel/oil: n/a
Weight full load: 1900 kg. (4189 lbs.)
Weight flying: 6100 kg. (13448 lbs.)
Wing load: 32 kg./sq.m. (6.5 lbs./sq.ft.)
Power load: 6.9 kg./hp. (15.3 lbs./hp.)
Load ratio %: 31.2
Max. speed: 137 km./hr. (85 mi./hr.)
Landing speed: 93 km./hr. (56 mi./hr.)
Time to height: 1000 m./10 min. 2000 m./
  25 min. 3000 m./48 min. (3281 ft./10 min)
  (6562 ft./25 min.) (9843 ft./48 min.)
Practical ceiling: 4000 m. (13123 ft.)
Duration hrs.: 4
Range: 540 km. (336 mi.)
Take-off run: 350 m. (1148 ft.)
Landing run: 300 m. (948 ft.)

GOLDEN AGE

Model: S-29-A
Type: Landplane-sesquiplane
Year: 1924
Manufacturer: Sikorsky Aero Engineering
  Corp.
Engine(s): Liberty x 2
BHP/RPM: 400/
Propeller: 3.15 m. (10 ft. 4 in.) x 2 /2 blades
Length: 15.19 m. (49 ft. 10 in.)
Height: 4.11 m. (13 ft. 6 in.)
Wing span(s) upper/lower: 21.03 m./19.05 m.
  (69 ft./62 ft. 6 in)
Wing chord(s) upper/lower: 3.12 m./1.78 m.
  (10 ft. 3 in./5 ft. 10 in.)
Aspect ratio(s) upper/lower: 6.97/12.8
Wing area(s) upper/lower: 63.36 sq.m./28.33
  sq.m. (682 sq.ft./305 sq.ft.)
Stabilizer area: 5.39 sq.m. (58 sq.ft.)
Elevator area: 3.53 sq.m. (38 sq.ft.)
Rudder(s) area: 3.53 sq.m. (38 sq.ft.)
Fin area: none
Weight empty: 3526.68 kg. (7775 lbs.)
Gross weight: 5443.1 kg. (12000 lbs.)
Low speed: 90.1 km./hr. (56 mi./hr.)
High speed: 185.1 km./hr. (115 mi./hr.)
Service ceiling: 3749 m. (12300 ft.)
Rate of climb: 1524 m./8.8 min. 3048 m./
  23 min. (5000 ft./8.8 min. 10000 ft./23 min.)
Duration hrs.: n/a
Range: n/a
No. built: 1

Model: S-31
Type: Landplane-sesquiplane
Year: 1925
Manufacturer: Sikorsky Manufacturing Corp.
Engine(s): Wright J-4 x 1
BHP/RPM: 200/1600
Propeller: 2.44 m. (8 ft.) x 1 /2 blades
Length: 7.92 m. (26 ft.)
Height: 3.15 m. (10 ft. 4 in.)
Wing span(s) upper/lower: 13.72 m./9.75 m.
  (45 ft./32 ft.)
Wing chord(s) upper/lower: 1.83 m./1.01 m.
  (6 ft./3 ft. 4 in.)
Aspect ratio(s) upper/lower: 7.9/11.25
Wing area(s) upper/lower: 24.15 m./8.92 sq.m.
  (260 sq.ft./96 sq.ft.)
Stabilizer area: 3.16 sq.m. (34 sq.ft.)
Elevator area: 3.16 sq.m. (34 sq.ft.)
Rudder(s) area: .65 sq.m. (7 sq.ft.)
Fin area: .28 sq.m. (3 sq.ft.)
Weight empty: 771.1 kg. (1700 lbs.)
Gross weight: 1315.42 kg. (2900 lbs.)
Low speed: 56.3 km./hr. (35 mi./hr.)
High speed: 199.6 km./hr. (124 mi./hr.)
Service ceiling: 4572 m. (15000 ft.)
Rate of climb: 4572 m./45 min. (15000 ft./
  45 min.)
Duration hrs.: 6
Range: n/a
No. built: 1

Model: S-32
Type: Land/seaplane-sesquiplane
Year: 1926
Manufacturer: Sikorsky Manufacturing Corp.
Engine(s): Liberty x 1
BHP/RPM: 400/1600
Propeller: 3.05 m. (10 ft.) x 1 /2 blades

Length: 10.97 m. (36 ft.)
Height: 4.57 m. (15 ft.)
Wing span(s) upper/lower: 17.78 m./11.58 (58 ft.
  4 in./38 ft.)
Wing chord(s) upper/lower: 2.54 m./1.27 m.
  (8 ft. 4 in./4 ft. 2 in.)
Aspect ratio(s) upper/lower: 7.4/9.78
Wing area(s) upper/lower: 44.59 m./11.61 sq.m.
  (480 sq.ft./125 sq.ft.)
Stabilizer area: 4.27 sq.m. (46 sq.ft.)
Elevator area: 1.3 sq.m. (14 sq.ft.)
Rudder(s) area: 1.86 sq.m. (20 sq.ft.)
Fin area: none
Weight empty: 1496.85 kg. (3300 lbs.)
Gross weight: 2449.4 kg. (5400 lbs.)
Low speed: 64.4 km./hr. (40 mi./hr.)
High speed: 214 km./hr. (133 mi./hr.)
Service ceiling: 4877 m. (16000 ft.)
Rate of climb: 4877 m./min. (16000 ft./52 min.)
Duration hrs.: 4
Range: n/a
No. built: 1

Model: S-33/S-33A
Type: Landplane-sesquiplane
Year: 1926/1927
Manufacturer: Sikorsky Manufacturing Corp.
Engine(s): Anzani x 1 or Lawrence x 1
BHP/RPM: 70/1400 60/1800
Propeller: 1.93 m. (6 ft. 4 in.) x 1 /2 blades
Length: 5.79 m. (19 ft.)
Height: 2.24 m. (7ft. 4 in.)
Wing span(s) upper/lower: 9.75 m./6.1 m.
  (32 ft./20 ft.)
Wing chord(s) upper/lower: 1.22 m./.76 m.
  (4 ft./2 ft. 6 in.)
Aspect ratio(s) upper/lower: 7.75/9.78
Wing area(s) upper/lower: 11.15 m./4 sq.m.
  (120 sq.ft./43 sq.ft.)
Stabilizer area: .84 sq.m. (9 sq.ft.)
Elevator area: .46 sq.m. (5 sq.ft.)
Rudder(s) area: .33 sq.m. (3.5 sq.ft.)
Fin area: .14 sq.m. (1.5 sq.ft.)
Weight empty: 362.87 kg. (800 lbs.)
Gross weight: 544.31 kg. (1200 lbs.)
Low speed: 56.3 km./hr. (35 mi./hr.)
High speed: 185.1 km./hr. (115 mi./hr.)
Service ceiling: 4572 m. (15000 ft.)
Rate of climb: 4572 m./58 min. (15000 ft./
  58 min.)
Duration hrs.: 2.5
Range: n/a
No. built: 2 (total all types of S-33s)

Model: S-34
Type: Amphibian-sesquiplane
Year: 1926
Manufacturer: Sikorsky Manufacturing Corp.
Engine(s): Wright J-4 x 2
BHP/RPM: 200/1600
Propeller: 2.44 m. (8 ft.) x 2 /2 blades
Length: 10.36 m. (34 ft.)
Height: 3.23 m. (10 ft. 7 in.)
Wing span(s) upper/lower: 17.07 m. /3.66 m.
  (56 ft./12 ft.)
Wing chord(s) upper/lower: 2.13 m./1.32 m.
  (7ft./4 ft. 4 in.)
Aspect ratio(s) upper/lower: n/a
Wing area(s) upper/lower: 36.79 m./4.46 sq.m.
  (396 sq.ft./48 sq.ft.)

Stabilizer area: 3.16 sq.m. (34 sq.ft.)
Elevator area: 1.67 sq.m. (18 sq.ft.)
Rudder(s) area: 2.69 sq.m. (29 sq.ft.)
Fin area: none
Weight empty: 1315.42 kg. (2900 lbs.)
Gross weight: 2041.16 kg. (4500 lbs.)
Low speed: 72.4 km./hr. (45 mi./hr.)
High speed: 201.2 km./hr. (125 mi./hr.)
Service ceiling: 4572 m. (15000 ft.)
Rate of climb: 4572 m./45 min. (15000 ft./
  45 min.)
Duration hrs.: 3
Range: n/a
No. built: 1

Model: **S-35**

Type: Landplane-sesquiplane
Year: 1926
Manufacturer: Sikorsky Manufacturing Corp.
Engine(s): Gnome-Rhone Jupiter 9A x 3
BHP/RPM: 425/1600
Propeller: 3.2 m. (10 ft. 6 in.) x 3 /2 blades
Length: 13.41 m. (44 ft.)
Height: 4.88 m. (16 ft.)
Wing span(s) upper/lower: 30.78 m./23.16 m.
  (101 ft./76 ft.)
Wing chord(s) upper/lower: 2.54 m./1.32 m.
  (8 ft. 4 in./4 ft. 4 in.)
Aspect ratio(s) upper/lower: 12.83/19.2
Wing area(s) upper/lower: 73.76 m./27.96 sq.m.
  (794 sq.ft./301 sq.ft.)
Stabilizer area: 5.11 sq.m. (55 sq.ft.)
Elevator area: 3.44 sq.m. (37 sq.ft.)
Rudder(s) area: 4.55 sq.m. (49 sq.ft.)
Fin area: none
Weight empty: 4399.84 kg. (9700 lbs.)
Gross weight: 9071.84 kg. (20000 lbs.)
Low speed: 104.6 km./hr. (65 mi./hr.)
High speed: 233.4 km./hr (145 mi./hr.)
Service ceiling: 5121 m. (16800 ft.)
Rate of climb: 5121 m./min. (168000 ft./
  70 min.)
Duration hrs.: 7
Range: n/a
No. built: 1

Model: **S-36 (general service version)**

Type: Amphibian-sesquiplane
Year: 1927
Manufacturer: Sikorsky Manufacturing Corp.
Engine(s): Wright Whirlwind x 2
BHP/RPM: 200/
Propeller: 2.39 m. (7 ft. 10 in.) x 2 /2 blades
Length: 10.36 m. (34 ft.)
Height: 3.66 m. (12 ft.)
Wing span(s) upper/lower: 18.9 m./8.53 m. (62
  ft./28 ft.)
Wing chord(s) upper/lower: 2.54 m./1.27
  (8 ft. 4 in./4 ft. 2 in.)
Aspect ratio(s) upper/lower: n/a
Wing area(s) upper/lower: 43.57 m./10.78 sq.m.
  (469 sq.ft./116 sq.m.)
Stabilizer area: 4.38 sq.m. (47.2 sq.ft.)
Elevator area: 2.13 sq.m. (22.9 sq.ft.)
Rudder(s) area: 3.77 sq.m. (40.6 sq.ft.)
Fin area: none
Weight empty: 1542.21 kg. (3400 lbs.)
Gross weight: 2449.4 kg. (5400 lbs.)
Low speed: 74.8 km./hr. (46.5 mi./hr.)
High speed: 193.1 km./hr. (120 mi./hr.)

Service ceiling: 4877 m. (16000 ft.)
Rate of climb: 182.88 m. per min. (600 ft.
  per min.)
Duration hrs.: n/a
Range: n/a
No. built: see long range version

Model: **S-36 (long range version)**

Type: Amphibian-sesquiplane
Year: 1927
Manufacturer: Sikorsky Manufacturing Corp.
Engine(s): Wright Whirlwind x 2
BHP/RPM: 200/
Propeller: 2.39 m. (7 ft. 10 in) x 2 /2 blades
Length: 10.36 m. (34 ft.)
Height: 3.66 m. (12 ft.)
Wing span(s) upper/lower: 21.95 m./8.53 m.
  (72 ft./28 ft.)
Wing chord(s) upper/lower: 2.54 m./1.27 m.
  (8 ft. 4 in./4 ft. 2 in.)
Aspect ratio(s) upper/lower: n/a
Wing area(s) upper/lower: 51.28 m./1078 sq.m.
  (552 sq.ft./116 sq.ft.)
Stabilizer area: 4.38 sq.m. (47.2 sq. ft.)
Elevator area: 2.13 sq.m. (22.9 sq. ft.)
Rudder(s) area: 3.77 sq.m. (40.6 sq. ft.)
Fin area: none
Weight empty: 1587.57 kg. (3500 lbs.)
Gross weight: 2721.55 kg. (6000 lbs.)
Low speed: 74.8 km./hr. (46.5 mi./hr.)
High speed: 193.1 km./hr. (120 mi./hr.)
Service ceiling: 4877 m. (16000 ft.)
Rate of climb: 182.88 m. per min. (600 ft.
  per min.)
Duration hrs.: n/a
Range: n/a
No. built: 6 (total all types of S-36s)

Model: **S-37B**

Type: Land/seaplane-sesquiplane
Year: 1927
Manufacturer: Sikorsky Manufacturing Corp.
Engine(s): Pratt & Whitney Hornet x 2
BHP/RPM: 525/1900
Propeller: 3.2 m. (10 ft. 6 in.) x 2 /2blades
Length: 13.72 m. (45 ft.)
Height: 4.93 m. (16 ft. 2 in.)
Wing span(s) upper/lower: 30.48 m./17.78 m.
  (100 ft./58 ft. 4 in.)
Wing chord(s) upper/lower: 2.54 m./1.52 m.
  (8 ft. 4 in./5 ft.)
Aspect ratio(s) upper/lower: n/a
Wing area(s) upper/lower: 74.13 sq.m./
  25.64 sq.m. (798 sq. ft./276 sq. ft.)
Stabilizer area: 7.9 sq.m. (85 sq. ft.)
Elevator area: 3.72 sq.m. (40 sq. ft.)
Rudder(s) area: 3.44 sq.m. (37 sq. ft.)
Fin area: none
Weight empty: n/a
Gross weight: 6441 kg. (14200 lbs.)
Low speed: 91.7 km./hr. (57 mi./hr.)
High speed: 206 km./hr. (128 mi./hr.)
Service ceiling: 4572 m. (15000 ft.)
Rate of climb: 228.6 m. per min. (750 ft.
  per min.)
Duration hrs.: n/a
Range: n/a
No. built: 2 (total all types of S-37s)

Model: **S-38C**

Type: Amphibian-sesquiplane
Year: 1928
Manufacturer: Sikorsky Aviation Corp.
Engine(s): Pratt & Whitney Wasp x 2
BHP/RPM: 420
Propeller: 3 m. (9 ft. 10 in.) x 2 /2blades
Length: 12.32 m. (40 ft. 5 in.)
Height: 4.12 m. (13 ft. 6 in.)
Wing span(s) upper/lower: 21.84 m./10.97 m.
  (71 ft. 8 in./36 ft.)
Wing chord(s) upper/lower: 2.54 m./1.5 m. (8 ft.
  4 in./4 ft. 11 in.)
Aspect ratio(s) upper/lower: n/a
Wing area(s) upper/lower: 53.32 sq.m./
  13.56 sq.m. (574 sq. ft./146 sq. ft.)
Stabilizer area: 4.09 sq.m. (44 sq. ft.)
Elevator area: 2.42 sq.m. (26 sq. ft.)
Rudder(s) area: 1.86 sq.m. (20 sq. ft.)
Fin area: 1.39 sq.m. (15 sq. ft.)
Weight empty: 3107.1 kg. (6850 lbs.)
Gross weight: 4753.64 kg. (10480 lbs.)
Low speed: 88.5 km./hr. (55 mi./hr.)
High speed: 201.2 km./hr. (125 mi./hr.)
Service ceiling: 5486 m. (18000 ft.)
Rate of climb: 228.6 m. per min. (750 ft.
  per min.)
Duration hrs.: n/a
Range: 957.6 km. (595 mi.)
No. built: 111 (total all type S-38s)

Model: **S-39**

Type: Amphibian-monoplane
Year: 1930
Manufacturer: Sikorsky Aviation Corp.
Engine(s): Pratt & Whitney Wasp Jr. x 1
BHP/RPM: 300/200
Propeller: 2.69 m. (8 ft. 10 in.) x 1 /2 blades
Length: 9.73 m. (31 ft. 11 in.)
Height: 4.32 m. (14 ft. 2 in.)
Wing span(s) upper/lower: 15.85 m. (52 ft.)
Wing chord(s) upper/lower: n/a
Aspect ratio(s) upper/lower: n/a
Wing area(s) upper/lower: 32.52 sq.m.
  (350 sq. ft.)
Stabilizer area: 2.77 sq.m. (29.8 sq. ft.)
Elevator area: 1.72 sq.m. (18.5 sq. ft.)
Rudder(s) area: 1.91 sq.m. (20.6 sq. ft.)
Fin area: .45 sq.m. (4.8 sq. ft.)
Weight empty: 1214.72 kg. (2678 lbs.)
Gross weight: 1814.37 kg. (4000 lbs.)
Low speed: 87 km./hr. (54 mi./hr.)
High speed: 193.1 km./hr. (120 mi./hr.)
Service ceiling: 5486 m. (18000 ft.)
Rate of climb: 228.6 m. per min. (750 ft.
  per min.)
Duration hrs.: n/a
Range: n/a
No. built: 21 (total all type S-39s)

Model: **S-40A**

Type: Amphibian-monoplane
Year: 1931
Manufacturer: Sikorsky Aviation Corp.
Engine(s): Pratt & Whitney Hornet x 4
BHP/RPM: 660
Propeller: 3.2 m. (10 ft. 6 in.) x 4 /2 blades
Length: 23.37 m. (76 ft. 8 in.)
Height: 7.26 m. (23 ft. 10 in.)

Wing span(s) upper/lower: 34.75 m. (114 ft.)
Wing chord(s) upper/lower: 4.88 m. (16 ft.)
Aspect ratio(s) upper/lower: n/a
Wing area(s) upper/lower: 161.65 sq.m.
  (1740 sq. ft.)
Stabilizer area: 13.85 sq.m. (149.05 sq. ft.)
Elevator area: 9.72 sq.m. (104.66 sq. ft.)
Rudder(s) area: 5.35 sq.m. (57.54 sq. ft.)
Fin area: 4.6 sq.m. (49.52 sq. ft.)
Weight empty: 1084.85 kg. (23900 lbs.)
Gross weight: 15694.28 kg. (34600 lbs.)
Low speed: 104.6 km./hr. (65 mi./hr.)
High speed: 209.2 km./hr. (130 mi./hr.)
Service ceiling: 4115 m. (13500 ft.)
Rate of climb: 217 m. per min. (712 ft. per min.)
Duration hrs.: n/a
Range: 1448.4 km. (900 mi.)
No. built: 3 (total all types of S-40s)

Model: **S-41**

Type: Amphibian-monoplane
Year: 1931
Manufacturer: Sikorsky Aviation Corp.
Engine(s): Pratt & Whitney Hornet x 2
BHP/RPM: 575/1950
Propeller: 3.2 m. (10 ft. 6 in.) x 2 /2 blades
Length: 13.79 m. (45 ft. 2¾ in.)
Height: 5.38 m. (17 ft. 7½ in.)
Wing span(s) upper/lower: 24.03 m. (78 ft.
  9¼ in.)
Wing chord(s) upper/lower: 2.92 m. (9 ft. 7 in)
Aspect ratio(s) upper/lower: n/a
Wing area(s) upper/lower: 67.72 sq.m.
  (729 sq. ft.)
Stabilizer area: 6.34 sq.m. (68.2 sq. ft.)
Elevator area: 1.17 sq.m. (12.6 sq. ft.)
Rudder(s) area: 2.56 sq.m. (27.6 sq. ft.)
Fin area: 3.34 sq.m. (36 sq. ft.)
Weight empty: 3505 kg. (7727 lbs.)
Gross weight: 5806 kg. (12800 lbs.)
Low speed: 106.2 km./hr. (66 mi./hr.)
High speed: 210.8 km./hr. (131 mi./hr.)
Service ceiling: 5550 m. (18210 ft.)
Rate of climb: 266.7 m. per min. (875 ft.
  per min.)
Duration hrs.: n/a
Range: n/a
No. built: 7 (total all types of S-41s)

Model: **S-42B**

Type: Flying boat-monoplane
Year: 1934
Manufacturer: Sikorsky Aviation Corp.
Engine(s): Pratt & Whitney Hornet x 4
BHP/RPM: 750/
Propeller: 3.5 m. (11 ft. 6 in.) x 4 /3 blades
Length: 21.03 m. (69 ft.)
Height: 6.63 m. (21 ft. 9 in.)
Wing span(s) upper/lower: 36.02 m.
  (118 ft. 2 in.)
Wing chord(s) upper/lower: 4.93 m. (16 ft. 2 in.)
Aspect ratio(s) upper/lower: n/a
Wing area(s) upper/lower: 124.49 sq.m.
  (1340 sq. ft.)
Stabilizer area: 13.56 sq.m. (146 sq. ft.)
Elevator area: 6.5 sq.m. (70 sq. ft.)
Rudder(s) area: 6.69 sq.m. (72 sq. ft.)
Fin area: 6.78 sq.m. (73 sq. ft.)
Weight empty: 10886.2 kg. (24000 lbs.)

Gross weight: 19050.86 kg. (42000 lbs.)
Low speed: 104.6 km./hr. (65 mi./hr.)
High speed: 305.8 km./hr. (190 mi./hr.)
Service ceiling: 4877 m. (16000 ft.)
Rate of climb: 243.84 m. per min. (800 ft. per min.)
Duration hrs.: n/a
Range: 1802.5 km. (1120 mi.)
No. built: 10 (total all types of S-42s)

Model: **S-43**

Type: Amphibian-monoplane
Year: 1935
Manufacturer: Sikorsky Aircraft Corp.
Engine(s): Pratt & Whitney Hornet x 2
BHP/RPM: 750/
Propeller: 3.5 m. (11 ft. 6 in.) x 2 /3 blades
Length: 15.6 m. (51 ft. 2 in.)
Height: 6.17 m. (20 ft. 3 in.)
Wing span(s) upper/lower: 26.21 m. (86 ft.)
Wing chord(s) upper/lower: 3.5 m. (11 ft. 6 in.)
Aspect ratio(s) upper/lower: n/a
Wing area(s) upper/lower: 72.52 sq.m. (780.6 sq.ft.)
Stabilizer area: 8.03 sq.m. (86.4 sq.ft.)
Elevator area: 3.87 sq.m. (41.7 sq.ft.)
Rudder(s) area: 3.4 sq.m. (36.6 sq.ft.)
Fin area: 3.29 sq.m. (35.4 sq.ft.)
Weight empty: 5806 kg. (12800 lbs.)
Gross weight: 9071.84 kg. (20000 lbs.)
Low speed: 104.6 km./hr. (65 mi./hr.)
High speed: 293 km./hr. (182 mi./hr.)
Service ceiling: 5334. (17500 ft.)
Rate of climb: 304.8 per min. (1000 ft. per min.)
Duration hrs.: n/a
Range: 1247.2 km. (775 mi.)
No. built: 53 (total all types of S-43s)

Model: **S-44/XPBS-1**

Type: Flying boat-monoplane
Year: 1937
Manufacturer: Sikorsky Aircraft Corp.
Engine(s): Pratt & Whitney Wasp x 4
BHP/RPM: 1050/2700
Propeller: 3.66 m. (12 ft.) x 4 /3 blades
Length: 23.22 m. (76 ft. 1 1/2 in.)
Height: 8.41 m. (27 ft. 7 1/4 in.)
Wing span(s) upper/lower: 37.8 m. (124 ft.)
Wing chord(s) upper/lower: 6.12 m. (20 ft. 1/2 in.)
Aspect ratio(s) upper/lower: 9.22
Wing area(s) upper/lower: 155.14 sq.m. (1670 sq.ft.)
Stabilizer area: 10.87 sq.m. (117 sq.ft.)
Elevator area: 6.22 sq.m. (67 sq.ft.)
Rudder(s) area: 5.42 sq.m. (58.3 sq.ft.)
Fin area: 8.55 sq.m. (92 sq.ft.)
Weight empty: 11978 kg. (26407 lbs.)
Gross weight: 22252.77 kg. (49059 lbs.)
Low speed: 103.5 km./hr. (64.3 mi./hr.)
High speed: 357.3 km./hr. (222 mi./hr.)
Service ceiling: 6340 m. (20800 ft.)
Rate of climb: 1524 m./8 min. 4572 m./25 min. (5000 ft. /8 min. 15000 ft. /25 min.)
Duration hrs.: 30
Range: 6485.6 km. (4030 mi.)
No. built: 1

Model: **VS-44A**

Type: Flying boat-monoplane
Year: 1942
Manufacturer: Vought-Sikorsky Aircraft
Engine(s): Pratt & Whitney Wasp x 4
BHP/RPM: 1200/
Propeller: 3.83 m. (12 ft. 7 in.) x 4 /3 blades
Length: 23.24 m. (76 ft. 3 in.)
Height: 8.4 m. (27 ft. 7-1/4 in.)
Wing span(s) upper/lower: 37.79 m. (124 ft.)
Wing chord(s) upper/lower: 6.12 m. (20 ft. 1/2 in.)
Aspect ratio(s) upper/lower: 8.9
Wing area(s) upper/lower: 155.14 sq.m. (1670 sq.ft.)
Stabilizer area: 13.67 sq.m. (147.2 sq.ft.)
Elevator area: 6.95 sq.m. (74.8 sq.ft.)
Rudder(s) area: 5.42 sq.m. (58.3 sq.ft.)
Fin area: 8.55 sq.m. (92 sq.ft.)
Weight empty: 13173.67 kg. (29043 lbs.)
Gross weight: 26864 kg. (59225 lbs.)
Low speed: 116 km./hr. (72 mi./hr.)
High speed: 362.1 km./hr. (225 mi./hr.)
Service ceiling: 5060 m. (16600 ft.)
Rate of climb: 1524 m./8 min. 4572 m./32 min. (5000 ft./8 min. 15000 ft./32 min.)
Duration hrs.: 44.1
Range: 7902 km. (4910 mi.)
No. built: 3 (total all types of VS-44s)

VERTICAL FLIGHT

Model: **VS-300 (final variant)/S-46**

Type: Helicopter
Year: 1941
Manufacturer: Vought-Sikorsky Aircraft
Engine: 1 Franklin 4AC-199
BHP/RPM: 100
Fuselage length: 8.5 m. (27 ft. 10 in.)
Fuselage width: 1.2 m. (4 ft.)
Overall height: 2.4 m. (8 ft.)
Main rotor diam.: 8.5 m. (28 ft.)
Tail rotor diam.: 2.3 m. (7 ft 8 in.)
Landing gear tread: 3 m. (10 ft.)
Passenger cabin length: n/a
Passenger cabin width: n/a
Passenger cabin height: n/a
Weight empty: 473.3 kg. (1043.5 lbs.)
Weight useful load: 112.3 kg. (247.5 lbs.)
Gross weight: 601 kg. (1325 lbs.)
High speed: s.l.: 96.2 km./hr. (52 kn./hr.) (59.8 mi./hr.)
Cruise speed s.l.: 79.7 km./hr. (43 kn./hr.) (49.5 mi./hr.)
Rate of climb: n/a
Service ceiling: n/a
Hovering ceiling IGE: n/a
Hovering ceiling OGE: n/a
Cruise fuel: n/a
Range: n/a
No. built: 1 (6 variants)

Model: **R-4/VS-316A/S-47**

Type: Helicopter
Year: 1942
Manufacturer: Vought-Sikorsky Aircraft
Engine: 1 Warner R-550-N
BHP/RPM: 200/2475

Fuselage length: 1.9 m. (35 ft. 5 in.)
Fuselage width: n/a
Overall height: 3.8 m. (12 ft. 5 in.)
Main rotor diam.: 11.6 m. (38 ft.)
Tail rotor diam.: 2.3 m. (7 ft. 8 in.)
Landing gear: 3 m. (10 ft.)
Passenger cabin length: 2.2 m. (7 ft. 3 in.)
Passenger cabin width: 1.2 m. (3 ft. 11 in.)
Passenger cabin height: n/a
Weight empty: 911.8 kg. (2010 lbs.)
Weight useful load: 240.4 kg. (530 lbs.)
Gross weight: 1152.1 kg. (2540 lbs.)
High speed: s.l.: 131.5 km./hr. (71 kn.) (817 mi./hr.)
Cruise speed s.l.: 103.8 km./hr. (56 kn.) (64.5 mi./hr.)
Rate of climb: 198.1 m./min. (650 ft./min.)
Service ceiling: 2438 m. (8000 ft.)
Hovering ceiling IGE: n/a
Hovering ceiling OGE: 152.4 m. (500 ft.)
Cruise fuel: 32.7 kg./hr. (72 lbs./hr.)
Range: 370.5 km. (200 naut. mi.) (230.2 mi.)
No. built: 131 (total all types)

Model: **R-5/VS-327/S-48**

Type: Helicopter
Year: 1943
Manufacturer: Vought-Sikorsky/Sikorsky Aircraft
Engine: 1 Pratt & Whitney R-985-AN-5
BHP/RPM: 450/
Fuselage length: 12.4 m. (40 ft. 10 in.)
Fuselage width: n/a
Overall height: 3.9 m. (12 ft. 9 in.)
Main rotor diam.: 14.6 m. (48 ft.)
Tail rotor diam.: 2.5 m. (8 ft. 4 in.)
Landing gear tread: 3.7 m. (12 ft.)
Passenger cabin length: 2.5 m. (8 ft. 4 in.)
Passenger cabin width: 1.2 m. (3 ft. 11 in.)
Passenger cabin height: n/a
Weight empty: 1715 kg. (3781 lbs.)
Weight useful load: 505.8 kg. (1115 lbs.)
Gross weight: 2220.8 kg. (4896 lbs.)
High speed: s.l.: 144.5 km./hr. (78 kn./hr.) (89.8 mi./hr.)
Cruise speed s.l.: 127.8 km./hr. (69 kn./hr.) (79.4 mi./hr.)
Rate of climb: 265/2 m./min. (870 ft./min.)
Service ceiling: 4298 m. (14100 ft.)
Hovering ceiling IGE: n/a
Hovering ceiling OGE: 426.7 m. (1400 ft.)
Cruise fuel: 99.8 kg./hr. (220 lbs./hr.)
Range: 370.5 km. (200 naut. mi.) (230.2 mi.)
No. built: 65 (total all types)

Model: **R-6/VS-316B/S-49**

Type: Helicopter
Year: 1943
Manufacturer: Vought-Sikorsky/Sikorsky Aircraft
Engine: 1 Franklin 0-405-9
BHP/RPM: 245/
Fuselage length: 11.7 m. (38 ft. 3 in.)
Fuselage width: 1.1 m. (3 ft. 8 in.)
Overall height: 3.2 m. (10 ft. 5 in.)
Main rotor diam.: 11.6 m. (38 ft.)
Tail rotor diam.: 2.5 m. (8 ft. 2 in.)
Landing gear tread: 2.7 m. (9 ft.)

Passenger cabin length: 2.1 m. (7 ft.)
Passenger cabin width: 1.1 m. (3 ft. 6 in.)
Passenger cabin height: n/a
Weight empty: 922.6 kg. (2034 lbs.)
Weight useful load: 267.2 kg. (589 lbs.)
Gross weight: 1317.2 kg. (2904 lbs.)
High speed: s.l.: 161.1 km./hr. (87 kn./hr.) (100.1 mi./hr.)
Cruise speed s.l.: 120.4 km./hr. (65 kn./hr.) (74.8 mi./hr.)
Rate of climb: 237.7 m./min. (780 ft./min.)
Service ceiling: 3048 m. (10000 ft.)
Hovering ceiling IGE: n/a
Hovering ceiling OGE: 457.2 m. (1500 ft.)
Cruise fuel: 35.4 kg./hr. (78 lbs./hr.)
Range: 185.2 km. (100 naut. mi.) (115.1 mi.)
No. built: 229 (total all types)

HISTORICAL AND TECHNICAL NOTES

Amphibian. An airplane that is capable of operation on land or on water by use either of floats or of a boat hull fuselage and a special set of wheels that can usually be retracted.

Autogiro. First flown successfully in 1923, the autogiro was the first significant rotary-wing achievement. It is an aircraft that derives lift from a free-turning rotor which rotates as a result of motion through the air. This motion comes from an engine-driven propeller. While the autogiro is not capable of hovering or vertical flight, it can make extremely short takeoffs and landings.

Cantilevered wing. A wing without any external bracing. This design significantly reduces drag and improves the overall performance of an aircraft.

Collective pitch control. A control in helicopters whereby the pitch of all blades in the lifting rotor or rotors is changed simultaneously, thereby controlling the rate of climb or descent of the helicopter. The collective control is a lever mounted alongside the pilot seat.

Coaxial. Rotor configuration in which two rotors revolve on coincident axes, one above the other, each turning in opposite directions to counteract torque.

Cruciform tail. An empennage or tail in which the surfaces intersect one another to form a symmetrical cross. Early airplanes were equipped with cumbersome multiple surfaces, often more than one surface for each horizontal and vertical plane. By the end of World War I, many aircraft were fitted with single-surface, cruciform tails. The single vertical rudder of the airplane found its counterpart in the single tail rotor of the helicopter, rotating in a vertical plane.

Cyclic pitch control. The control that changes the pitch of the rotor blades individually during a cycle of revolution to control the tilt of the rotor disc and, therefore, the direction and velocity of horizontal flight. The cyclic control stick protrudes from the cockpit floor immediately ahead of the pilot seat.

Downwash. The flow of air through revolving helicopter rotor blades, which pulls air down from above and exhausts it below the aircraft. Eddies and cross currents of turbulent air are sometimes generated as downwash encounters the fuselage of the helicopter.

Escadra vozdushnykh korablei. The EVK, or Squadron of Flying Ships, was a unique, self-contained organization. The large amount of supplies and technical complexity associated with supporting the Il'ya Muromets under combat conditions necessitated the organization of a mobile unit equipped with its own workshops, motor pool, railcars, and technical staff.

Fédération Aéronautique Internationale (F.A.I.). Founded on October 14, 1905, the initial purpose of the organization was to promote and regulate flying around the world and it became the official organization responsible for sanctioning and validating record-setting aircraft flights.

Fixed-wing. An aircraft, powered or unpowered, whose wings are attached to the fuselage, in contrast to rotor-wing aircraft with wings that rotate, like the helicopter and autogiro.

Imperial All-Russian Aero Club (IRAC). The IRAC was founded in January 1908. It encouraged the development of both lighter-than-air and heavier-than-air flying machines. It was the only Russian aeronautical organization empowered to license pilots. The IRAC not only set up a flying school but sponsored international aviation meets and exhibitions which were held throughout Russia.

Kiev-Pechersk Monastery. One of the most sacred sites in Russia, the monastery was founded in 1051 by the monks Anthony and Theodosius. It is now a complex of buildings and caves and some of the structures date back to the twelfth century.

Outriggers. Primary structural members supporting main or auxiliary rotors outboard of the aircraft fuselage centerline.

Petrograd. Originally known as St. Petersburg, the city's name was Russianized in 1914 to Petrograd in an expression of war-induced nationalism. In 1924 this former Imperial capital was renamed Leningrad.

Robert J. Collier Trophy. Award presented by the National Aeronautic Association (established in 1922) for the greatest achievement in aeronautics or astronautics in America.

Romanov dynasty. The ruling family of Russia from 1613 to 1917.

Russo-Baltic Wagon Company. The Russo-Baltiiskiy Vagonnyy Zavod (R-BVZ) built railroad cars, rolling stock, airplanes, and automobiles. The main R-BVZ factory was located on the Baltic Sea in the city of Riga and the aviation branch was located in St. Petersburg.

Sesquiplane. A biplane with one wing, most often the lower one, markedly smaller than the other wing. In some cases the smaller wing is only half the area of the larger wing.

Short-haul helicopter airlines. Commercial passenger-carrying operations where the longest distance flown is approximately 100–150 miles.

Sikorsky *Grand*. The world's first four-engine airplane. It evolved into three variants which have led to the mistaken assumption that more than one *Grand* was built. The original name for the aircraft was the *Bolshoi Baltiskiy* [Great Baltic]. Constructed in 1913 as a twin-engine tractor airplane, it was later modified to a four-engine, tractor/pusher layout with two engines in tandem (one behind the other) attached to the lower wing on either side of the fuselage. The name *Grand* came into use at this time. In June 1913, the aircraft was modified again and the third and final variant appeared. The official name was also changed to the *Russkiy vityaz* [Russian knight]. In this version all four engines were of the tractor-type mounted on the leading edge of the lower wing. The use of the popular name *Grand* has endured as the most common designation for the aircraft.

Sikorsky Il'ya Muromets. The Murometsy (plural for Il'ya Muromets) airplanes were built between 1914 and 1918. A number of versions were built, each one assigned a different type designation suffix. The type B was the first production Murometsy built, hence the aircraft was officially listed as the IM B. The B was followed by type V, designed specifically for military use. Further improvements and modifications led to the G subtypes, the G-1, G-2, G-3, and G-4. The G-2 was equipped with the first machinegun to be mounted in the tail of an aircraft. Next in the series was the type D, an attempt to produce an airplane with four engines in tandem. This design was lighter and smaller than any of the other Il'ya Muromets. The final variant was the E, the largest and most advanced of the Murometsy.

Single-rotor configuration. A helicopter with a single main rotor and a single tail rotor. Single-main rotor function is similar to the fixed wing of an airplane—rotor motion through the air generates lift for the helicopter, while forward motion produces lift for the fixed-wing of the airplane. The tail rotor counteracts main rotor torque, adjusting this force to swing the helicopter left or right for lateral directional control. The tail rudder of the airplane deflects the air left or right for lateral control.

Torque. As derived from Newton's third law of motion—"for every action there must be an equal and opposite reaction"—torque causes the fuselage of a helicopter to rotate in a direction opposite the rotation of its power-driven main rotor. The single-rotor helicopter employed a tail rotor to counteract torque, while the autogiro suffered no torque effects due to its unpowered rotor.

Transmission. A gearbox that converts the high-speed revolutions of the engine to a reduced speed for efficient operation of the tail rotor and main rotor.

White Nights. Also known as the midnight sun, when the sun does not appear to fully set, this phenomenon is common to the northern latitudes and results from a tilt in the earth's axis during the summer months.

Wing-Loading. The amount of weight supported by the wing of an aircraft in flight; determined by taking the gross weight of an airplane and dividing it by the area in square feet of the wing. The gross weight of the Sikorsky S-42 (38,000 pounds) divided by the the area of its wing (1,330 square feet) results in a wing-loading of 28.5 square feet, a very high figure compared with other flying boats of the time.

BIBLIOGRAPHY

This bibliography was compiled to provide a reference source on the career of Igor I. Sikorsky. The list is comprehensive, covering Sikorsky's entire life, with his own writings and titles drawn from Russian and English language sources. This compilation includes articles and books and is divided into five sections.

The first section is a listing of articles and books written by Igor Sikorsky in English. The second section, "General Works," contains titles dealing with broad themes associated with Sikorsky. A third section, including both Russian and English language materials, provides a selected list of titles that focus on his Russian years. At the end of this section, there is a list of Russian language periodicals, old and modern, that refer to the theme of aviation. Most of the items appearing in the fourth section, "The Golden Age," are articles that appeared in the aviation press from 1923 to 1941. A fifth section covers vertical flight and contains books and articles dealing with Sikorsky's pioneering work with the helicopter. A valuable reference on helicopters can be found in *Vertiflite* magazine, volume 34 number 1 (January/February 1988). This is an annotated list by E. K. Liberatore which contains 132 items, one of which is a multi-volume study of the history of vertical flight up to 1950. Volume 18 of this history is a general bibliography containing over five thousand entries. It covers the history, design descriptions, analysis, and patents on rotary wing aircraft.

WORKS BY IGOR I. SIKORSKY
(chronological)

"What Can Aircraft Do in the Next War," *Independent*, vol. 115, pp. 521–23, 1925. Illus.

"Aeronautics in Europe," *Aero Digest*, vol. 15, no. 1, pp. 63, 278, 280, 1929. Illus.

"Some Aspects of the Seaplane and the Amphibian," *Mechanical Engineering*, vol. 51, no. 11, 1929.

"Airplanes of the Future," *Aero Digest*, vol. 15, no. 6, pp. 54–56, 1929.

"The 'Clipper Ship' S-42," *U. S. Air Services*, vol. 19, no. 5, pp. 12–14, 1934. Illus.

"The Long-Range Flying Boat: Its Development and Characteristics." Precis of a lecture delivered by Igor Sikorsky, *Flight*, vol. 26, no. 1352, p. 1259, 1934.

"The Development and Characteristics of a Long-Range Flying Boat," *J. of R.A.S.*, vol. 39, pp. 263–75, 1935.

"Design Problems and Methods for Large Flying Boats," *J. Soc. Automotive Engineers*, vol. 37, no. 1, pp. 247–49, 1935. Illus.

"Problems of the Transoceanic Airplane," *J. Aeronautical Sciences*, vol. 3, no. 9, pp. 318–21, 1936. Illus.

"Tomorrow's Clippers," *Aviation*, vol. 35, no. 10, pp. 15–17, 49, 1936. Illus., tables.

The Story of the Winged-S: An Autobiography. New York: Dodd, Mead and Company, 1938 (rev. ed. 1958).

"Commercial and Military Uses of Rotating Wing Aircraft," *Proceedings*, Second Annual Rotating Wing Aircraft Meeting, Institute of Aeronautical Sciences, 1939.

"Future of the Helicopter," *Aero Digest*, vol. 38, pp. 120–21, 1941.

"Recent Developments in Direct Lift Aircraft," *Tool Engineer*, pp. 37–39, June 1941.

The Message of the Lord's Prayer. New York: Charles Scribner's Sons, 1942.

"Shape of Things to Come," *Skyways*, pp. 11–13, Feb. 1942.

"Helicopters of Tomorrow," *Aviation*, vol. 41, p. 90, 1942. Illus.

"Technical Development of the VS-300 Helicopter During 1941," *J. Aeronautical Sciences*, vol. 9, pp. 309–11, 1942. Illus.

"Helicopter Convertible to Autogyro Principle," *J. Soc. Automotive Engineers*, Sup. 46, Apr. 1943.

"Progress of the Vought-Sikorsky Helicopter Program in 1942," *Aeronautical Engineering Review*, vol. 2, pp. 41, 43, 1943. Illus.

"Every Spot on Earth Made Accessible by Helicopter," *J. Soc. Automotive Engineers*, pp. 18–20, May 1943.

The Invisible Encounter. New York: Charles Scribner's Sons, 1947.

"Recollections and Thoughts of a Pioneer," a lecture presented to The Wings Club, Nov. 16, 1964.

GENERAL WORKS

Bartlett, Robert M. *Sky Pioneer: The Story of Igor I. Sikorsky* (New York: Charles Scribner's Sons, 1947)

Delear, Frank J. *Igor Sikorsky: His Three Careers in Aviation*. New York: Dodd, Mead & Company, 1969.

Finne, Konstantin Nikolayevich. *Igor Sikorsky: The Russian Years*. Edited by Carl J. Bobrow and Von Hardesty. Washington, D.C.: Smithsonian Institution Press, 1987.

Finne, Konstantin Nikolayevich. *Russkiye vozdushnyye bogatyri I.I. Sikorskogo* [Russian air warriors of I. I. Sikorsky]. Belgrade, Yugoslavia, 1930.

Gibbs-Smith, Charles H. *Aviation: An Historical Survey from Its Origins to the End of World War Two*. London: HMSO, 1970, 1985.

Hallion, Richard P. *Test Pilots: The Frontiersmen of Flight*. Washington, D.C.: Smithsonian Institution Press, 1988 (revised ed.).

Lindbergh, Charles A. *The Wartime Journals of Charles A. Lindbergh*. New York: Harcourt Brace Jovanovich, 1970.

Pisano, Dominick A., and Cathleen S. Lewis. *Air and Space History: An Annotated Bibliography*. New York: Garland Press, 1988.

RUSSIAN PERIOD

Baldwin, S. *Vozdukhoplavatel'nyye dvigateli* [Aero engines]. St. Petersburg, 1909.

Barsh, G. V. *Vozdukhoplavaniye v yevo proshlom i nastoyashchem* [Aeronautics past and present]. St. Petersburg, 1903.

Belizhev, A. A. *40 let sovetskoi aviatsii* [Forty years of Soviet aviation]. Moscow: Znaniye, 1958.

Bobrow, Carl. "Early Aviation in Russia," *W.W. I Aero*, no. 114, pp. 18–29, 1987. Illus.

Boreyko, D. A. *Ukhod za aeroplanami i gidroplanami* [Maintenance of airplanes and seaplanes]. Petrograd: A. N. Lavrov, 1916.

Boreyko, D. A. *Osnovy aviatsii* [Foundations of aviation]. Petrograd: A. N. Lavrov, 1917.

Borozdin, N. *Zavoyevaniye vozdushnoi stikhii* [Conquest of the airways]. Warsaw, 1909.

Borozdin, N. *Zavoyevaniye i letaniye, Russkiye letuny* [Aeronautics and flight: Russian aviators.] St. Petersburg: Tipographiya A. S. Suvorina, 1911.

Boyd, Alexander. *The Soviet Air Force Since 1918*. London: Macdonald and Jane's, 1977.

Burche, Ye. F. "Nesterov." Part of a series on the lives of famous people. Molodaya gvardiya, 1955.

Bychkov, V. "Russia's flying warrior," *Krylya Rodiny*, no. 2 (reprinted and translated in *Bulletin of the Russian Aviation Research Group of Air-Britain*, vol. 26, no. 91), 1987.

Cain, Claude W. "Flying for the Czar: Alexander Riaboff, Imperial Russian Air Service. A Photo Essay," *Cross and Cockade*, vol. 11, no. 4, pp. 305–32, 1970.

Chaplygin, S. A. *Bibliografiya pechatnykh trudov* [A bibliography of printed works]. Moscow: TsAGI, 1968.

Cheremnykh, N., and I. Shipilov. *A. F. Mozhaiskiy-sozdatel' pervogo v mire samoleta* [A. F. Mozhaiskiy: Creator of the first airplane]. Moscow: Voyenizdat, 1955.

Duz', P. D. *Istoriya vozdukhoplavaniya i aviatsii v SSSR, do 1914–1918* [A history of aeronautics and aviation in the USSR for the period 1914–1918]. Moscow: Oborongiz, 1944, 1960, and 1979.

Duz', P. D. *Istoriya vozdukhoplavaniya i aviatsii v SSSR, do 1914 g.* [A history of aeronautics and aviation in the USSR, pre-1914 period]. Moscow: Mashinostroyeniye, 1981.

Ferber, F. *Aviatsiya, yeye nachaloi razvitiye* [Aviation: Its beginnings and development]. Kiev, 1910.

Frank, M. L. *Istoriya vozdukhoplavaniya i yego sovremennoye sostoyaniye* [The history of aeronautics and its current situation]. St. Petersburg: Izdatel'stvo Vozdukhoplavaniye, 1910.

Frank, M. L. *Istoriya i aviatsii* [History of aviation]. St. Petersburg, 1911.

Glagolev, N. *K'zvezdam, Istoriya vozdukhoplavaniya, Kn.1* [To the stars: History of aeronautics, Book I]. St. Petersburg, 1912.

Glagolev, N. *Vozdushnyy flot, Istoriya i organizatisya voyennogo vozdukhoplavaniya* [The air fleet: History and organization of military aeronautics]. Petrograd: "Viktoriya," 1915.

Glavneyshiye dannyye razlichnykh samoletov (po 15 avgusta 1917 g.) Samolety, primenyayemyye na fronte tablitsy. Certain data on various aircraft at the front. Petrograd: Uvoflot, 1917.

Golubev, V. V. *Sergei Alekseyevich Chaplygin*. Moscow: TsAGI, 1947.

Hardesty, Von. Red Phoenix: The Rise of Soviet Air Power, 1941–1945. Washington, D.C.: Smithsonian Institution Press, 1982.

Hardesty, Von. "Aeronautics Comes to Russia: The Early Years, 1908–1918," Research Report, National Air and Space Museum, pp. 23–44. Washington D.C.: Smithsonian Institution Press, 1985. Illus.

Istoriya SSSR, ukazatel' sovetskoy literatury za 1917–1967 gg. [History of the USSR, guide to Soviet literature for the years 1917–1967]. Moscow: Nauka, 1977.

Ivanov, N. I. *Aeroplanovdeniye* [Data on airplanes]. Moscow: MOV, 1915 and 1916.

Jackson, Robert. *Red Falcons: Soviet Airmen in Action, 1919–1969*. New York: International Publications Service, 1970.

Jones, David R. "The Birth of the Russian Air Weapon." *Aerospace Historian*, vol. 21, no. 3, pp. 169–71, 1974.

Karinskiy, Nikolai S. "The Story of Aerostation and Aviation in Russia." Manuscript in New York Public Library.

Khalyutin, S. *Sbornik statei po vozdukhoplavaniya (pod redaktsiei S. Khalyutin)* [Collection of articles about aeronautics]. Kiev, 1910.

Kilmarx, Robert A. *A History of Soviet Air Power*. New York: Frederick A. Praeger, 1962.

Kilmarx, Robert A. "The Russian Imperial Air Forces of World War I," *Airpower Historian*, vol. 10, no. 3, pp. 90–95, 1963.

Kritskiy, P. *Podvigi russkikh aviatorov* [Heroic deeds of Russian aviators]. Yaroslav: n.p., 1915.

Kryl'ya rodiny: Sbornik [Wings of the motherland: A collection]. Moscow: DOSAAF, 1983.

Lelase, L., and R. Mark. *Problema vozdukhoplavaniya* [Problems of aeronautics]. St. Petersburg, 1910.

Naidenov, V. F. *Aviatsiya v 1909 godu* [Aviation in the year 1909]. St. Petersburg: Tipographiya Usmanova, 1910.

Naidenov, V. F., ed. *Vozdukhoplavaniye, ego proshloye i nastoyashcheye* [Aeronautics: Its past and its contemporary status]. St. Petersburg, 1911.

Naidenov, V. F. *Zapiski po aviatsii* [Notes on aviation]. St. Petersburg, 1911–12.

Naidenov, V. F. *Aeroplany* [Airplanes]. St. Petersburg, 1911–12.

Nowarra, H. J., and G. R. Duval, eds. *Russian Civil and Military Aircraft, 1884–1969*. London: Fountain Press, 1971.

Pamyati Professora Nikolaya Yegorovicha Zhukovskogo [Recollections of Professor Nikolai Yegorovich Zhukovskiy]. Moscow, 1922.

Piotrovskiy, G. *Zavoyeraniye vozdukha* [Conquest of the air]. Vitebsk, 1910.

Popov, V. A., ed. *Vozdukhoplavaniye i aviatsii v Rossii do 1907 g. Sbornik dokumentov i materialov* [Aeronautics and aviation in Russia up to 1907: A collection of documents and materials]. Moscow: Oborongiz, 1956.

Prepodavaniye vozdukhoplavaniya v institute Putey soobshcheniya imperatora Aleksandra I [Teaching of aeronautics in the Alexander I Institute of Transportation]. St. Petersburg, 1911.

Riaboff, Alexander. *Gatchina Days: Reminiscences of a Russian Pilot*. Edited by Von Hardesty. Washington, D.C.: Smithsonian Institution Press, 1985.

Rodnykh, A. A. *Istoriya vozdukhoplavaniya i letaniya v Rossii* [History of aeronautics and flying in Russia]. 2 vols. St. Petersburg: Gramotnost', 1911.

Rodnykh, A. A. *Voyna v vozdukhe v byloye vremya i teper'* [The war in the air, past and present]. Petrograd: Delo, 1915.

Roustem–Bek, B. *Aerial Russia*. London: John Lane, 1916.

Russkiy morskoi i vozdushnyy flot, sooruzhennyy na dobrovol'nyye pozher-tvovaniya [The Russian Naval and Air Fleet: Building through voluntary support]. St. Petersburg, 1913.

Rynin, N. A., and V. F. Naidenov, eds. *Russkoye vozdukhoplavaniye, istoriya i uspekhi* [Russian aeronautics: Its history and successes]. St. Petersburg, 1911–13.

Shavrov, V. B. *Istoriya konstruktsii samoletov v SSSR do 1938 g.* [History of aircraft design in the USSR for the period before 1938]. Moscow: Mashinostroyeniye, 1969; 3d ed., 1985.

Sher, A. S. *Kul'turno-istoricheskoye znacheniye vozdukhoplavaniya* [Cultural and historic significance of aeronautics]. St. Petersburg, 1912.

Shipilov, I. F. *Vydayushchiisya russikiy voyennyy letchik P. N. Nesterov* [Peter Nesterov: Outstanding Russian military pilot]. Moscow, 1951.

Strizhevsky, S. *Nikolai Zhukovsky, Founder of Aeronautics.* Moscow: Foreign Language Publishing House, 1957.

Tiraspol'skiy, G. L. *Vozdukhoplavaniye i vozdukholetaniye* [Aeronautics and flight]. St. Petersburg, 1910.

Trunov, K. I. *Petr Nesterov* [Peter Nesterov]. Moscow: Sovetskaya Rossiya, 1971.

Uteshev, N. I. *Zapiski po istorii voyennogo vozdukhoplavaniya* [Notes on the history of military aeronautics]. St. Petersburg, 1912.

Veygelin, K. Ye. *10−15 iyulya 1911 g. perelet S. Petersburg-Moskava* [Flight from St. Petersburg to Moscow]. St. Petersburg, 1911.

Veygelin, K. Ye. *Azbuka vozdukhoplavaniya* [ABCs of aeronautics]. St. Petersburg, 1912.

Veygelin, K. Ye. *Zavoyevaniye vozdushnago okeana, istoriya i sovremennoye sostoyanye vozdukhoplavaniya* [Conquest of the air, ocean history, and contemporary state of aeronautics]. St. Petersburg: Knigoizdatel'stvo P. P. Soikina, 1912.

Veygelin, K. Ye. *Vozdushnyy spravochnik. Yezhegodnik Imp. vseross. aerokluba* [Air directory: Annual publication of the Imperial All-Russian Aero Club]. St. Petersburg: P. P. Soikina, 1912−16.

Veygelin, K. Ye. *Put'letchika* Nesterova [Path of the flier *Nesterov*]. Moscow and Leningrad, 1939.

Veygelin, K. Ye. *Ocherki po istorii letnogo dela* [Reflections on the history of flight]. Moscow: Oborngiz, 1940.

Vladimirov, L. *Sovremennoye vozdukhoplavaniye i yego istoriya* [Contemporary aeronautics and its history]. Kiev: n.p., 1909.

Vorob'yev, B. *Vozdukhoplavaniye v nashe vremya* [Aeronautics in our time], 1912.

Vozdukhoplavaniye i letaniye, Russkiye letuny [Aeronautics and flight: Russian aviators]. St. Petersburg: Tipographiya A. S. Suvorina, 1911.

Woodman, Harry. "Les Bombardiers geants d'Igor Sikorsky," *Le Fanatique de l'aviation*, nos. 150 and 151, May and June 1982.

Woodman, Harry. "Il'ya Muromets Type 'B' of WW I," *Airfix Magazine*, May 1985.

Yankevich, P. *Aerofotographiya Rukovodstvo vozdushnoi fotographii* [Aerial photography]. Petrograd: A. N. Lavrov, 1917.

Zaustinskiy, M. V. *Vozdukhoplavatel'nyye dvigateli* [Aero engines]. St. Petersburg, 1910.

Zhabrov, A. A. *Annotirovannyy ukazatel' literatury na russkom yazyke po aviatsii i voz-dukhoplavaniya za 50 let, 1881−1931* [Annotated guide to Russian-language literature on aviation and aeronautics for fifty years, 1881−1931]. Moscow, 1931.

Zhukovskiy, N. E. *Iz neopubilovannoi perepiski* [From unpublished notes]. Moscow: TsAGI, 1957.

Zhukovskiy, N. E. *Bibliografiya pechatnykh trudov* [A bibliography of printed works]. Moscow: TsAGI, 1968.

PERIODICALS

Aero, 1909−10.
Aero-i-automobil'naya zhizn', 1910−14.
Aeromobil', 1912.
Armiya i flot Niva, 1897−1917.
Automobil' i vozdukhoplavaniye, 1911−12.
Automobil'naya zhizn'i aviatsiya, 1913−14.
Biblioteka vozdukhoplavaniya, 1909−10.
Byulleten' Moskovskogo obshchestva vozdukhoplavaniya, 1910.

K'sport!, 1911−17.
Letaniye, 1910.
Morskoi sbornik, 1908−16.
Sevastopol'skiy aviatsionnyy illustrirovannyy zhurnal, 1910−.
Vestnik letchikov i aviatsionnykh motoristov svobodnoi Rossii, 1917.
Vestnik vozdukhoplavaniya, 1910−13.
Vestnik vozdukhoplavaniya i sporta, 1913.
Vestnik vozdushnogo flota, 1918−38.
Voyenno-vozdushnyy flot, 1914.
Voyennyy letchik, zhurnal Sevastopol'skoi aviatsionnoi shkoly, 1917.
Voyennyy mir, 1912−14.
Voyennyy sbornik, 1908−17.
Vozdukhoplavaniye, nauka i sport, 1910.
Vozdukhoplavaniye i sport, 1910.
Vozdukhoplavatel', 1903−16.
Vozdushnyy put', 1911.

THE GOLDEN AGE

"America's Fast Trans-Atlantic Liner," *Aeroplane*, vol. 53, no. 1364, pp. 43−44, 1937. Diagrs.

"America's Latest Amphibian," *Flight*, vol. 27, no. 1382, pp. 665−66, 1935, Illus., diagrs.

"Amphibie Sikorsky S-36," *La Nature*, no. 2781, p. 281, 1928. Illus.

"Amphibium Sikorsky S-43," *Flugsport*, vol. 27, no. 3, p. 50, 1935. Illus.

"Atlantic Routine," *Flight*, vol. 32, no. 1490, pp. 68−72, 1937. Illus.

"Avion Sikorsky S-37," *La Nature*, no. 2782, p. 329, 1928.

Bender, Marylin, and Selig Altschul. *The Chosen Instrument, Pan Am Juan Trippe: The Rise and Fall of an American Entrepreneur.* New York: Simon and Schuster, 1982.

"Big Flying Boats," *Aeroplane*, vol. 48, no. 1232, pp. 16−19, 1935. Illus.

"A Bigger Sikorsky," *Flight*, vol. 28, no. 1404, p. 530, 1935.

Burns, Fred. "Sikorsky S-41," *Air Transportation*, vol. 14, no. 9, p. 13, 1930. Illus.

"Chose Sikorsky Plane for Long Trade Flight," *Aviation*, vol. 26, p. 733, 1929.

Cleveland, R. M. "Aircraft Grow Larger," *Scientific American*, vol. 155, pp. 72−74, 1936. Illus.

"Control of Sikorsky Acquired by United," *Aviation*, vol. 27, p. 236, 1929.

Daley, Robert. *An American Saga: Juan Trippe and His Pan Am Empire.* New York: Random House, 1980.

Dawson, John R. "A Complete Tank Test of the Hull of the Sikorsky S-40 Flying Boat—American Clipper Class." N.A.C.A. Technical Notes No. 512, Dec. 11, 1934, 16 pages. Illus., diagrs., tables.

"Delivering Several Sikorskys," *Aviation*, vol. 27, p. 1224, 1929.

Derham, A. F. "Sikorsky Trans-Atlantic Airplane: A Redesigned Freighter," *Automotive Industries*, vol. 55, no. 12, pp. 462−63, 1926.

"Design and Construction Details of the New Sikorsky S-43 Amphibian," *Aero Digest*, vol. 21, no. 1, pp. 54−58, 1935. Illus., diagrs.

"Double Crossing the Atlantic," *Aeroplane*, vol. 53, no. 1364, pp. 39–40, 1937. Illus.

Fonck, René. "My New York–Paris Flight," *Aero Digest*, vol. 8, no. 6, 1926.

Franchimont, H. A. "Basic Design Features of the Sikorsky S-42," *Aero Digest*, vol. 25, pp. 54–56 (Aug.), 24–26 (Sept.) 50, 52 (Oct.), 1934.

"Le Frein Sikorsky á disques multiples," *L'Aeronautique*, vol. 12, no. 128, p. 14, 1930. Illus.

French, R. "Sikorsky, the Invincible," *National Aeronautic Magazine*, vol. 13, no. 11, pp. 11–12, 1935. Illus.

"Il Freno a dischi multipli Sikorsky," *Riv. Aeron.*, vol. 6, no. 2, pp. 360–61, 1930. Illus.

"A Future British Flying Boat," *Aeroplane*, vol. 50, no. 1297, pp. 409–12, 1936.

Garber, Paul E. "Trans-Atlantic Trip Fails," *U.S. Air Services*, vol. 11, no. 11, pp. 42–43, 1926.

"Giant Flying Boats for Pan American," *Aviation Engineering*, vol. 8, pp. 25–26, 1933.

"Giant Sikorsky Amphibian for Pan American Airways," *Airway Age*, vol. 11, no. 4, p. 558, 1930.

"Giant Sikorsky Amphibian for Pan American Airways," *Aviation Engineering*, vol. 3, no. 2, p. 28, 1930.

"Giant Sikorsky Amphibian for Pan American Airways," *Flight*, vol. 22, no. 4, pp. 154–55, 1930.

"Giant Trans-Atlantic Flying Boats According to Plans of the Consolidated Aircraft, Sikorsky and United Aircraft," *National Aeronautics Magazine*, vol. 15, no. 1, pp. 16–18, 1937. Diagrs.

Gillette, Leslie S. "Safety Is Outstanding Feature of Sikorsky Plane Design," *Automotive Industries*, Apr. 2, 1925.

Gluhareff, M. E. "Seaplane or Landplane for Transoceanic Service," *Aviation*, Mar. 1941.

"Hailing the American Clipper, Our Biggest Plane," *Literary Digest*, vol. 111, p. 36, 1931. Illus.

Hartney, Harold E. (Lt. Col.), "Sikorsky Air Transport," *Aero Digest*, vol., p. 204, 1925. Illus.

"Hertz Buys Sikorsky." *Aviation*, vol. 29, p. 1990, 1928.

Hoffman, M. L. "Sikorsky 41-Passenger S-40 Amphibian," *Air Transportation*, vol. 10, no. 13, pp. 34, 45, 1930. Diagrs.

"L'Hydravion Sikorsky S-42," *L'Aerophile*, vol. 43, no. 7, p. 202, 1935. Illus.

"Igor I. Sikorsky," *U.S. Air Services*, vol. 14, no. 1, pp. 52–54, 1929. Illus.

Klemin, Alexander. "Sikorsky's Contribution to Huge Amphibians: The S-40," *Aviation Engineering*, vol. 5, no. 4, pp. 18–21, 1931. Illus., diagrs., tables.

Klemin, Alexander. "The Sikorsky S-29 Twin Engine Transport Plane," *Aviation*, p. 84, Feb 16, 1925.

Klemin, Alexander. "Test Flights of the S-42," *Scientific American*, vol. 151, pp. 37–38, 1934. Illus.

Knott, Richard C. *The American Flying Boat: An Illustrated History*. Annapolis Maryland: Naval Institute Press, 1979.

Lindbergh, Anne Morrow. *The Flower and the Nettle: Diaries and Letters of Anne Morrow Lindbergh, 1936–1939*. New York: Harcourt Brace Jovanovich, 1976.

"Long Range Flying Boat," *Flight*, vol. 26, no. 1352, p. 1259, 1934.

McLaughlin, George F. "The All Metal Sikorsky," *Aero Digest*, vol. 8, no. 6, pp. 331, 394, 1926. Illus.

McReynolds, C. F. "Clipper Wing Grows Larger," *Aviation*, vol. 35, no. 8, pp. 38–39, 42, 45, 1937. Illus.

Mayborn, Mitch. "The Sikorsky S-35 and the First New York to Paris Attempt," *American Aviation Historical Society Journal*, vol. 3, no. 2, Spring 1958.

Mayborn, Mitch. "The Ugly Duckling, Sikorsky's S-38," *American Aviation Historical Society Journal*, vol. 4, no. 3, Fall 1959.

Millar, John. "The Sikorsky S-43 Amphibian Flying Boat," *Aeroplane*, vol. 53, no. 1370, pp. 38–39, 75, 1937. Illus.

"More about the Sikorsky S-42," *Aviation*, vol. 33, pp. 106–8, 1934. Illus.

"Mrs. Hoover Christens the 'American Clipper,' " *U.S. Air Services*, vol. 16, no. 11, pp. 17–18. 1931.

"Multiple Disc Brakes Devised by Sikorsky," *Aviation*, vol. 27, p. 1083, 1929.

Neville, Leslie E. "The Sikorsky S-38: New Amphibian Powered with Two Pratt & Whitney 'Wasp' Engines," *Aviation*, vol. 25, pp. 328–29, 343, 348, 1928. Illus., specs, 3-view.

Neville, Leslie E. "Sikorsky S-38," *Aviation*, vol. 25, no. 5, pp. 328–29, 343–347, 1928. Illus.

"The New Sikorsky Flying Boat," *Aviation*, vol. 23, no. 10, p. 522–24, 1927. Illus.

"New Sikorsky Flying Boat Creates Sensation," *U.S. Air Services*, vol. 19, no. 9, pp. 20–21, 1934. Illus.

"New Sikorsky Powered With Wasp Junior, Sikorsky S-39 Amphibian," *Southern Aviation*, vol. 2, no. 1, p. 44, 1930. Illus.

"The New Sikorsky S-39," *Airway Age*, vol. 11, no. 5, pp. 696–97, 1930. Illus., Tables.

"A New Twin-Engine Amphibian," *Aviation*, vol. 20, p. 603, 1926.

"A New Type of Wheel Brake," *Aeroplane*, vol. 38, no. 5, pp. 169–70, 1930. Illus.

"On the Proposed Trans-Atlantic Flight: The Sikorsky S-35 Special Three-Engine Plane Nearing Completion for Flight This Month," *Aviation*, vol. 21, no. 8, pp. 318–19, 1926. Illus.

"On Various Sorts of Flying Boats. Parts I-II," *Aeroplane*, vol. 48, nos. 1245, 1248, pp. 382–83, 471–75, 1924. Illus.

"Pan American S-42 Flying Boat," *Aero Digest*, vol. 24, no. 4, pp. 56–57, 64, 1934. Illus.

"Pan American's Super Clipper," *Aviation*, vol. 33, p. 96, 1934. Illus.

"Patrol Bomber," *Flight*, vol. 32, no. 1497, p. 234, 1937. Illus.

"Performance Plus," *Aviation*, vol. 33, pp. 246–49. Illus.

"Planes for the Sportsman: Sikorsky S-39 Amphibian," *Sportsman Pilot*, vol. 4, no. 3, pp. 24–25, 1930. Illus., diagrs.

"Products of the Sikorsky Manufacturing Corporation," *Aviation*, vol. 19, no. 14, pp. 439–40, 1925. Illus.

"Projected Non-Stop Flight from New York to Paris," *Scientific American*, vol. 135, pp. 146–48, 1926.

"Projected Sikorsky Amphibian," *Scientific American*, vol. 142, pp. 389–90, 1930. Illus.

"Propeller Brakes and Their Use in Multi-Engined Aircraft: Installation on the Sikorsky S-42," *Aero digest*, vol. 27, p. 30, 1935. Diagrams.

Rogers, William A. "The S-35 Is Flight Tested," *Aero Digest*, vol. 9, no. 3, 1926.

Sergievsky, Boris V. "The Problem of Flying in Colombia: Sikorsky Seaplane Proves Indispensible to Andean National Corporation," *Aviation*, vol. 22, pp. 715–16, 1927.

"S-42," *Aero Digest*, vol. 24, no. 4, pp. 56–57, 1934.

"S-42," *Aeroplane*, pp. 723-724, Apr. 25, 1934.

"S-42," *Aviation*, vol. 33, no. 4, pp. 106–8, 1934.

"S-42," *U.S. Air Services*, vol. 18, no. 5, pp. 13–14, 1934.

"S-42 Designed for Maintenace," *Aviation*, vol. 33, p. 273, 1934. Illus.

"Sikorsky Addition Begun at Bridgeport," *Aviation*, vol. 27, p. 758, 1929.

"The Sikorsky Airliner," *Aviation*, vol. 20, no. 14, pp. 508B-8C, 1926.

"Sikorsky 'American Clipper,' " *Aircraft Age*, vol. no. 7, pp. 10–11, 1932.

"Sikorsky Amphibian," *Scientific American*, vol. 138, pp. 354–56, 1928. Illus.

"Sikorsky Amphibian Makes Cross-Country Trip," *Airway Age*, vol. 9, p. 47, 1928. Illus.

"Sikorsky Amphibian S-41," *Aero Digest*, vol. 17, p. 70, 1930.

"Sikorsky Amphibian S-41," *Airway Age*, vol. 11, no. 10, p. 1353, 1930.

"The Sikorsky Aviation Corporation," *Aviation*, vol. 32, no. 5, p. 152, 1933.

"Sikorsky Bridgeport Production Starts Nov. 1," *Aviation*, vol. 27, p. 900, 1929.

"Sikorsky Concern in Re-Organization," *Aviation*, vol. 29, p. 1193, 1928.

"Sikorsky Forms Company," *Aviation*, p. 401, Apr. 9, 1923.

"The Sikorsky 'Guardian,'" *Aviation*, vol. 24, no. 3, pp. 148–50, 1928.

"Sikorsky Hopes to Have America Lead World in Passenger Airplanes," *Sunday Eagle Magazine* (Brooklyn, N.Y.), p. 79, Dec. 28, 1924.

"The Sikorsky Multiple Disc Brake," *Flight*, vol. 21, no. 51, pp. 1325–26, 1929. Illus.

"Sikorsky Occupies New Factory," *Aviation*, vol. 21, p. 1002, 1926.

"Sikorsky Passenger Carrying" (re: the S-29A), *Aviation*, vol. 20, p. 26, 1926.

"Sikorsky Patrol and Bombing Flying Boat," *Aero Digest*, vol. 31, no. 3, p. 68, 1937. Illus.

"Sikorsky Projects Include Wind Tunnel," *Aviation*, vol. 27, p. 1273, 1929.

"The Sikorsky S-29A Commerical Biplane," *Flight*, vol. 17, no. 20, pp. 285–86, 1925. Illus.

"The Sikorsky S-29A Twin-Engined Transport Biplane," *Aviation*, vol. 18, no. 7, pp. 182–84, 1925. Illus., specs.

"The Sikorsky S-35, the Three-engined (Jupiter) Transatlantic Biplane," *Flight*, vol. 18, no. 39, pp. 638–40, 1926. Illus.

"The Sikorsky S-35 Trans-Atlantic Plane," *U.S. Air Services*, vol. 11, no. 9, pp. 26–27, 1926.

"The Sikorsky S-36B Amphibian," *Flight*, vol. 19, no. 42, pp. 738–39, 1927. Diagrs.

"The Sikorsky S-38 Amphibian," *Aeroplane*, vol. 36, no. 18, p. 714, 1929. Illus.

"Sikorsky S-38-BH," *Western Flying*, vol. 8, no. 5, p. 84, 1930.

"The Sikorsky S-39," *Air Transportation*, vol. 11, no. 14, p. 27, 1930. Illus.

"The Sikorsky S-39 Amphibian," *Aviation*, vol. 28, no. 16, pp. 803–5, 1930. Illus.

"Sikorsky S-39B," *Western Flying*, vol. 9, no. 3, p. 80, 1931.

"The Sikorsky S-39 Light Amphibian," *Aero Digest*, vol. 16, no. 5, p. 125, 1930. Illus., tables.

"Sikorsky S-40," *Aero News and Mechanics*, p. 52, Apr. 1930. Diagrs.

"Sikorsky S-40," *Flight*, p. 1135, Nov. 13, 1931.

"Sikorsky S-40," *Les Ailes*, Nov. 5, 1931.

"Sikorsky S-40 Amphibian," *Aviation*, vol. 3, no. 4, p. 89, 1931.

"Sikorsky S-40 Amphibian," *National Glider*, vol. 3, no. 5, pp. 7–8, 1931. Illus.

"Sikorsky S-40 Amphibian," *Southern Aviation*, vol. 3, no. 4, p. 33, 1931.

"Sikorsky S-40 Amphibian," *Western Flying*, vol. 10, no. 6, p. 58, 1931.

"The Sikorsky S-40 Amphibion, A Giant for the Pan American Air Fleet," *Aviation*, vol. 30, no. 10, pp. 594–98, 1931. Illus., 3-view.

"The Sikorsky S-40 Amphibion," *Aero Digest*, vol. 19, no. 3, pp. 66–67, 1931. Illus.

"Sikorsky S-40 and S-42," *Aero Digest*, vol. 26, p. 96, 1935. Diagrs.

"Sikorsky S-40 Flying Boat," *Aero Digest*, vol. 16, no. 2, pp. 126–127, 1930. Illus.

"Sikorsky S-40 Flying Boat," *Canadian Air Review*, vol. 22, no. 11, pp. 28–29, 1930.

"Sikorsky S-41," *U.S. Air Services*, vol. 15, p. 41, Oct. 1930.

"Sikorsky S-41A," *Western Flying*, vol. 9, no. 6, pp. 76–77, 1931. Illus.

"The Sikorsky S-41 Amphibian," *Aviation*, vol. 29, no. 5, p. 302, 1930. Illus.

"The Sikorsky S-42," *Aeroplane*, vol. 46, no. 17, pp. 723–24, 1934. Illus.

"Sikorsky S-42," *Air World*, pp. 8–11, Sep. 1934.

"Sikorsky S-42A Flying Boat," *Interavia*, no. 332, June 15, 1936.

"Sikorsky S-42 description détaillée de cet hydravion de transport quadrimoteur," *Les Ailes*, p. 1, May 31, 1934. Illus.

"Sikorsky S-43 Amphibian," *Southwestern Aviation*, pp. 14–15, July 1935.

"Sikorsky S-43 Amphibian Seaplane," *Aviation*, vol. 33, no. 12, p. 412, 1934. Diagrs., table.

"Sikorsky S-43 Amphibion," *Southwestern Aviation*, vol. 4, no. 1, pp. 14–15, 1935. Illus.

"Sikorsky S-43 and S-42-A," *Aero Digest*, vol. 28, p. 92, 1936. Illus., diagrs.

"Sikorsky S-43 and S-42B," *Aero Digest*, vol. 30, p. 90, 1937. Diagrs.

"Sikorsky S.H.O.," *La Science Aerienne*, vol. 1, no. 2, p. 158, 1932. Illus.

"Sikorsky Sales," *Aviation*, vol. 20, p. 592, 1926.

"Sikorsky's Latest," *Aviation*, vol. 34, no. 7, pp. 34–36, 1935. Illus.

"Sikorsky's Latest: The XPBS-1," *Popular Aviation*, vol. 22, no. 5, p. 21, 1937. Illus.

"Sikorsky 'Super Clipper,' " *Aviation*, vol. 33, no. 3, p. 96, 1934. Illus.

"Sikorsky 'Super Clipper,' " *Sportsman Pilot*, vol. 8, no. 3, p. 33, 1932.

"The Sikorsky Trans-Atlantic Plane," *Aviation*, vol. 29, no. 22, pp. 834–35, 1926. Illus., specs., 3-view.

"The Sikorsky Twin-engined Amphibian Type S-38 Model, 1928," *N.A.C.A.*, Aircraft Circular No. 79, p. 13, 1928. Illus.

"The Sikorsky Type S-36-B Twin Engined Amphibian," *Aero Digest*, vol. 11, no. 3, pp. 284–85, 1927. Diagrs., Illus.

"The Sikorsky Type S-38 Wasp-Engined Amphibian," *Aero Digest*, vol. 13, no. 2, pp. 248, 250, 1928. Illus.

"Sikorsky X PBS," *Luftwehr*, vol. 4, no. 12, p. 511, 1937. Illus., table.

"Six Sikorsky Planes Ordered by Colonial," *Aviation*, vol. 26, p. 731, Mar. 9, 1929, pg. 731.

"Tests of Sikorsky-35," *Aero Digest*, vol. 9, no. 4, p. 231, 1926.

"The Twin-motored Sikorsky Model S-37," *Aero Digest*, vol. 11, no. 4, pp. 422–24, 1927. Illus., diagrs.

"A 200 M.P.H. Amphibian," *Flight*, vol. 27, no. 1361, p. 90, 1935. Illus.

"Use of Rubber on the Brazilian Clipper, Sikorsky S-42," *Rubber Age*, vol. 36, pp. 15–16, 1934. Illus.

van Mounier, P. J. J. "Igor Sikorsky en Zijn Amphibie-vliegtuigen," *Het Vliegveld*, vol. 15, no. 1, pp. 25–28, 1931. Illus.

von Gosslau, F. "Amphibian-flugzeuge mit Schwimm und Fahreinrichtungen," *Zeitschrift des V.D.I.*, vol. 72, no. 5, pp. 157–59, 1928. Illus., diagrs.

von Hans, Herrmann. "Das Handels-seeflugzeug," *Werft-reedereihafen*, vol. 12, no. 15, pp. 277–81, 1931. Illus.

"Whitney and Walgreen Buy Sikorsky Planes," *Aviation*, vol. 29, p. 939, 1928.

Woodman, Harry. "Le Sikorsky S.29A," *Le Fanatique de l'aviation*, no. 174, May 1984.

"Work Starts on Largest Amphibian," *Aircraft*, vol. 9, no. 9, pp. 8–9, 1931.

"World's Largest Amphibian: Sikorsky S-40," *Scientific American*, vol. 145, p. 406, 1931. Illus.

Young, E. E. "Wings for Our Foreign Trade: Trade Mission Flight of the Brazilian Clipper," *Aero Digest*, vol. 25, pp. 18–19, 1934. Illus.

Vertical Flight

Apostolo, Giorgio. *The Illustrated Encyclopedia of Helicopters*. New York: Bonanza, 1984.

Boyne, Walter J., and Donald S. Lopez. *Vertical Flight: The Age of the Helicopter*. Washington, D.C.: Smithsonian Institution Press, 1984.

"Details of Sikorsky Helicopter," *Engineer*, p. 248, Oct 18, 1940.

"Details of the Sikorsky Helicopter," *Aero Digest*, vol. 36, no. 6., pp. 56–57, 1940.

"Details of the Sikorsky Helicopter," *Aviation*, vol. 39, no. 7, pp. 65, 122, 1940. Illus.

Everett-Heath, John. *Soviet Helicopters: Design, Development and Tactics*. London: Jane's Publishing, 1983.

Fay, John. *The Helicopter: History, Piloting, and How It Flies*. New York: Hippocrene, 1987.

Gablehouse, Charles. *Helicopter and Autogiros: A Chronicle of Rotating-Wing Aircraft*. Philadelphia: J.B. Lippincott, 1987.

Gregory, H. Franklin. "Army's Flying Windmill," *Air Force*, p. 6 ff., Mar. 1943.

Gregory, H. Franklin. "Helicopter," *Air Trails Pictorial*, p. 13, 1944.

Gregory, H. Franklin. "Helicopter Outlook," *Aviation News*, Dec. 27, 1943.

Gregory, H. Franklin. "Recent Air Corps Developments in Rotating Wing Aircraft," *J. Aeronautical Sciences*, Aeronautical Engineering Review Section, pp. 9–11, 1942.

Gunston, Bill. *An Illustrated Guide to Military Helicopters*. New York: Arco, 1981.

Gunston, Bill. *Helicopters of the World*. New York: Crescent, 1983.

"Helicopter Flown Successfully," *Popular Science*, vol. 137, no. 3, p. 50, 1940. Illus.

"Helicopter Joins Army as Courier Ambulance," *Popular Mechanics*, p. 16, May 1943.

"Helicopter Proves Worth as Anti-Submarine Weapon," *Aero Digest*, p. 311, June 1943.

"Igor Sikorsky Demonstrates His Helicopter," *U.S. Air Services*, vol. 25, no. 7, p. 15, 1940.

Kastner, J. "Sikorsky's Helicopter: A Flying Machine Which May Some Day Be Everyman's Airplane," *Life*, pp. 80–84, June 21, 1943.

Klemin, A. "Sikorsky's Helicopter," *Scientific American*, vol. 163, p. 189, 1940. Illus.

Klemin, A. "Helicopter Records: Rotary Aircraft Operates as Seaplane or Amphibian Helicopter," *Scientific American*, p. 34, July 1941.

Klemin, A. "Latest Helicopter Is a Two-Seater with Enclosed Cockpit," *Scientific American*, p. 275, June 1943.

Lambermont, Paul M., and Anthony Pirie. *Helicopters and Autogyros of the World*. New York: A.S. Barnes, 1970 (rev. ed.).

Loening, G. "U.S. Leads World in Helicopter but Big Problems Remain," *Aviation News*, pp. 13–14, Dec. 6, 1943.

Macauley, C. B. F. *The Helicopters Are Coming*. New York: McGraw Hill, 1944.

Morris, Charles Lester. "Dawn of a New Era," *Air Force*, p. 7 plus, Mar. 1943.

Morris, Charles Lester. *Pioneering the Helicopter*. Alexandria, Va.: Helicopter Association International, 1985.

Nikolsky, Alexander A. *Notes on Helicopter Design Theory*. Princeton, N.J.: Princeton University Press, 1944.

Nikolsky, Alexander A. *Helicopter Analysis*. New York: Wiley, 1951.

Painton, F. C. "Coming Air Age," *Atlantic*, pp. 33–39, Sep. 1942.

Perry, H. W. "Return to Old Love," *Flight*, pp. 569–570, June 27, 1940.

Sikorsky, Sergei and Allen Andrews. *Straight Up*. Sikorsky Aircraft, United Technologies, 1984.

"Sikorsky, Stout Back Greyhound Plan For 14-Passenger Helicopter Buses," *Aviation News*, p. 10, Oct. 25, 1943.

"Sikorsky Helicopter," *Automotive and Aviation Industries*, vol. 86, p. 37, 1942. Illus.

"Sikorsky Helicopter: The Air World's Runabout?" *Civil Aeronautics J.*, vol. 4, pp. 76–77, 1943. Illus.

"Sikorsky Helicopter Sets Endurance Record," *Science Digest*, p. 82, June 1941.

"Sikorsky Helicopter Streamlined," *Popular Science*, p. 73, Aug. 1942.

"Sikorsky Sells Army on Future of His Helicopter," *Newsweek*, p. 58, Mar. 8, 1943.

"Sikorsky's Flying Windmill Helps Celebrate Air Mail's Anniversary," *Life*, p. 28, May 31, 1943.

"Skyway Flivver: Sikorsky's Amphibian Helicopter Is Easier to Drive than an Auto," *Life*, pp. 45–46, Oct. 19, 1942.

Smith, Frank Kingston. *Legacy of Wings: The Story of Harold F. Pitcairn*. New York: Jason Aronson, 1981.

Townson, George. *Autogiro: The Story of "the Windmill Plane."* Fallbrook, Calif.: Aero Publishers Inc., 1985.

Volodko, A.M. *Vertolet-truzhenik i voin* [Helicopter as worker and warrior]. Moscow: DOSAAF, 1984.

"Vought-Sikorsky Helicopter VS-300," *Interavia*, no. 712, pp. 17–18, May 29, 1940.

"Vought-Sikorsky Helicopter," *Engineer*, vol. 175, p. 230, 1943. Illus.

INDEX